HOW TO DEVELOP

ESSENTIAL HR POLICIES

HR POLICIES

AND

PROCEDURES

HOW TO DEVELOP
ESSENTIAL
HR POLICIES
AND
PROCEDURES

John H. McConnell

AMACOM
American Management Association
New York • Atlanta • Brussels • Chicago • London • San Francisco
Shanghai • Tokyo • Toronto • Washington, D.C.

Special discounts on bulk quantities of AMACOM books are available to corporations, professional associations, and other organizations. For details, contact Special Sales Department, AMACOM, a division of American Management Association, 1601 Broadway, New York, NY 10019.
Tel.: 212-903-8316. Fax: 212-903-8083.
Web site: www.amacombooks.org

This publication is designed to provide accurate and authoritative information in regard to the subject matter covered. It is sold with the understanding that the publisher is not engaged in rendering legal, accounting, or other professional service. If legal advice or other expert assistance is required, the services of a competent professional person should be sought.

Library of Congress Cataloging-in-Publication Data

McConnell, John H.
    How to develop essential HR policies and procedures / John H. McConnell.
      p. cm.
    Includes bibliographical references and index.
    ISBN 0-8144-0827-3
    1. Personnel management—Handbooks, manuals, etc.   I. Title.

HF5549.17.M32 2005
658.3'01—dc22

2004002410

Printing number

10 9 8 7 6 5 4 3 2 1

To

Connie Zalewski, Jean Downs,

Georgina Halliday, and Betty Dunn

Contents

PART THREE

PART FOUR

List of Figures

The Advisory Board

TO ENSURE A WORK OF THIS TYPE has as broad an application as possible, an advisory board of human resources professionals was employed to assist in creating a book to meet the needs of a wide variety of organizations. The board members represent organizations with as few as 200 to as many as several thousand employees. They are from a variety of geographic locations with experience in financial services, manufacturing, retail, sales, government, technology, and service organizations. Their education varies, and their experience in human resources ranges from ten years to forty years. The single most important characteristic that each possesses is experience in developing and implementing a comprehensive set of HR policies and procedures.

The advisory board members contributed individually and collectively to the creation of the policy and procedure subjects covered in this book and the completeness of coverage. Their input created a thoroughness that probably could not have been realized by the author alone.

To all these advisory board members, AMACOM and the author express their appreciation. Their contributions of time and expertise have made this book a valuable tool that can be used in your efforts to continually improve your HR function.

KATHY BOFFA is currently human resources manager for Dicar, Inc., a manufacturer of urethane parts for the corrugated industry. One of her first assignments was to develop a complete set of HR policies and procedures for the company. Before joining Dicar, she held a similar position for a nonprofit organization. She has a master's degree in educational training and development from Montclair University.

ROBERT A. NOWACZYK is currently director of corporate services for John Wiley & Sons, Inc., a scientific, technical, and medical publisher. Previously, he held HR executive positions with Oppenheimer-Funds and The Vanguard Group. In all of his positions, he has been involved with the development and administration of HR policies and procedures and has assisted other HR professionals in developing policies and procedures for their own companies. He has a bachelor of science degree from the University of Delaware and a master of business administration from Widener University. He is past chairman of the Society for Human Resource Management's Employment Practices Committee and past president and founding member of the Greater Valley Forge Human Resources Association.

STAN T. PLONA has held several executive positions in human resources with Corporate Express, Inc.; GMAC Home Services, Inc.; Quest Diagnostics Incorporated; and Merrill Lynch & Co., Inc. In all these positions, he has been accountable for administering the companies' HR policies and procedures, and for one company, he developed its initial set of HR policies and procedures. He has a bachelor's degree in industrial psychology from Baruch College of the City University of New York (CUNY) and is currently working on a master's degree at the same school.

GEORGEANNE C. PRATT-KLINGENSMITH is currently vice president of human resources for Pliva, Inc., a pharmaceutical manufacturer. She developed the company's initial set of HR policies and procedures and is accountable for their maintenance and administration. Before joining Pliva, she held HR positions with Sidmak Laboratories, Continental Insurance Company, and Gasoline Marketers of America. She is a graduate of Glassboro State College and is currently pursuing a course of study at Centenary College.

FERDINAND J. SETARO is managing director of TLE Associates, a firm specializing in organizational development and improvement services. He has consulted with numerous companies to assist in their development of HR policies and procedures. Formerly, he was director of organizational and management development for The Vanguard Group; director of organizational and management development for Colonial Penn Group; director of human resources for CPG Data Group; and director of supervisory development for the American Management Association. He has a BA from Columbia University and is a graduate of the Advance Program in Organizational Development. He is past president and chairman of the board of directors for the Association of Internal Management Consultants and is a prolific author and seminar leader.

ROBERT A. STOTO is director of human resources and labor relations for County College of Morris in Randolph, New Jersey. Previously, he was a vice president of human resources and administration for Curtis-Wright Corporation and personnel manager for the Elizabeth New Jersey Housing Authority. In all of these positions, he has been involved in creating and implementing HR policies and procedures. He has a master's degree in industrial relations and human resources from Rutgers University and a bachelor's degree in psychology from Seton Hall.

Acknowledgments

WRITING A BOOK TO ASSIST ORGANIZATIONS in developing a comprehensive set of human resources policies and procedures requires a great many considerations. Fortunately, I had the assistance of a team of HR professionals—the advisory board acknowledged in the previous section—who represent a wide range of related knowledge and experience. Their combined wisdom contributed significantly to this book.

There are also four people with whom, over the years, I collaborated on the creation of policies and procedures for their organizations. Those experiences and their counsel provided an excellent basis for the initial development of this book. They are Sigmund Brody, Ralph Brown, Russell Glicksman, and William Pierce. These four individuals held corporate executive positions in organizations for which my consulting firm was developing policies and procedures. Although they do not represent the only organizations for which we did such work, each of them brought to the task an understanding of organizational realities and the desire to create policies and procedures that were flexible and addressed the needs of both their individual organizations and their employees. They did not contribute directly to the writing of this book, but their previous counsel, suggestions, questions, and insights gave this book practicality and relevance.

Also, I wish to acknowledge Rob Kaplan, who is both my friend and agent. As always, he made valuable contributions to my work because of his unique experience in the world of management books, coupled with an outstanding editor's eye. Adrienne Hickey, AMACOM's executive editor, has an unfailing ability to identify the professional needs a book of this type should be meeting, and her friendship and guidance was of considerable assistance, and Mike Sivilli, AMACOM associate editor, again made my manuscript more readable and useful. These three are colleagues in the best sense of the word and ensure that a project such as this is not only successful but also rewarding and enjoyable.

Finally, as I must in every book, I recognize and thank Ruth Long, who carefully reads and corrects my initial drafts.

John H. McConnell

HOW TO DEVELOP

ESSENTIAL HR POLICIES

AND

PROCEDURES

Introduction

"If you can't explain what you are doing in simple English, you are probably doing something wrong."
                                        —ALFRED KAHN

COMMON SENSE WOULD SEEM TO DICTATE the necessity of having written policies and procedures covering all aspects of the employee/organization relationship. "You've got to know the rules to play the game successfully," my high school basketball coach told me. Yet, there are organizations with few or no written policies and procedures. In fact, there are organizations that have never considered developing policies and procedures—written or otherwise. There are organizations with written policies and procedures that read well but have no relationship to the needs of the organization or its employees. There are organizations with elaborate sets of policies and procedures that no one seems to read, let alone follow, and there are organizations that appear to use their policies and procedures primarily as rules for identifying and punishing infractions.

In actuality, policies and procedures serve a number of purposes:

❑ They provide clear communication between the organization and its employees regarding conditions of employment.

❑ They form a basis for treating all employees fairly and equally.

❑ They are a set of guidelines for supervisors and managers.

❑ They create a basis for developing employee handbooks.

❑ They establish a basis for regularly reviewing possible changes affecting employees.

❏ They form a context for supervisor training programs and employee orientation programs.

A CASE STUDY

A number of years ago, my consulting firm was asked to produce a video case study depicting the importance of having and communicating policies and procedures. It was to be part of the organization's management training program. We wanted to produce a case study that was realistic and portrayed how a lack of policies and procedures can contribute to problems for both the organization and its employees, so in our research for the script, we spoke with a number of human resources professionals at several organizations. The final script was based on a type of situation that was described numerous times.

An employee is driving to work, and we hear his thoughts. He is planning on resigning that morning, but as he thinks through the words he will use, they seem to indicate he has not identified exactly why he is taking another job.

When he arrives at his office, he meets with his manager and submits his resignation. The manager is shocked. In the ensuing conversation, the manager refers to the employee as the best worker in the department and attempts to discover the reason for his leaving. As they talk, it becomes apparent there are policies and procedures in place that would have retained the employee, but they were never communicated or followed.

EMPLOYEE OPINION SURVEYS

Over the years, we conducted numerous employee opinion surveys for a variety of organizations. Those surveys used questionnaires, interviews, and focus groups to gain information about employee perceptions of their conditions of employment. One objective of the surveys was to discover what conditions of employment were important to employees, as well as how satisfied they were with all conditions of employment. Employees consistently identified fairness and equal treatment as being of major importance to them. Even at companies experiencing difficult times, employees were willing to accept a great deal of unpleasantness if all were sharing equally in the problems.

MISUNDERSTOOD POLICIES AND PROCEDURES

In this next example, it is interesting to consider how long the existing policies and procedures would have remained in place, and presumably used to make decisions regarding employees, if the development of a training program had not brought them to senior management's attention.

A Cleveland electronics firm hired a consultant to create a training program for newly appointed supervisors. One of the first sessions was to cover the company's policies and procedures. The consultant read the company's published manual and wrote the session.

The consultant's contract required the company's senior management committee to review and approve the contents of each session, so the consultant met with that group and described that session's subject matter.

As he completed his presentation, the company president said, "I'm afraid you're going to have to do a rewrite. Those are not our policies and procedures."

The human resources vice president said, "Yes, they are. He's got them right."

The other vice presidents began to chime in. Some thought they were correct. Some thought they were wrong, and some thought they were only partially correct. The president finally said, "Well, if they are what have just been described, we better change them."

The upshot was the training program was put on hold until all the policies and procedures could be reviewed and rewritten if necessary. In the end, more than 78 percent of the existing policies and procedures received major revisions, 8 percent were canceled as being unrelated to the company, and twelve new policies and procedures were created.

THE OBJECTIVE OF POLICIES AND PROCEDURES

These examples are provided to give some indication of the importance of having a comprehensive set of HR policies and procedures in every organization, no matter what its size. Not every organization has negative experiences such as these. Many have excellent policies and procedures that reflect the needs of the organization, are kept current, are communicated to all employees, and serve as a basis for fair and equal treatment.

Unless you are an independent contributor, working by yourself, you are probably working in some type of organization. Along with you are many different people with many different needs, and many different supervisors. To treat everyone equally and consistently, a set of policies and procedures specifically prepared for your organization is required, and it should be in writing and well communicated.

It is the position of this book that the objective of HR policies and procedures should be to provide clear and consistent statements of the organization's policies regarding all conditions of employment and procedures for their equal and fair implementation. To fulfill this objective, policies and procedures should:

❏ Be clear and specific, but provide adequate flexibility to meet changing conditions.

❏ Comply with all appropriate federal and state laws and regulations.

❏ Agree with one another and reflect an overall fair and equal approach to employees.

THE POLICY AND ITS PROCEDURE

It is important that the procedure should fulfill the policy, and the policy should clearly state the purpose and desire of the organization. Such is not always the case:

The United States Department of Veterans Affairs was formed in 1989, replacing the former Veterans Administration. Both departments credit Abraham Lincoln's Second Inaugural Address with providing their mission: "To care for him who shall have borne the battle and for his widow and orphan."

On a recent visit to one VA office—an office that prominently displayed a framed copy of the mission on its wall—I overheard the interaction between a clerk and a man who appeared to be a veteran submitting some type of application. The clerk said, "Can't you read? You filled the form out wrong. Now, you've got to do it all over again, and if you don't do it right this time, you'll have to do it again."

Somehow, the procedure being implemented did not seem to meet the stated policy.

PURPOSE OF THIS BOOK

Now that we know the objective of HR policies and procedures, what is the purpose of this "how to" book? It was written:

❐ To provide a methodology for identifying an organization's needed HR policies and procedures

❐ To review all elements for consideration in writing those policies and procedures

❐ To provide a format for their construction, review, and updating

What This Book Does

To fulfill that purpose, this book provides you with a methodology to:

❐ Identify the policies and procedures your organization needs.

❐ Collect the information necessary to write each policy and procedure.

❐ Develop a consistent format for all policies and procedures.

❐ Obtain appropriate approvals for each policy and procedure.

❐ Publish, distribute, and communicate all policies and procedures.

❐ Maintain the currency of all policies and procedures, and identify any newly required policies and procedures.

What This Book Does Not Do

Although this book considers all potential HR areas requiring policies and procedures, it is not meant to be a source of what policies and procedures an organization should have. Neither does it identify the best policies and procedures. Those can only be determined by the individual needs and situations of each organization.

This book does not prescribe one set of policies and procedures applicable to all organizations. Just as people differ, so do organizations. Each has its own culture, history, and needs. An organization's policies and procedures must recognize those specific needs and be developed within such a context.

This book cannot cover all details, rationale, strengths, and weaknesses of all conditions of employment to be addressed by policies and procedures. For example, there are numerous types of incentive compensation programs. Which program your organization should have is beyond the scope of this book, but once you have a compensation program, this book will lead you through a review of its elements to include in an appropriate policy and procedure.

Likewise, this book does not attempt to recommend management practices. For example, I have often questioned the appropriateness of using a temporary suspension (such as one week) as "punishment" for excessive absenteeism. (Why use time away from work to correct excessive time away from work?) Yet, many companies have such a practice. For organizations that use that approach, this book assists them in writing the best policy and procedure for it. It does not question the correctness of the approach.

The text does not include policies and procedures for you to copy and use. Rather than require you to make your organization's needs fit a standard format, this book gives you the tools to create policies and procedures to meet those specific needs. For readers who find sample policies and procedures useful, the accompanying disk provides them. These samples may be copied and adapted to fit your requirements.

This book does not require you to use a specific template. Instead, it provides a format as the basis for writing your policies and procedures, but like the policies and procedures themselves, that format must be customized to the requirements of your organization. Some organizations want their policies and procedures written directly to employees using pronouns such as "you" and "we." Others want purely objective statements. Some want separate documents for policies and separate documents for procedures. Others want a single document to describe both. Some want a standard policy for the entire organization with different procedures at different locations, but others want a standard policy and procedure applicable throughout the organization.

This book does not cover policies and procedures for all functional areas of an organization. It is a book for HR policies and procedures. Those required solely for use by other areas, such as legal, finance, marketing, and purchasing, are outside the scope of this book. The only exception is when another function's policy and procedure subject has an HR aspect. For example, a finance policy regarding reimbursement of travel expenses often has HR elements.

This book cannot cover every possible subject for a policy and procedure. For example, a chemical company may have a policy and procedure for employees purchasing used steel drums. That has very little general application, and there are thousands of such unique issues. This book concentrates on subjects that have wide application. Even so, the methodology provided can be used as the basis for developing policies and procedures not specifically covered by this book.

CONDITIONS OF EMPLOYMENT

There are many subjects that can serve as the basis for HR policies and procedures. As already mentioned, some are unique to a specific organization. Some can be treated separately, and others can be combined or grouped with other subjects. The approach used in this book is to develop a set of policies and procedures for the conditions of employment most often requiring them, and to do so in a manner that allows an organization to customize them by grouping or further subdividing the subjects.

Our advisory board identified the following conditions of employment as those most generally requiring policies and procedures:

Conditions of Employment	Examples
Internal Selection	Transfer, promotion, job posting, demotions, changing locations
External Selection	Advertising, applications, interviews, paid expenses, placing a new employee on the payroll, employee referrals, Immigration Reform and Control Act requirements, required forms, orientation, drug tests, physicals, performance and ability testing, use of search firms and employment agen-

	cies, fees, equal opportunity employment, hiring authority
Compensation	Salaries, wages, gain-sharing, commissions, annual reviews, merit increases, general increases, shift compensation, overtime compensation, compensation ranges, position valuation, piecework, bonuses, and all other cash compensation
Benefits	Insurance, including health, accidental death and dismemberment, dental, vision, life, disability, travel, workers compensation, unemployment, long-term care, prescription drug; retirement and pension plans, including contributory, noncontributory, organization contributions, vesting, benefits, retirement age, retirement planning and counseling; cafeteria benefit plans; and all other types of benefits
Terms of Employment	Employment at will, employee classifications, types of employment, employment of relatives, overtime, length of service (i.e., seniority)
Equal and Fair Treatment	Nondiscrimination, sexual harassment, remedies, fair treatment, grievance procedure, legal requirements, bulletin board notices, affirmative action, training
Time Away from Work	Personal days, holidays, vacation, sick days, family leave, paid and unpaid leave, eligibility
Attendance	Lateness, absenteeism, notification, abuse, remedies, guidelines, reporting, penalties for abuse
Training and Development	Tuition reimbursement, organization required, development counseling, individ-

	ual training plans, external seminars, internal meetings, counseling, career pathing, organization-paid training
Performance Evaluation	Standards and/or objectives, reviews, review frequency, record keeping, review factors, employee appeals
Performance Improvement	Positive discipline, progressive steps of discipline, disciplinary actions for misconduct, miscounts requiring immediate discharge, layoffs, recalls, resignations
Grievance Procedure	Steps, appeals, arbitration, representation, filing process
Code of Business Conduct	Gifts, prohibited relationships, external communications, meals, privileged information, publications, dealing with the media, whistle-blower protection

Our advisory board also identified labor relations as a key area, but felt it should not be included in this book. Labor relations are governed by many laws and regulations, and the resulting policies and procedures are the outcome of negotiations.

Although the board identified several other important subjects, they are not treated at length here because they are not formally established in the majority of organizations. These subjects are dealt with in Chapter 22 on Other Policies and Procedures.

CONTENTS

The major part of this book is divided into four sections. Each part, along with its chapters, is outlined below.

Part 1—Getting Started

Chapter 1: A Process for Developing a Comprehensive Set of Human Resources Policies and Procedures

Chapter 2: Identifying the Policies and Procedures Your Organization Requires

The disk accompanying this book contains all of the forms introduced in the chapters and a sample set of human resources policies and procedures—including some additional subjects not covered in the chapters. The forms on the CD are available for you to copy and use as is, or to revise to better meet your organization's requirements.

All policies and procedures in the book come from actual organizations. Some have been edited to remove identifying information.

TIME TO START

So that's what this book is all about. When you complete it, you will have identified the policies and procedures your organization requires and thoroughly reviewed any existing policies and procedures. And you'll have a plan and the ability to develop and administer a comprehensive set of policies and procedures.

So, with all that said, let's begin.

Getting Started

1

A Process for Developing a Comprehensive Set of Human Resources Policies and Procedures

"If you don't know where you are going, you will probably end up somewhere else."

—LAURENCE J. PETER

THIS CHAPTER INTRODUCES AN OVERALL PROCESS for developing a comprehensive set of human resources policies and procedures for your organization. The following chapters will describe each step of that process in detail.

First a few definitions for some of the terms used in this book:

DEFINITIONS

Organization. The overall entity—a company, government department, or division.

Human Resources. The function within the organization (no matter what its title) that is accountable for obtaining and maintaining a qualified productive workforce.

Senior Managers. Regardless of actual titles, the top management positions within the organization accountable for establishing the direction of the organization, its mission, strategic plan, and overall objectives.

Manager. Regardless of actual titles, any employee accountable for directing a function of the organization and/or has supervisors and managers reporting to it.

Supervisor. Regardless of actual titles, any individual accountable for directing the employees performing the actual work of a function or of the organization.

Management. All employees who function as senior managers, managers, and supervisors.

Employees. All people employed by the organization.

Conditions of Employment. All elements governing the relationship between the organization and its employees.

Policy. A statement of the organization's position regarding a specific condition of employment—what the organization believes is the correct approach to fulfilling that condition of employment. For example, the following are policy statements:

> "To treat all employees equally with respect to selection and promotions."

> "To pay employees 10 percent above the surveyed compensation rate for similar jobs in the community."

Procedure. The methods for accomplishing—or implementing—a policy. For example, if a policy provides all employees with two weeks' vacation each calendar year, the procedure would describe specific elements and actions such as:

- Eligibility for full vacation
- Eligibility for less than full vacation
- How to request specific time-off for vacation (e.g., identifying any required forms)
- Pay for the vacation time-off
- Conflict resolution when two or more employees request the same time-off period
- Pay in lieu of vacation
- Resolution of unused vacation days
- Identification of persons authorized to implement the elements of the procedure

Some organizations publish separate books or documents for these two items—one for the organization policies and another for organization procedures. In this book, a policy and its procedure will be presented in the same document to assist in ensuring the correct relationship is maintained.

An Ohio firm had a policy of promotion from within whenever possible. At one of its locations, all job opportunities were announced, and employees were allowed to apply for them. If no employee applied or none were qualified, an external search was begun.

At a second location of the same company, the management team reviewed its personnel files and decided whether one or more employees were qualified for the open position. If there were qualified employees, they were contacted for interviews. If there were none, an external search was begun.

Same company. Same policy. Two different procedures.

SUBJECTS FOR POLICIES AND PROCEDURES

Subjects for policies and procedures are basically classified as conditions of employment. However, they can also be grouped according to how they are identified as needed by the organization. For example:

❏ Mandated policies and procedures
❏ Recognized as needing policies and procedures
❏ Changes requiring policies and procedures

Mandated Policies and Procedures

These are subjects for which policies and procedures are required by federal, state, and local laws and regulations; by contracts; by memberships; and by licenses. For example, most organizations are required by law to have a formal policy and procedure regarding nondiscrimination in making employment decisions.

Contractual arrangements, memberships, and licenses may also require certain policies and procedures. For example, a pharmaceutical packaging firm had to develop a procedure regarding a certain type of compensation in order to meet a customer contract requirement. Another company had to provide specific employee benefit procedures to meet membership requirements in an industry association, and a license it was granted to provide certain products stipulated specific employee travel reimbursements procedures.

The common element is that these policies and procedures were all required by an external source, and such requirements usually are ones that have to be met. In these situations, failure to have and implement the required policies and procedures can lead to substantial costs, from fines to the loss of contracts, licenses, and memberships.

A Georgia insurance company had an overtime policy that allowed customer service telephone representatives to work overtime (over forty hours in one week) without pay. The employees "banked" their overtime hours to be used during the year for additional time-off with pay. The manager of the department initiating the policy and procedure claimed it was necessary to allow employees to complete telephone calls that occurred near the end of a shift. He also said it was good for morale and, at a department meeting, the employees agreed to this approach.

Approximately one year after initiating the practice, the manager discharged an employee for poor performance. The employee filed a complaint with the Department of Labor, claiming he had been required to work overtime without overtime (time and a half) compensation. The Department of Labor conducted an audit of the company and decided the employee was correct. The company's practice was in violation of U.S. law since the employee was classified as a nonexempt employee (i.e., nonexempt from the overtime pay requirements of the Wage and Hour Law).

The employee received back pay. All employees who had worked overtime under this practice received back pay. The company was instructed to discontinue the practice, and it received a significant fine.

Recognized as Needing Policies and Procedures

Subjects identified by the organization as requiring policies and procedures may, in some instances, already be written and published. In other cases, they may not exist as policies and procedures, but are covered by some other type of document. The important point is that they have been recognized as needed.

Surprisingly, some companies have published employee handbooks but no organizational policies and procedures. In effect, those handbooks are the only statements of the company's policies and procedures regarding conditions of employment.

A small conveyor manufacturer in Florida operated with no formal policies and procedures. Its president felt such an approach limited the company's ability to treat each employee as an individual. However, the company gave all newly hired employees a copy of the handbook that described their employment conditions.

A discharged employee filed a complaint against the company for discrimination. In the ensuing hearing, the handbook was accepted as representing the company's formal policy statement regarding discharges, and the company's actions were found in breach of that policy.

Changes Requiring Policies and Procedures

There are other subjects for which policies and procedures are identified as needed because of some type of change. A change in local regulations is one example. The point is that something has occurred that requires a new policy and procedure or the revision of an existing one. A new fringe benefit may require a new or revised benefits policy and procedure. A new contract may require a new or revised policy and procedure to comply with its terms.

Sometimes it is not a change or revision that's needed. Instead, it is the recognition of a requirement previously overlooked. For example, an exiting employee may give information that identifies a policy and procedure that is required to eliminate conflicting operations practices. Often these types of subject needs are identified through:

❐ Changes in jobs and/or systems
❐ Addition of new equipment
❐ Department performance reviews
❐ Employee opinion surveys, organizational studies, department meetings, and focus groups
❐ Exit interviews conducted with departing employees

Changes resulting from laws and regulations generally are subjects that mandate policies and procedures. For example, when the Occupational Safety and Health Administration (OSHA) was enacted, many employers had to revise their safety rules to meet the act's requirements.

Sometimes, on examination, subjects can turn out to be individual employee or department training needs rather than organizational ones and do not require an organization policy and procedure. It is still important to know about them.

A supervisor at a Philadelphia-based insurance company disagreed with the company's policy on paying overtime, so she wrote a separate one for her own department, but her policy was known only to the employees in her department.

Although the supervisor did not know it, her policy was in violation of the U.S. Wage and Hour Law, as well as company policy. By accident, the human resources director discovered the policy and immediately had it revised. The result was a thorough survey of the company to discover if any other such policies existed. The HR director was astounded by the number that were identified.

YOUR OBJECTIVE

Before examining the development process, let's consider your motivation and objective. If you are reading this book, you probably have an interest in creating or reviewing a set of HR policies and procedures for your organization. Perhaps you work in human resources and have recognized a need. Perhaps you have received an assignment from senior management, or perhaps you inherited an ongoing project. Whatever the initial motivation, you have an assignment, and as with all management tasks, the place to start is with an objective. What is it you want to accomplish?

In the book's Introduction, the objective for HR policies and procedures was stated as follows:

To provide clear and consistent statements of the organization's policies regarding all conditions of employment and procedures for their equal and fair implementation.

However, whatever prompted you to begin a review of your organization's policies and procedures may add to the original objective. It may even conflict with that objective. It is important that you recognized exactly what it is you are attempting to accomplish. Therefore, before beginning, see if you can clearly state your objective. State what you believe to be your objective in one sentence, beginning with the word "to." For example:

"To provide standard policies and procedures for managing employees."

"To ensure the organization meets all of its legal requirements with respect to its employees."

"To respond to employees concerns about a lack of consistent policies and procedures."

"To update existing policies and procedures."

Actually, these examples lack two of the conditions an objective should have. An objective should include a *measure* and a *time*. Take the last example: "To update existing policies and procedures." By inserting the word "all," the objective now contains a measure. By adding "by March 1," the objective has a time frame. The finished objective then reads as follows:

To update all existing policies and procedures by March 1.

If possible, always add a measure and time requirement to your objective. Then be sure that whoever gave you the assignment, or whomever you report to, agrees with the objective.

These examples are not necessarily the most appropriate ones for your organization, but they illustrate a point: You must understand what it is you are attempting to accomplish. However, this does not prohibit you from recommending another objective or making revisions to the one you have. If you are having difficulty identifying your objective, and including a measure and a time, you need to stop and clarify what it is you are attempting to do. Once that is accomplished, you are ready to begin. So let's turn our attention to a process for accomplishing your objective.

THE PROCESS

The process to develop a set of HR policies and procedures is like any other management process:

❑ Establish a clear objective (quantifiable with a time).

❑ Develop a plan to accomplish the objective.

❑ Implement the plan and ensure the results conform to both the plan and the objective.

Once you have established an objective to either review your organization's current policies and procedures or to develop a comprehensive set of new HR policies and procedures, you have taken the first action necessary to begin this management activity. With an objective established, you can move on to developing a plan for achieving that objective—determining the what, who, and when.

What Needs to Be Done?

The "what" of your plan for creating a comprehensive set of policies and procedures (or updating current ones) is to identify the tasks required to accomplish your objective. Those tasks, once identified, should be placed in an order for implementation. Basically, the tasks and their sequence are:

1. Identify a prioritized list of the policies and procedures your organization needs and obtain approval for their development and a development sequence.

2. Develop a policy statement for each identified subject and obtain approval for it.

3. Develop a procedure for each approved policy and obtain approval for it.

4. Publish and communicate the completed and approved policies and procedures.

5. Establish a process for a regular review of existing policies and procedures.

Each of the above tasks has subtasks, and those will be dealt with in subsequent chapters. However, these general statements of the tasks to accomplish in your plan provide a basis for identifying "who" should be assigned "what."

Who Does What?

The tasks of the project require several key assignments:

- ❏ Who is in charge?
- ❏ Who does the work?
- ❏ Who approves the work?
- ❏ Who publishes the completed policies and procedures?

Who's in Charge?

This project, like any other, needs someone in charge—someone accountable for its successful completion. Since you are reading this book, you may be that person. If you are, you must determine who fulfills the balance of the tasks. If your organization is relatively small, if you do not require a great number of new policies and procedures, or if you have considerable time to complete the assignment, you may be able to perform most of the tasks yourself. However, it is more likely that you will need to have the assistance of others. One approach is to form a team of those people who will perform the actual development work and identify a committee to approve the work completed.

Who Does the Work?

Gathering the necessary information and then writing the policies and procedures may require considerable time. Depending on the completion time for the project, you may have to delegate individual policies and procedures to other people. Those individuals, in effect, become a team for the project.

The team could be composed of HR people and/or representatives from various functional areas of the organization. Together you can design the project, process, and final formats. Then each person can be assigned a specific number of policies and procedures to develop. When completed, they are reviewed by the entire team. An additional benefit of creating a team is the advice and assistance that different people can provide—not only for the policies and procedures they are individually assigned, but also for the policies and procedures being developed by all team members.

Who Approves the Work?

So, who has final approval of the developed policies and procedures? Good question. This assignment has to be established at the beginning of the project. Generally, there is a senior management group accountable for approvals. Often it is an existing group (possibly the group that initially assigned you the project), and this task merely becomes an additional assignment for it. Some organizations require their boards of directors to approve HR policies and procedures.

Establishing a comprehensive set of HR policies and procedures is a significant management activity. It describes exactly how the organization will interact with its employees, which affects morale, hiring, retention, and even potential legal situations. It is such an important activity with such far-reaching implications that senior management should always be involved.

There are several others who may not give final approval but who should be involved before submission for final approval. Because of the legal implications and requirements of many policy and procedure subjects, either your organization's legal department or an external labor lawyer should review all proposed policies and procedures. Legal counsel should provide approvals, compliance advice, and recommendations, or raise any areas of concern and any possible problems. Approval should also be obtained from those who will be administering the policies and procedures, since these individuals can assess how practical they are and identify areas of potential abuse and problems.

A Michigan firm hired a local college professor to develop a new set of HR policies and procedures. He submitted them for approval to a senior management committee. The committee approved them, and the new policies and procedures were published. However, the professor had never reviewed the drafts with the supervisors who had to administer them.

When the supervisors received the newly published policies and procedures, they immediately recognized several that would not work as written, but since they had been left out of the development process, they elected to practice malicious obedience. "If that's what they want us to do, that's what we'll do," was their attitude.

The supervisors implemented the policies and procedures exactly as written. Problems developed. The policies and procedures had to be withdrawn and rewritten—this time with supervisory involvement.

Members of the approval group should have a wide range of knowledge of the organization so they can correctly evaluate and approve policies and procedures. Another consideration is their credibility. Employees will want to have confidence that the policies and procedures were developed by appropriate and knowledgeable people representing all areas of the organization and all functions.

Whatever approach you select for getting approvals, it is important to establish it in advance of the project.

Who Publishes the Completed Policies and Procedures?

Once the policies and procedures have been written and approved, they have to be published and communicated to all employees. Since these are HR policies and procedures, that activity normally is assigned to someone in human resources. Whoever is to be accountable should be aware of the assignment early in the process and, ideally, involved in the process. This person will also need to maintain a record of the policy and procedure development and any decisions and changes made that may require revisions.

Actual publication may use different formats for different employees. Management may receive a manual containing the actual documents. Employees may receive a handbook covering the policies and procedures but not the actual documents. Whatever format is used, some type of communication and/or training must accompany the distribution.

When Is the Work to Be Completed?

A completion time for the entire project should have been established as a part of the project's objective. Now that you have identified specific tasks and accountabilities, you need to assign a completion time to each task, and those deadlines must contribute to the entire project being completed on time.

If your objective is to revise existing policies and procedures, it will probably take less time than starting from scratch. If you have just one location, it will take less time than multiple locations demand. If you have a group of people working on the project, it will take less time than attempting to do everything yourself.

Most of the time required to complete the individual tasks is taken up by gathering the necessary information. Writing the policies and procedures, once you have the information, is generally not as time-consuming. However, obtaining the necessary approvals can sometimes be lengthy.

A plastics manufacturer in New Jersey decided it needed a set of policies and procedures. The company employed a person to perform that job on a temporary basis over the course of one year. The company had identified fourteen policies and procedures to develop—a task that was considered doable within the time frame.

Seven years later, this person was still employed (although her assignment was now human resources manager), but only 60 percent of the policies and procedures had been written. Why?

It took her longer than expected to obtain information about current company practices, but the real holdup was obtaining approval. On average, the senior management group took four months to approve a policy and procedure, with an average rewrite request requiring another month.

You are going to have to use what you know about the organization, the number of people assigned to the tasks, the amount of time each person can give, the number of policies and procedures to write, and the approval process to estimate individual task completion times. Keep in mind the necessity to complete the entire project by its due date.

You now have a plan. You have determined the what, who, and when. Now it's time to implement the tasks of the plan.

IDENTIFYING THE POLICIES AND PROCEDURES YOUR ORGANIZATION NEEDS

This first task is basically one of research and information gathering. What is required is a thorough knowledge of current practices, existing policies and procedures or other documents, mandated policies and procedures, and the direction the organization wants to pursue.

This activity should generate a list of subjects for policies and procedures, and those subjects should be prioritized in order of organization need. The prioritization also becomes the order for their development—that is, the most needed policy and procedure is developed first. When that list is approved, you have a schedule and can move on to the actual development.

WRITING THE POLICIES AND OBTAINING THEIR APPROVAL

Since the policy serves as a guide for the procedure, it is prudent to first develop the policy and have it approved before beginning to write the procedure. However, in identifying the needed policies and procedures, you most likely obtained some of the information required to write both.

A human resources manager at a utility company in Wisconsin was assigned the task of writing several policies and procedures. She gathered the necessary information, developed a sequence, and had it approved. She then began the actual writing of the policies and procedures.

Because she had a relative short time frame to complete the project, she wrote a policy and its procedure at the same time and submitted them for approval. Unfortunately, the management committee approving the work did not agree with the policy statement she had written. After considerable discussion, they wrote a new policy statement that made the already-written procedure unworkable.

WRITING THE PROCEDURES AND OBTAINING THEIR APPROVAL

Once a policy is approved, you can write the procedure to implement it. Using a standard format can simplify this task. When a policy is approved prior to writing the procedure and the appropriate information is obtained regarding implementation, approval of the procedure is also generally easy. However, make sure that the proper management is involved in the development and/or approval. You do not want to issue a policy and procedure and later discover it was incorrect.

PUBLISHING AND COMMUNICATING THE POLICIES AND PROCEDURES

In some cases, you may want to publish individual policies and procedures as they are written and approved. Other times you may want to wait and publish the complete set after they are all approved. Whatever the case, this step places the policies and procedures in the hands of those who will be implementing them. These individuals should also receive whatever training in their use is required. In most cases, it is the supervisors and managers of employees who are doing the actual administration, so they will require the fullest communication. In addition, all employees need to know about new policies and procedures and the impact they may have on them.

ESTABLISHING A PROCESS FOR REGULARLY REVIEWING POLICIES AND PROCEDURES

As previously noted, sometimes policies and procedures must be revised to deal with changes in the business environment or within the organization. Therefore, you need a system for regular and comprehensive reviews, including a method for retaining decisions made throughout the period that are not covered by the existing policy and procedure. For example:

An Illinois firm had a policy and procedure covering overtime. The policy was to offer equal amounts of overtime to all employees.

One employee was away from work due to illness for three months. When he returned, he felt that, under the policy, he should be given the first opportunities of working overtime until he caught up with the balance of the department. His supervisor referred to the policy and procedure, but it did not address that issue.

Eventually, a decision was jointly made by the supervisor, department manager, and human resources manager that an employee who is away from work for any reason is not to be considered for overtime during that period.

The human resources manager made a record of this decision. The next year a similar question developed. The record was referred to and a decision made that was consistent with the previous one. The next year the policy and procedure came up for review. It was revised to include the decisions made since its last rewriting and publication.

CONCLUSION

This chapter overviewed a process for developing a set of HR policies and procedures for your organization. The next chapter deals in detail with the first task of that process: identifying a prioritized list of the policies and procedures your organization needs and obtaining approval for their creation and a development sequence.

2

Identifying the Policies and Procedures Your Organization Requires

"The first step to finding something is knowing where to look."
—John Lubbock, quoted by Peter Porter

THE FIRST TASK OF THE PROCESS is to identify what policies and procedures your organization requires. This means considering the subjects from all three categories:

❐ Mandated policies and procedures
❐ Recognized as needing policies and procedures
❐ Changes requiring policies and procedures

It also means contacting appropriate people within your organization to obtain the necessary information. Usually, to identify requisite policies and procedures, you need input from a variety of sources, and that type of information gathering works best when you have a starting list of subjects to be considered. Even if the subjects on the list are not those in the final completed list, they serve as anchor points to begin the review process.

There are two basic approaches to developing a starting list. Which approach to use depends on whether your organization has an existing set of HR policies and procedures. If it does, they provide a starting point. If not, you have to create a starting point. You could begin by just asking managers what they feel should be covered, but generally, it is easier for them to provide information when you can give them an initial list.

In any event, once you have a list, you may need to add to it. If you are in human resources, you may have knowledge of additional subjects and other existing policies and procedures requiring revisions. You may know of new laws that mandate policies and procedures. You may have records of internal problems that can be corrected by having a policy and procedure. You may know of policies and procedures that are no longer applicable. Whatever the case, if you have such knowledge, you need to add those subjects to your list.

EXISTING POLICIES AND PROCEDURES

If your organization has an existing set of policies and procedures (even if it is not a complete set of the ones required), they provide a basis from which you can work. You can then obtain information about how well they are meeting the organization's needs, as well as what revisions and additional policies and procedures are required. The first thing to do, then, is make a list of any existing policies and procedures and/or subject matter.

You can use the titles of the policies and procedures, but in some cases you may have to add additional descriptions. For example, to understand exactly what a policy and procedure titled Employee Classifications covers, you might need explanations for the following terms:

- ❏ Exempt/Nonexempt
- ❏ Salaried/Hourly
- ❏ Senior Management/Management/Supervision/Nonmanagement
- ❏ Part-Time
- ❏ Full-Time
- ❏ Permanent
- ❏ Temporary
- ❏ Hourly
- ❏ Union Represented

Whenever policies and procedures deal with several subjects not completely identified in their titles, you need to explain. As another example, assume a policy and procedure titled Time-Off Pay covered vacations, holidays, and sick days. You probably want to identify these sub-subjects; however, they do not have to be listed as separate subjects. Instead, you can list the main subject followed by an explanation, as such:

Time-Off Pay—Includes vacations, holidays, and sick days.

There may be files or records of problems that have been encountered in the administration of existing policies and procedures. These problems may require revisions or additions. Also, situations may have developed that are not covered by the existing policies and procedures. If decisions had to be made to rectify those situations, you need to know about them, and the omissions that caused them, so that a revised policy and procedure can address them.

A Questionnaire

Once you have an initial list, you can use it to survey the organization to determine the effectiveness and importance of the subjects. Figure 2-1 is an HR policy and procedure review form. It can be used for such a survey (it is available on the accompanying disk for you to copy and use).

The form consists of three parts. For question one, you list existing policy and procedure subjects in the first column. The second column is for those being surveyed to rate the effectiveness of each of these policies and procedures. Question two asks the people you are surveying to identify subjects required but not currently in existence as policies and procedures and to rate their importance to the organization. The third question asks you to list any policies and procedures that may be required during the next year. Responses to these three questions provide initial input for the three types of subjects (i.e., mandatory, recognized as needed, and changes requiring policies and procedures).

NO EXISTING POLICIES AND PROCEDURES

If your organization does not currently have a set of HR policies and procedures, you need to take a slightly different approach, but you still need to develop a starting list and create a similar questionnaire. In that situation, you are asking recipients of the questionnaires to identify what

Figure 2-1. HR policies and procedures review (existing policies and procedures).

To: _____

Our organization is currently reviewing its existing policies and procedures to determine their effectiveness and identify any changes that are required. Your input will be of considerable assistance in this effort, so please answer the following questions and return the completed form to _____ by_____.

1. Listed below are the current human resources policies and procedures by subject. Indicate how satisfied you are with the effectiveness of each by placing a number on the appropriate line in the column following the title. Use a nine-point scale to indicate satisfaction: 1 = Not Satisfied; 5 = Satisfied; 9 = Very Satisfied. You may use all the numbers on the scale between these anchor points. Do not use fractions or decimals.

Policy and Procedure	Satisfaction with Effectiveness
_____	_____
_____	_____
_____	_____
_____	_____
_____	_____
_____	_____
_____	_____
_____	_____
_____	_____
_____	_____
_____	_____
_____	_____
_____	_____
_____	_____
_____	_____

2. List below any additional subjects you feel require HR policies and procedures. After you have listed them, rate the subjects according to how important you feel it is for them to be policies and procedures. Again, use a nine-point scale, but this time: 1 = Not Necessary; 5 = Important; 9 = Very Important. You may use all the numbers on the scale between these anchor points. Do not use fractions or decimals.

Subject	Importance
_____	_____
_____	_____
_____	_____

_____ _____

_____ _____

_____ _____

_____ _____

_____ _____

_____ _____

_____ _____

_____ _____

_____ _____

_____ _____

3. What additional policy and procedure requirements may develop within the next year?

_____

_____

_____

_____

_____

_____

_____

policies and procedures they believe are required. However, a starting list still makes the task much easier for those asked to supply information. Actually, there are several sources to assist you in developing a starting list of subjects.

Recommendations

Perhaps a consultant has suggested certain topics to you, or your organization's labor attorney has made recommendations. Both can be valuable sources you should consider. Also, you may have received an initial list of subjects from whoever gave you this assignment.

Internal Records

Review any existing records that may identify needed subjects. For example, if your organization has a disciplinary procedure and/or employee grievance procedure, examine what subject areas seem to be the sources of misunderstandings. Results of employee opinion surveys may also identify areas requiring improved understanding. Exit interviews, too, can reveal what's not working. Key questions to ask when reviewing records are:

❐ What issues developed that required decisions?

❐ What problems occurred between supervisors and employees?

❐ What complaints and grievances were filed?

❐ What questions did employees ask about conditions of employment?

❐ What misunderstandings were identified?

All of these are probable sources of subjects required for a policy and procedure manual.

Conditions of Employment

Consider each of the major conditions of employment and note what subjects within each would apply to your organization. The list of subjects from the Introduction to this book is one such source. These conditions of employment are listed below, with a few additions:

❐ External Selection

❐ Internal Selection

❐ Compensation

❐ Benefits

❐ Training and Development

❐ Performance Evaluation

❐ Grievance Procedures

❐ Equal and Fair Treatment

❐ Performance Improvement

❐ Time Away from Work

❐ Attendance

❐ Rules and Regulations

❐ Travel and Entertainment

❐ Safety and Health

❐ Security

❐ Information Technology

❐ Code of Business Conduct

❐ Terms of Employment

❑ Employee Relocation

❑ Labor Relations

Information-Gathering Questionnaire

Figure 2-2 is an information-gathering questionnaire that can be used when there are no existing policies and procedures. (It is also available on the accompanying disk.) The form is similar to the one used when there are existing policies and procedures. However, this form has only two parts: one to list and rate possible subjects, and one to identify subjects that may become necessary during the next year. Responses will still provide input for all three categories of subjects.

Enter your starting list in the first column of Part 1. If you already have some policies and procedures, list them first with a note stating they currently exist. If you use all the available lines for your list, add additional lines (at least ten) to the end of the list.

CONDUCTING THE SURVEY

When the questionnaire (whichever version) is prepared, you can send it to the appropriate people for completion. You can mail or e-mail it, or if you have a programmer available, it can be offered as an online questionnaire for completion.

Who needs to complete the questionnaire? Usually it is sent to senior management, operating management, and human resources. Some organizations also survey their employees.

Senior Management

Senior management is where you should start because this group has overall accountability for the organization and its direction. Senior managers may not be able to provide specific topics, but they can identify the major areas where they believe policies and procedures should exist.

If senior management provided you with an initial list at the time you received the assignment, you already have input from them. If not, you need to capture their perceptions of what is required. However, keep in mind that this group will most likely be approving your final list of policies and procedures.

Figure 2-2. HR policies and procedures review (no existing policies and procedures).

To: _____

Our organization is currently in the process of developing a comprehensive set of human resources policies and procedures for our organization. When completed, it will provide guidelines for the correct administration of all conditions of employment. Your input will be of considerable assistance in this effort. Please answer the following questions and return the completed form to _____ by _____.

1. Listed below are several subjects for a set of human resources policies and procedures. The list is not exhaustive. The subjects merely serve as a starting point. Review the list and then add, on the available lines, any additional subjects you feel our organization requires.

Once you have listed all subjects you think are required, rate the importance of each for our organization. Use a nine-point scale to indicate their importance: 1 = Not Important; 5 = Important; 9 = Very Important. You may use all the numbers on the scale between these anchor points. Do not use fractions or decimals.

Policy and Procedure   **Importance**

2. What policy and procedure requirements may develop within the next year?

_____

_____

_____

_____

_____

_____

_____

_____

_____

Operating Management

Operating management (i.e., managers and supervisors below the senior level) generally has a more detailed set of needs. They are the ones constantly interacting with employees, so they have knowledge and experience and know what areas require coverage.

In most cases, these two management groups (particularly the ones actually managing/supervising employees) are your best sources of information. They know what is working and what is not, and they know what is needed. An important by-product of involving operating managers is that they perceive they are part of the improvement process.

Human Resources

Like supervisors, human resources is involved in the administration of the subjects that require policies and procedures. If you are in the HR department, you already have experience and knowledge of what areas need to be covered, so you should identify what those are. If you are not in the HR function, then be sure to solicit information from someone who is. The HR department also usually retains records of problems associated with conditions of employment.

Other Functional Areas

Although human resources is the most likely source of information, you should survey other functional areas of the organization as well—for example, finance, purchasing, travel, and legal departments. Actually, some organizations make it a practice to contact every functional area.

Employees

Employees other than those in management have information, but it is somewhat more difficult to obtain. Employees tend to perceive things in terms of their individual needs rather than those of the entire organization. Even so, they can provide some insight into problem areas.

Other Information Sources

So far we have considered internal sources of information. There are other sources—many external to the organization—that can suggest additional areas to consider. You can simultaneously seek out these sources while surveying the people in the organization.

Experts

As previously mentioned, consultants and labor attorneys can be helpful. If your organization uses a human resources consultant, contact the consultant. This contact has knowledge of your organization and may have already submitted a recommend list of subjects and/or revisions.

Every organization should have a relationship with a labor attorney. The attorney can be someone in private practice or an internal function (department) within your organization. Whatever the relationship, a labor attorney may not be able to identify all subjects you need to cover, but at least you will receive information on those subjects you are mandated to cover.

Other Organizations

Other organizations can be an excellent source of information. Not only can they provide insights into what areas they identified as important, they can also contribute to your development of specific procedures.

Many organizations will allow you to read their policies and procedures manual. Some will even provide you a copy. In addition, industry groups or associations may be able to offer a sample policy and procedure manual or a list of topics obtained from a review of members' manuals. Often these associations collect such information from member organizations in the same industry and make it available to all.

Books and Publications

There are numerous books covering these HR topics. In some cases, you will find books dealing with a single subject, such as compensation or performance evaluation. General management and human resources books will cover many, if not all, topics. HR journals often include articles on policies and procedures, so a review of the available literature may also provide additional insight.

CHOOSING A SURVEY FORMAT

The format we have been considering is a questionnaire, but that is not the only one that can be used. Individual interviews and meetings are also an excellent way of gathering information.

Interviews

Interviews are very effective because you are able to collect questionnaire information and also explore the thinking behind the responses. You can ask additional questions to better understand the answers you receive.

To be successful, an interview should be planned and the question areas identified in advance. Completing a questionnaire with a starting list accomplishes much of that for you. Then you identify who needs to be interviewed.

In advance of the interview, the starting list subjects are written on small (3″ × 5″) index cards—one subject per card. These are given to the interviewee, and the interviewee is asked to arranged them on a table in order of importance. Once that is accomplished, the interviewee is asked what additional subjects are required, and the interviewer writes those subjects on separate cards. The interviewee is then allowed to insert the cards in their appropriate places. A record is then made of the sequence.

The final step is for the interviewee to rate the importance of each subject to the organization. The nine-point scale from the questionnaires (Figures 2-1 and 2-2) can be used. Other times, the interviewee is requested to place the cards in three piles—Not Important, Important, and Very Important. The interview concludes with the interviewer asking any questions about the interviewee's rating of subjects.

Although effective, individual interviews are more time-consuming than questionnaires (averaging one hour per interview), so they are only practical if you have relatively few people to survey. They also require someone with the necessary interviewing skills.

A more traditional interview approach is explained next.

Who to Interview

In most cases, you want to interview someone who has knowledge and experience in dealing with the subjects a set of HR policies and procedures covers. Generally, these people are managers and supervisors of nonmanagement employees. Senior managers can provide information, but their input is usually not as practical as what operating management can contribute. A mix of both types of interviews can be quite productive, however.

If the interviews are to be your sole or a major source of information, you want to interview enough people from enough areas to provide a full range of information. How many is enough? It's hard to say. To a large extent, it depends on the total size of the populations you are targeting, the managers' availability, and the number of separate locations you have to cover.

For example, if you have ten operating managers, you can easily interview all ten. However, if you have fifty managers, in several locations and working different schedules, you probably only want to interview a representative sample. The question then becomes how many, and who should be in the sample?

There are formulas, available in most statistics books, for determining a valid sample size. The main consideration is that you have a large enough sample to ensure the results represent the entire group. Figure 2-3 is one approach to sample size.

Figure 2-3. Sample size table.

Total Population	Sample Size
11–20	4–6
21–50	6–10
51–100	10–20
100 +	15 per 100

Once you have determined the number to represent the total, you next need a system for selecting the ones to make up the sample. If your organization has several locations, you need to divide the population and sample size by the number of locations and treat each separately. A random sample approach can then be used.

Creating a random sample is a technique for attempting to ensure the sample represents the entire population. This is accomplished by selecting sample participants randomly; that is, not using any predetermined criteria. A simple way of doing this is to write each person's name on a small card, place all the cards in a container, mix them, and then draw the required number of cards. A more professional method is to use a random numbers table.

To use a random numbers table, first assign a number to each person in the population. Start with one and then number them consecutively. Locate a random numbers table in a statistics book. If your total population is fifty and you are going to have a sample of fifteen, use the first fifteen numbers in the table: 17, 5, 33, 24, 8, 47, 13, 39, 43, 17, 35, 7, 27, 3, and 29. The fifteen people with those assigned numbers become your sample.

Interview Questions

Base the interview questions on the questionnaires already developed, but be prepared to also ask follow-up and clarification questions such as:

❏ What has caused this policy and procedure to require revisions?

❏ What makes this subject an important one for a new policy and procedure?

Questions should not be answerable in one word. If they are, it puts you in the position of having to push for an explanation. So, instead of asking, "Do you feel the current policy and procedure is too strict?" you might ask: "How would you change the current policy and procedure to make it more effective?"

The first question will only prompt a yes or no answer, and that type of answer provides little useful information. The second question not only solicits more information in the answer, but also creates the basis for a follow-up question. Do not use questions that communicate a desired answer. For example:

> Our company's president believes that employees should not be paid for their first day of absence due to illness. How do you feel about that?

Chances are people will agree with the president even if they think employees should be paid for their first day of illness.

You may discover that the interviewee has completely different objectives for the policies and procedures than you have. Even so, your role in the interview is to be objective. Don't argue. Accept the information given. Your role is to identify the subjects required for policies and procedures, not defend those the interviewee does not perceive as helpful.

Often such interviews can clear up misunderstandings as well as provide information. Whatever the case, you may want to conclude the meeting by telling the interviewee what happens next:

❏ Are you going to interview other involved managers?

❏ Are you going to put together a starting list of subjects and question other managers?

❏ Are you going to use input from your interviews as a basis for meetings?

❏ Will the interviewee be told the final outcome of this information-gathering process?

Whatever the case, tell all interviewees what you will do next and when they will be advised of the results.

Who Conducts the Interview

Ideally, the person conducting the interview should be perceived as positive, neutral, nonthreatening, and interested. In addition, the interviewer should be someone with knowledge about the organization's conditions of employment and any existing policies and procedures.

Meetings

Meetings also provide additional information and are highly effective, but like interviews, they require more time to conduct than questionnaires.

However, meetings offer an advantage: They allow sharing and discussion among information providers. This often speeds the entire process.

The following portion of this chapter is a detailed approach for conducting an information-gathering meeting. The questionnaire that you have already developed is used as the basis for the meeting.

General Considerations

Meetings allow participants to share opinions and question assumptions. The product is usually a list far more representative of the organization's needs than a single person might provide. However, meetings require more time than a mailed questionnaire. Generally, such a meeting runs between one and one-half to two hours.

The ideal size for a meeting of this type is six to fifteen people. More than twenty people makes it difficult to have a discussion. If there are that many participants, separate, smaller meetings are better. One or two meetings might include everyone, but if it is a larger number of people, or they are at several locations, the number of required meetings may escalate and become impractical. To determine who and how many should participate in a meeting, consider the same factors and methods suggested for interviews.

The people in a single meeting should have the same general degree of information and accountability for implementation of policies and procedures. If you are seeking information for a single organization location, the meeting participants should all be from that location. If you are seeking information regarding implementation of an attendance and punctuality policy and procedure, then participants should be those supervisors and managers accountable for implementing the policy and procedure.

If you are surveying different types of employees, such as employees of different organizational levels, different locations, and different job classifications, do not mix them in the same meeting. This is particularly true for mixing management and nonmanagement employees and employees with a reporting relationship. You also should consider any major differences that may exist between people and departments. If you know of mixed opinions among managers (e.g., some favoring a policy and procedure and some opposed), invite them all to a separate meeting to resolve the differing perceptions and discover any related problems.

At times, HR and financial employees and a labor attorney may be added to a group. These people can bring another dimension to the discussions. If you include HR representatives, be sure there are at least two in a group.

A conference atmosphere is most productive. Set up a square or U-shaped table with chairs around. The room should be private, and to limit interruptions, remove the telephone from the room. This format tends to promote discussion. You will also need a pencil and pad for each participant, a chart pad (two is better) with markers, and masking tape for posting charts on the wall.

Once you have established a location, date, and time, and selected participants, you need to notify them of the meeting and its purpose. Also, in advance of the meeting, send each participant one of the questionnaires. Ask each participant to complete it and bring it to the meeting.

Meeting Guide

Arrive at the meeting site early to ensure the room is set up as required and all materials are available. Bring extra questionnaires since it is not unusual for some participants to arrive without them. Also, write the starting list subjects on a chart pad.

When the participants have all arrived, state the objective for the meeting. Your opening statement will probably be similar to one of the following:

"We are here to review our organization's current policies and procedures, describe any needed revisions, and identify any additional subjects required for a comprehensive set of human resources policies and procedures."

Or, alternatively:

"This meeting's purpose is to identify the subjects required for a comprehensive set of human resources policies and procedures."

Check if anyone has any questions and then display the chart with the starting list subjects. Ask the participants if there are any other subjects to add to the list. If any are mentioned, add them to the list on the chart pad. If necessary, go to a second piece of chart paper, but as you complete one, post it on the wall where it is visible to all participants. Ask the participants to add the new subjects to the lists on their questionnaires and rate them as they did the original ones. Give them a few moments to finish this task.

Next, divide the participants into at least two groups. (You can have three or four groups.) Be sure there are between three and seven people in each group. Odd numbers per group are better than even ones for breaking deadlocks and reaching consensus. Try to ensure each group has a variety of potential inputs. You are going to assign each group a portion of the subjects to evaluate. Then you are going to reconvene the entire group and merge the subjects into a final prioritized list.

If you are dealing with existing policies and procedures, say: "Each of you has rated the effectiveness of our existing policies and procedures and identified additional policies and procedures and rated their importance for our organization. Now, you are to work in small groups and pool your thoughts."

If there are two groups, assign half of the existing policies and procedures and half of the additional subjects to each group. If you have three groups, assign a third of the existing policies and procedures and a third of additional subjects to each group, and if you have four groups, assign a quarter to each group. (If you have no existing policies and procedures, you make the same assignment but just leave out any reference to existing policies and procedures.) Be sure each group knows the subjects assigned to it. Then explain the assignment as follows:

❐ Each group considers just the subjects assigned to it and places them in order of importance for the organization to have as policies and procedures. List the most important subjects first, then the next most important and so on, until all subjects are listed. Afterward, the subjects of existing policies and procedures will be mixed with new subjects.

❐ For each existing policy and procedure the group must write an R next to it, if it requires revision, or an O, if it is okay in its present format.

❐ Next to each new subject, the group writes an M if it's "a must" for the organization; a W if it is a policy and procedure the group wants but is not a must; and an N if the subject is not necessary.

Check to make sure everyone understands your instructions. Circulate around the room while the groups are working on this assignment. Depending on the number of subjects, this activity will probably require fifteen to thirty minutes.

When the groups have completed the assignment, have each read its rank order. Write the subjects on a chart pad in descending order of importance. Do not place any ranking numbers in front of the subjects. Place each group's list on a separate chart pad or post the lists side by side on the wall. Do not have more than one list on a single piece of paper and do not place one group's list under another.

Then say, "Okay, you have individually rated all of the subjects and in small groups ranked a portion of the subjects. Now, we want to develop a final list of all the subjects."

Go to a chart and write the number 1 and ask, "Of all these subjects, which do you think is the most important for our organization to have as a policy and procedure?"

After asking this question, move to the side or back of the room and wait for a response. Sometimes there is an immediate answer, other times you have to wait while the participants think about their response. It is important for you to wait because that establishes the fact that the results of this meeting will reflect their input. In the unlikely event several minutes pass without an answer, ask the question again. (If you still do not receive an answer, you can reverse the question and ask the group to start with the least important policy and procedure for the organization.)

When you receive an answer, write it after the 1. Then cross out that subject from the group list and write a 2 after the first subject on the new list. Ask the group to identify the next most important policy and procedure. Proceed in this way until you have all the subjects ranked. Then say: "Now that we have ranked these subjects in their order of importance to our organization, let's see how you rated them."

Point to each existing policy and procedure on the list and ask the group to which it was assigned if it requires revision. Then write on the chart an R next to it, if it requires revisions, or an O if it is okay as-is.

Ask the balance of the participants if they agree. If not, encourage discussion to understand any differences, and encourage the participants to arrive at a group decision. Make note on a separate pad of any specifics regarding revisions. In some instances, you may discover that additional research following the meeting is necessary to determine if a policy and procedure actually requires revision.

Continue in this fashion until the entire group has considered all existing policies and procedures. Then turn to the new subjects. You are going to handle them the same way, looking for an evaluation of their importance to the organization as policies and procedures.

Start with the additional subject listed nearest the top of the list on the chart and ask the group to which it was assigned for their rating. Write it after the subject and then allow the other participants to agree or disagree or to discuss. Proceed in this manner for all additional subjects.

Tell the group this list and their ratings will be used to create a prioritized list for the development of new and/or revised policies and procedures. If their results will be combined with the findings of other groups, let them know that. If you are going to be sending the questionnaire to people who did not attend a group meeting, let them know that, too.

At the end of the meeting, ask if there are any final questions and thank the participants for their input.

Multiple Techniques

When there are many people to be surveyed, it may be best to use a combination of meetings, interviews, and questionnaires. The interviews can assist in establishing an initial subject list. In some organizations, individual interviews are used with senior managers. The meeting can involve more people, usually a selection of managers and supervisors, so you can refine the list and add supporting reasons from a representative number of people. A questionnaire based on the meeting results can then be used to obtain information from those not interviewed or participating in the meeting, thereby simultaneously make them part of the process.

COMBINING QUESTIONNAIRE RESPONSES

If you used the questionnaires as your sole information-gathering tool, the results from the individual questionnaires need to be combined. This is true whether you are evaluating existing policies and procedures, a list of possible policy and procedure subjects, or a combination.

First, you need to make a list of all subjects. Because you already have the ones you initially provided on the form, list those first. Then add any subjects that were suggested as required by the people completing the questionnaires. You can do this in the first column of the policy and procedure survey results form. A copy of that form appears in Figure 2-4, and also on the accompanying disk.

The next columns are for recording responses by the groups surveyed: senior managers and managers/supervisors. You may have to add additional columns if, for example, you also surveyed nonmanagement employees. The combining procedure is similar for each column.

Next, sort the questionnaires by surveyed group. Recall the scale used for rating has nine points (1 through 9). You need to determine the average rating for each subject. This requires you to total the individual ratings from the nine-point scale and divide by the number of raters. For example, assume you received the following ratings from six senior functional managers:

Figure 2-4. Policies and procedures survey results.

Subject	Senior Managers	Managers and Supervisors	Totals

Manager	Rating
Legal	8
Human Resources	3
Operations	7
Marketing	8
Purchasing	2
Security	3

These ratings total 31. Since there were six responses, the average senior manager rating is 5.2. However, all individuals in a group may not respond to all subjects. For example, if only four senior managers responded to a subject, and their total rating for that subject is 30, the average is calculated by dividing the total responses by four. In this instance, the average would be 7.5, but there were only four responders.

It is important to calculate both the average for a group and the number responding (i.e., the frequency of responses). An average of 5.7 for a group of 22 is more significant than an average rating of 2 with only one responder.

The report is completed by writing two numbers on each line: the average number for each group is the number on the left, and the number on the right is the number of responses for that subject (frequency). So, if four senior managers responded to a subject and their average rating = 3, the entries on the survey results form (Figure 2-4) would appear as:

3   4

ANALYZING DIFFERING LEVELS OF AGREEMENT

When existing policies and procedures receive consistent ratings from all groups, there is basically consensus regarding their usefulness. New subjects with consistent ratings from all groups also indicate there is agreement on whether or not the subjects are required as policies and procedures. However, there may be instances where there are wide differences among ratings. Those differences should be investigated to discover what is causing the varying perceptions and what might be done to obtain consensus.

Prioritizing Areas for Further Investigation

So, where do you start? Do you investigate differences in ratings for a subject first, or do you investigate those subjects perceived as needing improvement by all groups?

There is no one correct answer to that question. Both are important, and if either or both occur, they should be investigated and the differences corrected, if possible, before moving on. Figure 2-5 is a form you can use to separate subjects identified as needing improvement from those subjects on which there is little agreement.

Resolving Disagreements

Begin by reviewing the results and determining whether there are subjects with significant disagreements either between groups or within groups or both. Significant disagreements exist when the ratings for a single subject fall below and above 5. The ratings below 5 are stating the subject is not important for making into a policy and procedure, while the ratings above 5 are stating it is a very important subject. These differences need to be resolved or at least understood. However, there's one caveat.

The number of responses that differ also have to be considered. For example, if eighteen managers responded and seventeen rated the subject a 7, but one manager rated it a 3, you actually have received a very consistent rating with a difference of only about 0.6 percent. You might want to talk with the one manager who gave the subject a low rating, but as a general guideline, you can use the majority rating.

Another example is when you have only two responders and each rates the same subject at opposite ends of the scale—for example, two supervisors respond to a subject and one rates it a 2 and the other rates it an 8. This indicates the two responders perceive the same subject completely differently, so this situation, too, requires investigation.

If the disagreement in ratings is between groups (e.g., senior managers rate the subject a 3 and supervisors rate it a 7), contact members of each group. It could be that one group has possibly encountered issues related to that subject and the other has not. You efforts here are to determine what, if anything, needs to be done to resolve the difference.

If it turns out only one group or a small number of people give a subject a very low rating, that alone may not mean it should not be a policy and procedure. It may mean there's a misunderstanding or a train-

Figure 2-5. Summary of policies and procedures survey results.

Subject	Senior Managers	Managers and Supervisors	Totals
_____	_____	_____	___
_____	_____	_____	___
_____	_____	_____	___
_____	_____	_____	___
_____	_____	_____	___
_____	_____	_____	___
_____	_____	_____	___
_____	_____	_____	___
_____	_____	_____	___
_____	_____	_____	___
_____	_____	_____	___
_____	_____	_____	___
_____	_____	_____	___
_____	_____	_____	___
_____	_____	_____	___
_____	_____	_____	___
_____	_____	_____	___
_____	_____	_____	___

Subjects Needing Improvement

_____
_____
_____
_____
_____
_____
_____
_____
_____

Subjects with Little Agreement

_____
_____
_____
_____
_____
_____
_____
_____
_____

ing need. It may mean the subject relates only to a specific department or area. If you are unable to clarify the situation, you will want to identify that subject as one requiring resolution. If there is a subject for which the senior managers' ratings are significantly higher than those of the other managers and supervisors, you want to ask questions such as:

❑ How did the senior managers decide on their ratings—that is, what is the basis of their ratings?

❑ What is the basis of the ratings of the managers and supervisors?

❑ What is the basis for the different ratings?

❑ Are both groups involved in the implementation of the policy and procedure?

❑ What actions are required to produce similar ratings?

Asking questions such as these may reveal performance facts of which you were unaware. The answers may also uncover incorrect information about the subject and/or the policy and procedure. You may discover that it is actually a training problem and not a policy and procedures one. Whatever the answers, you will have information that will allow you to take corrective action.

Analyzing Low Ratings

Next, you need to identify those subjects that were identified consistently as not necessary or not important. If they are not mandatory subjects, you need to determine if, in fact, policies and procedures are not required. Here you need to ask questions such as:

❑ What was the reason for adding this subject to the initial list?

❑ Is this policy and procedure mandated by laws, licenses, memberships, or contracts?

❑ What will be the consequences if no policy and procedure exists for this subject?

❑ What was the basis for the low ratings this subject received?

You may discover that although everyone rated the policy and procedure as not necessary, each did so for different reasons. If that is the situation, you have two problems to contend with. First, you are going to have to take action to ensure everyone has the same correct information, and then you must act to improve performance in the implementation of that policy and procedure.

When you resolve any disagreements, you can place those subjects among those similarly rated. Any disagreement you are unable to resolve needs to be kept separate.

COMBINING INTERVIEW RESPONSES

Interview responses are treated exactly the same way as questionnaires. However, with interviews you generally have more information since you were able to ask follow-up questions. You may still encounter differences between responders that require resolving, but you probably already know why any existing policies and procedures were identified as needing improvement.

COMBINING MEETING RESPONSES

Meeting responses, like interview responses, also usually provide the reasons existing policies and procedures may be identified as needing improvement. In addition, meeting responses generally have few differences since they were worked out at the meeting. However, if you are combining results from multiple meetings, you may discover differences between meetings. If that occurs, you need to resolve them as described in the sections on combining questionnaire responses and resolving questionnaire disagreements.

You also need to convert the letter ratings to numbers. For existing policies and procedures, an R (revision required) and an O (okay as-is) were used. Convert each R to a 3, and convert each O to a 7. For new subjects, three letter ratings were used: M (must have), W (wanted), and N (not necessary). Convert each M to a rating of 7, each W to a 5, and each N to a 3.

Use the group ratings from a meeting as the averages for subjects. For the frequencies, use the number of people in the group meeting.

COMBINING MULTIPLE TECHNIQUE RESPONSES

The results from more than one information-gathering technique can be combined using the basic procedure described for questionnaire results.

However, when you are calculating an average for a meeting and one or both other techniques (i.e., interviews or questionnaires), you first need to transform the group results into a total number for all members.

For example, assume there were ten people in a group meeting. Their average rating for a subject was 7. To change that to a total for all members of the group you multiply the frequency (10) by the average rating (7). The product is 70. You can use that total number and the frequency to calculate an average for the meeting and the other inputs.

PRIORITIZING THE LIST

Once you have resolved any disagreements or discovered the basis for them, and calculated all the averages and frequencies for each subject, you are ready to prepare a list of policies and procedures requiring development or revision. Priorities are based on several factors. You can use the form shown in Figure 2-6 for this purpose (this form is also available on the disk accompanying this book).

Start with subjects that are mandatory policies and procedures. List the existing ones requiring revision first. Then list any new mandatory subjects. For each group, list the one with the lowest average first; then the next lowest average; and so on for all subjects in each group. Do not list any policies and procedures not requiring revisions just yet.

Next, list the nonmandated, existing policies and procedures requiring revisions. List these by average: the lowest average first; then the next lowest average; and so on for all subjects in each group.

Then, list the new subjects. List them by average, but this time, list highest average first; then the next highest average; and so on for all those in each group.

Next, list subjects requiring resolution. These are the subjects for which there are conflicting ratings that you have been unable to resolve. If there are some identified reasons, note them.

Existing policies and procedures not requiring revisions are listed next. Finally, make a list of the subjects for policies and procedures that were suggested but not rated as important.

The final step is to combine all these subjects into a single list—a list of the priorities for development. It is probably best to begin, again, with the existing mandatory policies and procedures requiring revision. Next, come the new mandatory subjects; then the nonmandatory existing poli-

Figure 2-6. HR policies and procedures priority.

Mandatory Policies and Procedures: Our organization is required to have written policies and procedures covering the following subjects. Requirements are based on laws and/or contractual obligations.

1. _____ _____
2. _____ _____
3. _____ _____
4. _____ _____
5. _____ _____
6. _____ _____
7. _____ _____
8. _____ _____
9. _____ _____
10. _____ _____

Policies and Procedures Needed   **Agreement**

1. _____ _____
2. _____ _____
3. _____ _____
4. _____ _____
5. _____ _____
6. _____ _____
7. _____ _____
8. _____ _____
9. _____ _____

Existing Policies and Procedures Requiring Resolution

1. _____ _____
2. _____ _____
3. _____ _____
4. _____ _____
5. _____ _____
6. _____ _____

Existing Policies and Procedures Not Requiring Revision   **Totals**

1. _____ _____ _____
2. _____ _____ _____
3. _____ _____ _____
4. _____ _____ _____
5. _____ _____ _____
6. _____ _____ _____

(continues)

Figure 2-6. (Continued.)

7. _____   _____   _____
8. _____   _____   _____
9. _____   _____   _____
10. _____   _____   _____
11. _____   _____   _____
12. _____   _____   _____
13. _____   _____   _____
14. _____   _____   _____
15. _____   _____   _____
16. _____   _____   _____
17. _____   _____   _____
18. _____   _____   _____
19. _____   _____   _____

Existing Policies and Procedures Not Needed

1. _____   _____   _____
2. _____   _____   _____
3. _____   _____   _____
4. _____   _____   _____
5. _____   _____   _____
6. _____   _____   _____
7. _____   _____   _____
8. _____   _____   _____

cies and procedures; and finally the nonmandatory new subjects. However, before submitting the list for approval, have it reviewed by people who may have reason to suggest changes to it.

CHECKING MANDATORY SUBJECTS

Although you have surveyed the organization for the needed policies and procedures, the employees contacted—even those in top management—may not be aware of everything. Before you submit your prioritized list, you need to ensure these subjects have been properly considered.

Check with Legal

If you did not earlier consult the appropriate legal professionals, you need to do so now. You want to be confident that all the required subjects have been identified and included in your list. Chapter 3 lists the major federal laws that have to be considered, but not all state and local laws. Covering all state and local requirements is beyond the scope of this book. Also, federal laws and their accompanying regulations are constantly being changed, so you need input from someone current in that field.

Check with Human Resources

Again, if you did not check with human resources earlier and HR representatives were not a part of your information gathering, check with them now. HR needs to review the list before it is submitted for approval. If your organization has multiple divisions or multiple locations, you want to be sure to obtain input from each human resources area. Sometimes one may have requirements significantly different from the others.

Check with Functional Areas

Any functional area within the organization that might have related policies and procedures, or is referenced in any of the subjects on your list, needs to have an opportunity to review it. This is generally most true of the finance function. In some organizations, the list is also sent to everyone who contributed to it for their input before seeking approval.

When these reviews are completed and any necessary adjustments to your list are made, you are ready to submit it for approval.

OBTAINING APPROVAL

The last step in this process is to obtain approval for the subjects on the list and their order. Here you want approval of the subjects you are using for policies and procedures and the sequence in which you propose to develop them. Generally, this approval should be made by the senior management of the organization or a special senior management group appointed to direct the activity.

If you obtain approval by mail, you may want to use a cover memo similar to the following:

To: _____

As a result of our recently conducted survey of human resources policy and procedure requirements, including input from our labor attorney, the attached is a list of subjects required. These subjects have been listed in order of priority. Please review the list and submit any comments you have to _____ by _____. Our plan at this time is to begin to implement the policy and procedure developments on _____.

You can also elect to request approval with a simpler statement:

Please indicate your approval of the list, or the changes you feel should be made, by _____.

The most efficient approach is to submit the list to the individual or group from whom you are seeking approval. Then follow it up with a meeting to explain the subjects requiring resolutions and to answer any questions. However, the main purpose of the meeting is to obtain approval of the list so development can begin.

CONCLUSION

Before moving on to the actual writing of policies, the next chapter reviews some of the legal conditions with which you should be familiar.

CHAPTER 3

Laws and Regulations

"That which is necessary is never a risk."   —PAUL DE GONDI

ONE PURPOSE OF HUMAN RESOURCES POLICIES and procedures is to ensure the organization complies with appropriate federal, state, and local laws and regulations, some of which actually require written policies and procedures.

The last two decades have seen the passage of a number of laws and regulations that affect the relationship between employers and employees. In addition, the risk of litigation has further stressed the importance of having correct policies and procedures.

In many, if not all, hearings and lawsuits regarding employees, the organization's policies and procedures become a key piece of evidence (sometimes for the employee and sometimes the employer). Their absence also can affect a court's decision.

An employee filed a charge that she was discriminated against by her employer with respect to a promotion. She claimed the discrimination was based on her age, sex, and race.

The company claimed it had not discriminated and cited its policy of fair and equal treatment of all employees without regard to sex, race, and age. However, the only document the company could produce to support its claim was a bulletin board statement and a required poster.

The judge ruled in favor of the employee and stated the company was at fault for not having a published policy and procedure and for not training its management in the correct implementation of it.

MAJOR LAWS AND REGULATIONS

It is beyond the scope of this book to identify all of the HR-related laws and regulations. Many apply to specific industries, and some are applicable to specific geographic locations. It should be the role of your legal department and/or labor attorney to know the laws and regulations specific to your business, but you should be aware of the major federal and state ones as you embark on the process of developing a set of policies and procedures. The laws have different definitions of what organizations are covered by them. You need to consult with your labor attorney or legal department to determine exactly which apply to your organization and what their provisions are.

Age Discrimination in Employment Act. This act applies to employers of twenty or more employees in most industries. It prohibits discriminating on the basis of age (specifically, individuals forty years and older).

Americans with Disabilities Act. This act prohibits discrimination on the basis of physical and mental disabilities.

Civil Rights Act—Title VII. This is the federal equal employment opportunity law. Employers with fifteen or more employees may not discriminate in conditions of employment based on race, color, religion, sex, or national origin.

Consolidated Omnibus Budget Reconciliation Act (COBRA). Employers of twenty or more people must offer employees and their dependents the right to continue group health and dental coverage for eighteen to thirty-six months beyond when it would otherwise terminate.

Employee Polygraph Protection Act. This law prohibits employers from using a lie detector test for job candidates and employees.

Employee Retirement Income Security Act (ERISA). This act establishes requirements for employee benefit plans.

Equal Pay Act. This act prohibits paying different wages for equal work based on sex.

Fair Labor Standards Act. Also referred to as the Wage and Hour Law, it deals with minimum wage and payment of overtime. It also establishes minimum ages for certain work.

Family and Medical Leave Act. Employers of fifty or more employees must offer up to twelve weeks of unpaid but job-protected leave in any twelve-month period for the birth and care or the placement or adoption of the employee's child; for the care of a spouse, parent, or child with a serious health condition; and for a serious health condition of the employee.

Immigration Reform and Control Act. Employers are required to ensure, by obtaining acceptable evidence, that an employee is eligible to work in the United States. For employers of four or more people, this act prohibits discrimination based on national origin or citizenship.

Juror's Protection Act. This act protects employees from any form of disciplinary action for serving on jury duty.

Occupational Safety and Health Act (OSHA). This act establishes the requirements for a safe and healthy workplace and prohibits discharge of an employee who exercises rights under this act.

Older Workers Benefit Protection Act. This act prohibits the reduction of benefits on the basis of age.

Pregnancy Discrimination Act. This law prohibits disparate treatment of pregnant women solely based on their condition.

Sarbanes-Oxley Act of 2002. This act provides protection for employee "whistle-blowers," mandates that publicly held corporations establish procedures for their protection, and prohibits retaliation and discrimination.

MILITARY SERVICE LAWS

There are both federal and state laws dealing with military service. Generally, they require organizations to give employees in the National Guard and reserves time-off to meet their service requirement. This covers both annual training and activation. (Some states require employers to pay normal wages for up to fourteen days.) Employees returning from such service are to be returned to their jobs or ones of equal status. Their return is to be "timely," which is usually defined as ninety days after completing activated service. However, if the person was injured while on duty the timely return requirement may be extended for as much as one year plus thirty-one days.

OTHER LAWS AND REGULATIONS

The laws outlined are but a few of those that affect employers. There are others that are specific to federal contractors, and still others that deal with unions and union-organizing attempts. There are state and local regulations, and there are laws in other areas, such as the Internal Revenue Code, that also affect conditions of employment.

The previous list simply summaries the most common laws affecting HR policies and procedures. It is not meant to imply that you should be a legal expert, only that you become aware of the types of concerns you should address. Your labor attorney should provide you with specific advice on ensuring your compliance with all appropriate laws.

CONCLUSION

Let's now return to the results of identifying the policies and procedures your organization needs. Now that a list of them and a sequence for their development has been established, you can begin to create appropriate policy statements and have them approved.

PART TWO

Developing Human Resources Policies and Procedures

CHAPTER 4

Writing Policies and Obtaining Their Approval

"You can have everything in life you want if you will just help enough other people get what they want."
— ZIG ZIGLAR

WHEN YOU HAVE AN APPROVED, prioritized list of subjects for your organization's needed policies and procedures, you are ready to begin their actual development. First, you create and obtain approval for a policy statement for each subject, and then you write a procedure for the approved policy and have the procedure approved.

Some organizations treat these as two separate steps. Others combine information gathering for the procedure along with the information for the policy, believing it is a more efficient approach and eliminates having to keep questioning the same people. This book treats the two information gatherings separately. However, there is no one correct way. You should use the method that best meets your organization's culture and the assignment objective you received. However, if you wish to gather information for both the policy and procedure at the same time, you can easily combine the methods provided.

INFORMATION FOR A POLICY STATEMENT

To write a policy statement, you need to know:

- ❐ Current Policy (used within your organization)
- ❐ External Policies (policies of similar organizations)
- ❐ Legal Considerations (any specific policy requirements stemming from laws, contracts, licenses, and/or memberships)

❏ Financial Considerations (requirements resulting from your organization's financial situations)

❏ Survey Results (any input regarding the organization's policy identified through an employee opinion survey)

❏ Recommendations (any recommendations from your labor attorney and consultants)

CURRENT POLICY

If your organization currently has a policy and procedure in a subject matter, you have a starting point—the existing policy statement. Even if your organization does not have an existing policy statement, in all probability there is an unwritten policy being followed. In some cases where there is an existing policy statement, there may also be areas within the organization that are practicing a different policy.

A Colorado resort hotel did not have any written policies and procedures for its 250 employees. "All of our employees know the rules and follow them," the general manager said.

However, an employee opinion survey conducted to identify any problem areas for employees discovered major differences in how employees were treated. Employees in one department were allowed to take up to five personal days off per year with pay. In another department it was three days, and in another no days.

Employees in one department were allowed to arrive up to ten minutes late and then make up the time at the end of the day. Employees in another department were not paid for any time they were late and were not allowed to make the time up. Arrival time was not recorded for employees in another department.

As one employee wrote on his survey, "I don't get it. I work five feet from someone in another department. We both work for the same company, but she works under an entirely different set of rules than I do."

You need to discover what the current policy is in both writing (if any) and in practice. As with the identification of required subjects (see Chapter 2), your internal approach to this step depends on whether your organization already has a published policy and procedure for a subject.

Existing Policy and Procedure

If a policy and procedure exists, the first activity is to determine how well the policy statement meets the needs of the organization. Since a policy states what the organization wishes to accomplish in a specific subject, senior management and human resources are usually the two major sources of information. Here you want answers to questions such as:

❏   Does this policy statement represent what our organization desires to accomplish?

❏   How well does this policy statement meet the needs of our organization?

❏   Does this policy statement require any revision to better meet the needs of our organization?

❏   Does this policy statement apply to all employees, departments, and locations of our organization?

Managers and supervisors are generally implementation-oriented. If they are asked similar questions, you will probably receive answers that have more to do with procedure than policy. Even so, you need to discover if the policy is being correctly communicated to employees. You can use a short questionnaire for that purpose. A sample questionnaire is shown in Figure 4-1 (and on the accompanying disk).

Of course, you can obtain information from any of these groups through interviews and meetings as well as by questionnaires. We will consider these other techniques later in this chapter.

No Existing Policies and Procedures

If there are no existing policies and procedures, you still need to use senior management and human resources as your primary sources of information for developing a policy statement. Both of these groups tend to have a total organizational approach—senior managers as an extension of their overall management role and HR as the internal function primarily accountable for conditions of employment.

Figure 4-1. HR questionnaire (existing policies and procedures).

To: _____

We are currently reviewing our organization's existing policies and procedures to identify any changes that are required. One such policy and procedure is _____ (a copy is attached).

Read the policy statement on page _____ of that policy and procedure and then answer the following questions:

1. How well does the policy statement agree with what employees have been told?
   _____
   _____

2. What changes, if any, do you feel need to be made to the policy statement?
   _____
   _____

3. What other suggestions do you have for improving this policy statement?
   _____
   _____

When you have answered the questions, please return this questionnaire to _____.

_____
(Your name)

_____
(Date)

The task can be best accomplished by providing a format for their responses. Figure 4-2 is a questionnaire you can use that establishes such a format. It requests the policy statement to be written in one sentence beginning with the word "to." The advantages of this format are that it requires the person to use as few as words as possible, it structures the syntax of the sentence, and it makes it easier for people to respond.

Again, you can accomplish the same result through interviews and meetings. Whether an interview or questionnaire, or some combination of the three, eventually you need to create a policy statement based on all the inputs you have received.

Figure 4-2. HR questionnaire (no existing policies and procedures).

To: _____

We are currently developing a comprehensive set of human resources policies and procedures. A list of subjects for these policies and procedures has been created and approved. We are now beginning the actual development, and the first task is to create a policy statement.

For our purposes, a policy is what the organization wishes to accomplish with the specific subject matter of a policy and procedure. It is the purpose of the accompanying procedure.

On the lines below, write in one sentence what you believe to be the purpose the organization wishes this policy and procedure to fulfill. Begin your one-sentence statement with the word ''to.''

TO

_____

_____

_____

_____

When complete, return this questionnaire to _____.

_____

(Your Name)

_____

(Date)

1. How well does the policy statement agree with what employees have been told?

_____

_____

2. What changes, if any, do you feel need to be made to the policy statement?

_____

_____

3. What other suggestions do you have for improving this policy statement?

_____

_____

When you have answered the questions, please return this questionnaire to _____.

_____

(Your name)

_____

(Date)

The Interview Method

Chapter 2 described the general approach to an interview. Although in that chapter the primary focus was identifying needed policies and procedures, the same considerations apply to preparing for and conducting a policy information-gathering interview. Again, you use the questionnaire as the basis for the questions, keeping in mind that the outcome you want is a policy statement.

The Meeting Method

A meeting of appropriate people can be an ideal method for creating a policy statement, particularly if it is possible to conduct a meeting with all appropriate participants. For example, if senior management and HR are your key information and approval sources, and they total less than twenty people, use the meeting format.

A meeting provides an opportunity for a statement to be constructed with full participation of all appropriate parties. Ideally, you send the questionnaire in advance of the meeting to each participant and then have them bring their completed questionnaires to the meeting. The meeting can begin with participants sharing their statement. The balance of the meeting can be a discussion where the aim is to produce a single, final policy statement.

If the meeting is composed of senior managers, and they are also the ones who approve the final statement, you can accomplish both elements of the task—writing the policy and having it approved—at the same time.

The same considerations mentioned for an information-gathering meeting (see Chapter 2) apply, and the same guidelines can be used. The difference is that you have the small groups develop policy statements, and then the entire group discusses, revises, and approves a final policy statement.

A meeting of this type takes approximately a half-hour if you are working with an existing policy statement and an hour if you are creating a new policy statement. You can do more than one statement per meeting, but the meeting should be kept to less than three hours unless you have devoted the entire day to developing policy statements.

POLICY CONSIDERATIONS

If you do not use a meeting, you have to combine the statements you have received in the form of completed questionnaires. This requires reading all of them and identifying any common elements and directions. From those you form a statement. If there is an existing policy and procedure, the statement can serve as a basis for the new one, and you can use the inputs you have received to revise it.

More specifically, review the responses you have received. In most cases, there will be more similarities than differences, but when you encounter significant differences, you need to investigate. You may need to contact the individuals to determine why there are differences. Sometimes they may be due to a misunderstanding about your request. Sometimes you may discover areas or departments within the organization that have differing policies. When that occurs, you need to discover what the organization wants. Does it want a common policy, or can different areas have different policies? A meeting with whomever is accountable for approving the policies may be required to resolve this issue.

As a general rule, it may be helpful to use senior managers' input for developing the policy statement and then adjust it as necessary with the information collected from others. If you have a great number of inputs, it may help to begin by writing a statement that you feel best summarizes the overall direction. Then you can identify any significant differences and resolve them. Eventually, you will have resolved most or all differences among the responses. That's when it is time to develop a single policy statement.

The Initial Policy Statement

The policy statement describes the purpose of the policy and procedure, so it is important that senior management agrees with it. This can be accomplished through written or electronic communications. However, the most efficient approach is to have a meeting of senior managers, or a representative group of senior managers, to create the statement.

Whichever approach you use, the outcome should be the same: You must determine exactly what the organization's position is regarding the subject. If you use a meeting, a recommended agenda is as follows:

❐ Describe and define the subject.

❐ If there is an existing policy and procedure, describe the survey concerns about it.

❐ Describe any input from the legal department and human resources.

❐ Hold a discussion to ensure there is a common understanding of the subject, any legal requirements, and the identified internal requirements.

❐ Then create a policy statement.

Before creating a policy statement, you should establish some guidelines for writing it. Those guidelines answer the questions:

❐ What style should be used?

❐ How long should the policy statement be?

❐ What is the scope of the policy statement?

What Style Should You Use?

The answer to this question provides a consistent approach to structuring policy statements. In the examples supplied in this book, the policy statements are all written in an objective format. No pronouns, dates, or proper names are used. As a general rule, short is better than long, and clear, concise statements are better than ones with equivocating words. Here are examples:

EXAMPLE 1

Our compensation policy is to pay all employees based on their individual performance.

EXAMPLE 2

Our policy is to pay the majority of employees based on their levels of performance except in cases when management elects to pay via another method.

Clearly, the first example is better than the second.

How Long Should the Policy Statement Be?

The examples provided in this book are relatively short statements. They are not meant to be detailed. They are meant to provide overall guidance and direction for the creation and implementation of procedure development. They describe what the procedure is to accomplish—the objective it is to fulfill.

Some organizations prefer a very detailed policy statement. The following are statements from two organizations. Both describe a policy on compensation:

ORGANIZATION 1

It is the policy of the organization to compensate employees at a rate competitive with compensation levels for similar jobs in the community.

ORGANIZATION 2

It is the policy of the organization to compensate employees competitively with rates of other organizations in the community, and to do so by annually surveying rates of compensation in the community, publishing survey results, and establishing and adjusting compensation to be within 5 percent of survey rates.

Either approach is acceptable. Whichever you use should represent your organization's desires and be consistent with all policies and procedures.

What Is the Scope of the Policy Statement?

Here the question to answer is, Does this policy apply to all functional units, locations, and employees of the organization or only some? For example, if the organization consists of several divisions at different geographic sites, there might be some variations. This needs to be addressed.

Multiple Subjects

For some subjects, it may take considerable time to develop a policy statement. They may require multiple meetings. Other times they may proceed quite fast. A recommended approach is to provide a draft statement and then allow the group to adjust it. That statement should answer the following questions:

❏ Does this statement accurately describe our organization's purpose for this subject?

❏ Does this statement represent fulfillment of any legal requirements regarding this subject?

❏ Does this statement agree with the organization's mission and objectives?

Mandatory Policy Considerations

In most cases, you probably do not need to consult your attorney or legal department at this time. However, if you know of something that may impact a policy—a new or revised law, results of a court or arbitration proceeding, or a recently awarded contract, for example—you should then obtain appropriate advice. Also, if you feel a policy statement in any way might have legal problems the way it is written, contact legal counsel for advice. Even if you do not resolve the issue with them at this time, you will be requesting their advice on the final policy and procedure.

A California restaurant chain hired only young and what it believed to be attractive people. The establishment wanted to project a specific image and believed that a certain type of employee would project the right image.

An experienced waitperson with excellent references applied for a job and was not hired. Instead a younger, less experienced person was selected. When asked why, the company spokesperson told the experienced candidate that she was too heavy to fit their image.

The person filed a complaint, which was upheld at the hearing. The ruling stated the restaurant could provide no evidence to support its policy, so it was in violation of federal law.

The Approved Policy Statement

Once you have a final, written policy statement, it can then be submitted to those accountable for approving it. A meeting that you attend tends to work best. Otherwise, you may find yourself in back-and-forth memo or e-mail exchanges that can greatly prolong the approval process.

Multiple Policies

In the approach described so far, the task has been developing and obtaining approval for a single policy statement. If you are working on several policies at once, you may want to consider grouping them. If so, consider also the order in which you are scheduled to develop the policies; the relationship of the policies to each other; the common elements in the policies; and whether similar people should be involved in the development and/or approval of the policies.

Also, you will probably discover it is easier and more efficient to have people focus on more than one policy at a time.

CONCLUSION

Once you have a statement of the organization's policy for a subject, you can move ahead with creating the procedure to implement that policy. That process is covered in the next chapter.

CHAPTER 5

Writing Procedures and Obtaining Their Approval

"If you have an important point to make, don't try to be subtle or clever."

—Sir Winston Churchill

Generally, writing the procedure requires more time than developing the policy statement. Your task here is to discover exactly what is occurring, ensuring it meets the policy statement and applies to all elements of the organization included in its scope. Even when there are no existing policies and procedures, it is very probable that some type of procedure is being implemented for the majority of human resources conditions of employment. Numerous questionnaires, interviews, meetings, and follow-up conversations may be required just to discover whether any "unwritten" policies and procedures are being followed.

For example, there may not be a published policy and procedure on absenteeism. However, departments and supervisors confront absenteeism, so they probably have their own way of dealing with it—which may differ by department and even by supervisors within the same department. If that is the case, you have the added assignment of changing some current practices.

There are two starting points. One is with the existence of policies and procedures in a specific subject. The second is when there are no existing policies and procedures. Still, in both cases, what you need is information.

Once you have a policy statement acceptable to senior management, you can write the procedure. With an existing policy and procedure, you have not only a starting point, but at least some information on required revisions, either from the management surveyed and/or your labor attorney. Even so, you are most likely going to have to obtain additional, specific information from a number of sources. You need someone who knows what current practices—written or unwritten—are. You may need several people or, in some cases, just one knowledgeable person to serve as this content expert. You also need someone who's accountable for actually writing the procedure. And, here again, you need to establish the style of writing the procedure.

One approach is to establish teams for the various policies and procedures. This can be a team of two or several individuals. Their assignment is to identify the procedure steps required to implement the policy. Exactly how detailed the procedure steps need to be is something you determine beforehand.

ASSIGNMENTS

To get started, one individual should be placed in charge of developing a single policy and procedure, although others may assist. That person should be someone who has personal knowledge about, or at least is well acquainted with, the areas affected the most.

Then, identify and make a list of everyone who is accountable for administering the policy and procedure. These people then need to be contacted for their input.

Information Sources

Generally, you will be obtaining information from more sources than were necessary for developing the policy. Since you need to contact everyone involved in implementing the procedure, in most cases they will be supervisors and managers. Senior managers probably will not know the details of implementation.

You can use any of three methods to gather information: questionnaires, interviews, and meetings. These same techniques were used in identifying your policy and procedure subjects (Chapter 2) and in writing the policy statements (Chapter 3). This chapter describes the development of a questionnaire, since it requests the same information you would seek from any type of information-gathering technique.

You have to obtain information that explains why the policy and procedure was perceived as necessary and what current practices are. As mentioned already, even when there are no published policies and procedures, there may be other documents that describe how supervisors and managers are currently handling situations. Employee handbook, memos, bulletin board notices, and letters to all employees are just a few sources. However, there also may be standard implementation practices for which there are no records. For example, supervisors may regularly assign employees with the greatest length of service to certain jobs. This may be a common practice but never documented. Likewise, some departments may allow employees to schedule their own starting times, and again it has never been formalized.

Certain subjects, however, are not open for individual supervisor interpretation, among them vacation, benefits, and compensation. These are generally overall approaches. However, investigation must deal with even these subjects. Sometimes you may discover that in spite of an overall policy and procedure, some supervisors are operating in violation of it.

EXISTING POLICIES AND PROCEDURES NEEDING REVISIONS

One of the first groups to contact are any employees (as indicated in your initial survey) who can identify what policies and procedures your organization needs written. They will tell you whether existing policies and procedures require revision or are not serving the organization well. You want these individuals to be able to answer questions such as:

- ❐ Are there any problems with the implementation of the existing policy and procedure?
- ❐ Is the procedure being implemented as written?
- ❐ If not, what is occurring?
- ❐ Should something be added?
- ❐ Is something no longer needed?

Figure 5-1 is a policy and procedure development questionnaire (a copy of which is also on the accompanying disk). The actual wording of your questionnaire will vary depending on whether it is the sole informa-

Figure 5-1. Policy and procedure development questionnaire (existing policy and procedure).

To: _____

We are currently in the process of updating our human resources policies and procedures. One of those is _____ (a copy of the current one is attached). This is a subject that you implement, so your information will be of considerable assistance.

Please answer the following questions and return the questionnaire to _____ by _____. Thank you for your assistance.

If you have any questions, call _____ at _____.

The former policy statement has been revised. The new policy of our organization appears below:

_____
_____
_____

Next review the procedure and answer the following questions:
Have you encountered any difficulties in the area covered by this subject? _____ If yes, describe below:

_____
_____
_____
_____
_____

Is there anything other than this policy and procedure, currently in writing regarding this subject, that governs your actions and decisions? _____ If yes, indicate below what it is:

_____
_____

Does the procedure, as written, provide you the directions needed for implementation? _____ If no, what needs to be added, removed, or revised? Write your responses on the lines below or mark the copy of the actual procedure to reflect your needs.

_____
_____
_____
_____

What else would assist you in the implementation of this policy and procedure?

_____
_____
_____
_____
_____

_____
(Your name)

_____
(Date)

tion-gathering technique or it is used in concert with one or more other approaches.

The questionnaire refers to a new policy statement. If the existing one has not been changed, you do not need that reference. Some organizations ask respondents to comment on the revised policy statement and its applicability to their areas. This is seen as providing another good source of information. However, if the policy statement has already been approved, asking for comments may create a problem.

NO EXISTING POLICIES AND PROCEDURES

Figure 5-2 is a second policy procedure development questionnaire. This one is for use when there are no existing policies and procedures. The two questionnaires are very similar, but when there are no existing policies and procedures, you need to discover not only what policies and procedures need to be written, but also what people are currently (if informally) doing to handle a specific work situation.

Sometimes an investigation of this type discovers policies and procedures that are unknown to senior management and human resources.

A North Carolina textile plant was a unit of a Tennessee corporation. The corporation had a set of HR policies and procedures applicable to all locations. One of those policies and procedures covered length of service

Figure 5-2. Policy and procedure development questionnaire (new policy and procedure).

To: _____

We are currently in the process of developing a set of human resources policies and proce-dures. One subject is ————. This is a subject that you must deal with, so your information will be of considerable assistance.

Please answer the following questions and return the questionnaire to _____ by _____. Thank you for your assistance.

If you have any questions, call _____ at _____.

The following is the organization's policy regarding this condition of employment:

_____

_____

We want to develop a procedure that describes how this policy will be implemented within our organization. Since it is a subject related to your area of accountability, we wish to know what practices you are currently following and what you feel is required. Answer the following ques-tions:

Have you encountered any difficulties in the area covered by this subject? ———— If yes, de-scribe below:

_____

_____

_____

_____

_____

Is there anything other than this policy and procedure, currently in writing regarding this sub-ject, that governs your actions and decisions? _____ If yes, indicate below what it is:

_____

_____

Now consider what actions and decisions you are required to make in this subject area. List them below. If they must occur in a certain order, list them in that order.

_____

_____

_____

_____

_____

Is there anything currently in writing regarding this subject that governs your actions and decisions? _____ If yes, indicate below what it is:

_____

_____

_____

_____

What additional considerations are there for developing this policy and procedure?

_____

_____

_____

_____

_____

_____

(Your name)

_____

(Date)

---

with the company. It stated: "If an employee's employment with the company is terminated for any reason and the employee is later rehired, there will be no credit given for any service prior to the most recent hire date."

The manager at the North Carolina plant interpreted that condition to apply only to employees discharged by the company. He decided it did not apply to employees who voluntarily quit, were in good standing at the time of their departure, and who returned to employment within a year. In those conditions, prior service was combined with new service. This interpretation was written, included in new employee materials, and practiced by human resources at the North Carolina facility.

Over five years, only eight employees received prior service credits under its terms. However, no one at the corporate office knew of the policy's existence until a grievance was filed by an employee who had been transferred from the Tennessee plant to another location of the company. At the new location, this employee's length of service was recalculated based on the corporation's policy and procedure.

The grievance eventually was submitted to arbitration. The arbitrator's ruling was for the employee. Not only was her length of service returned to the amount calculated under the Tennessee plant's policy and procedure, but several adjustments to other employees' lengths of service had to be made.

Sometimes such practices are not written, but when they are informally known and consistently administered, they can become as binding as those correctly written, approved, and communicated.

OTHER INFORMATION-GATHERING METHODS

The questionnaire is usually sufficient when there are existing policies and procedures and there are no major changes affecting their implementation. Interviews are also often used if there are not too many people to contact. However, in trying to develop new procedures, make major revisions to existing ones, or combine many different practices, particularly when there are a number of people from whom to seek the information, a meeting is usually more effective and efficient.

Interviews

If you interview someone, you can use the questions from the questionnaire as a starting point and then add questions based on the responses you receive.

In some cases you may find it easier to write the steps a supervisor follows on individual index cards—one step per card—and have the interviewee arrange them face-up on a table, in sequence. Then the person can identify redundancies, missing steps, and any other needed changes.

Whatever the case, always follow good information-gathering interview techniques as described in Chapter 2.

Meetings

Meetings allow you to develop a procedure with numerous inputs at one time, so they are quite effective and efficient. In many ways, group meetings are similar to interviews since you are again gathering information. You can follow the basic meeting guide provided in Chapter 2. However, instead of attempting to identify subjects for policies and procedures, you want to describe existing or proposed procedures.

In the meeting, assign each small group a separate topic or, if there is only one subject being considered, a portion of that subject. Have them describe what they are currently doing to handle the work situation and/ or what is needed. Then have each group report their findings, followed by a discussion of the whole group. You want to reach agreement among the participants regarding the information or identify areas in which the subject has to be treated differently.

Multiple Techniques

For example, assume you have a number of supervisors to contact regarding a policy and procedure. You could begin with a few interviews to obtain basic knowledge of what is occurring in practice and what is needed. Now you have a basis for a meeting of a number of supervisors to detail the information. Then, to ensure all are involved, you can distribute a questionnaire based on the group meeting to anyone not at that meeting.

Combining Results

Combining responses can take considerable time, depending on the number of responses received and the degree of variations among them. The best first step is to sort the responses into similar groups—that is, similar by their implementation procedures. Then identify the significant difference between groups. If your organization wants a consistent procedure, you need to resolve these differences. To accomplish that, you may need to hold a separate meeting if all inputs were from several sources.

If the organization does not prefer any one approach and will allow implementation to accommodate individual departments and managers, the meeting should include all approaches so they can be discussed and a final procedure agreed on and developed. However, if the differences are unacceptable to the organization, you need a meeting to revise those procedures to acceptable ones. This requires the development, understanding, and acceptance of the organization's requirements by all supervisors and managers.

Avoid requesting information and then telling the responders, "Thanks, but that is the way it's going to be." That type of approach is self-defeating.

Once the major differences are resolved, you then need to determine the number of subprocedures. For example, a policy and procedure covering internal selection may have separate subjects of job postings, management recommendations, and file searches. Each of these has a separate set of steps.

Next, list the steps of the procedure and/or each subprocedure in sequence. In the process, you will sometimes discover areas requiring additional information or where there are conflicting details. Along with each step you need to identify three things:

❐ Who is accountable for implementing the step?

❐ What, if any, form is required to accomplish the step?

❐ To what other policy and procedure does the step relate?

Who Is Accountable for Implementing the Step?

Be sure that someone is accountable for each step. Also be sure that there is a unity of command—that is, two different people are not assigned accountability for implementing a single step.

A New Jersey department store had a procedure covering the creation of the annual holiday window display. One of the steps was to order the display. However, three individuals were accountable for the ordering: the store manager, the display supervisor, and the advertising manager.

It should not be too surprising to learn that one year three displays were ordered—one by each of the three accountable people.

"It could have been worse." the store manager said. "At least we had a display. We could have had none if each manager thought one of the other two had placed the order."

What, If Any, Form Is Required to Accomplish the Step?

Often a form can greatly simplify a step. If it is an existing form, review it to ensure it does the job. If it is a form that does not exist, identify what it should include and have someone familiar with form design create one.

Sometimes you may discover there are forms in use that are the creation of a single department, and they may be ones you decide to incorporate for use across the entire company. In other cases, they may be forms to eliminate.

There is a story (or maybe a legend) that during World War II a bored company clerk, as a joke, created a monthly report on the quantity of flypaper being used. He sent the report to headquarters every month for more than a year.

When he was rotated to the States, the reports stopped. Actually, no one else knew anything about them. However, a month later the company received a communication requesting the previous month's flypaper report.

To What Other Policy and Procedure Does the Step Relate?

Engineering drawings often include a note, "All dimensions given once." The idea is to avoid problems when a revision is needed and a dimension appears in more than one place. A dimension may be changed, but if it is not known every place it appears, all of them may not be changed. Then you risk ending up with two different dimensions for the same design, which can create confusion and costly mistakes.

It is a good rule to follow in writing procedures. Write a step only one time. If it relates to another procedure or subprocedure, indicate the relationship. For example, a travel reimbursement policy and procedure might have a step that states:

5. Upon completion of the Travel Expense Form, submit it to the Accounting Department.

Another step in another procedure might also describe what to do with the completed form. Rather than repeating the direction, it could state:

Refer to Step 5 in the Travel Reimbursement Policy and Procedure.

Are All Steps Required?

You also need to ensure that you have identified all the required steps and eliminated unnecessary ones. For example, assume you have identified the following steps for requesting vacation time-off:

1. Employee completes a Request for Vacation Time-Off form.
2. Upon approval, the employee may schedule the time-off.

Omitted from these steps are what the employee does with the completed form and how approval is obtained. To make the procedure complete, those steps need to be added.

On the other hand, if not questioned, steps may be included that are not necessary.

In London, there are several volunteer artillery companies that appear at military events and provide cannon salutes. Their procedures duplicate those of the regular army.

A new member going through training asked, "Why, just before we fire the cannon, does one of the crew run back two paces and kneel facing away from the cannon?"

No one knew, but after some research they discovered the answer. In days when the cannons had been pulled by horses, one member of the crew was assigned to hold their reins to keep the horses from bolting when the cannon was fired. Although horses were no longer used in the ceremony, the assignment was still in existence

MANDATORY POLICIES AND PROCEDURES

Subjects that require mandatory policies and procedures generally have an initial source of information. In some cases, the law or a contract indicating the requirements has specified wording and descriptions of content you must use. So for mandatory policies and procedures, your first source is whomever indicated the need. This source might not have all the information you require, but is at least a starting point and may be able to guide you to another source, if necessary, for answers to these questions:

❐   Do our practices differ from the required policy and procedure?
❐   Has something outdated the policy and procedure?

For example, you may be told there are too many instances of employee absenteeism that are not covered by the existing policy and procedure. If that's the case, you need to find out what those instances are.

WRITING THE PROCEDURE

Some organizations detail all steps of a procedure. However, most deal with the major assignments and allow specific steps to be developed in the areas accountable for implementation.

For example, one organization may describe the steps of approving a salary increase as follows:

1. The supervisor of the employee initiates a salary increase recommendation.

2. The manager of the supervisor approves the salary increase.

3. The approved salary increase is submitted to human resources.

4. Human resources ensures the salary increase is within the policy and procedure, and approves and submits the salary increase to payroll.

5. Payroll implements the salary increase and notifies the initiating supervisor of the effective date.

6. The supervisor notifies the employee of the increase and its effective date.

Here is another, more detailed version of the same procedure:

1. The supervisor of the employee initiates a salary increase recommendation. Form HR-47 is used for this purpose. All areas of the form must be completed, and any increase must be within the approved department budget and within thirty days of the employee's anniversary date.

2. The manager of the supervisor approves the salary increase. Approval must be made on the basis that all preconditions have been met.

3. The approved salary increase is submitted to human resources.

4. Human resources ensures the salary increase is within the policy and procedure, and approves and submits the salary increase to payroll.

5. Payroll implements the salary increase and notifies the initiating supervisor of the effective date.

6. The supervisor notifies the employee of the increase and its effective date.

The outcome of this effort is a procedure. The next steps are to present it to the total management group for approval and then to your labor attorney for final review. At that point, you will have created a policy and procedure.

When you have the steps listed in order, you can then write the procedure or, in most cases, procedures. Many procedures have a number of separate processes.

What Style Should Be Used?

This answer should provide a consistent approach and generally should complement the style used for the policy statements. The examples supplied in this book are all written in an objective format. No pronouns, dates, or names are used. As a general rule, short is better than long, and clear, concise statements are better than ones with equivocating words. Also, do not attempt to detail every possible step in a procedure. If you do, you will discover the policies and procedures are always requiring revisions.

For example, the steps for initiating a salary increase could be stated as follows:

1. The employee's supervisor initiates a Form HR-289 recommending the increase.

2. The supervisor's department manager ensures the recommended increase is within the approved department budget and then approves the increase by signing Form HR-289 and submitting it to human resources. If not approved, it is returned to the supervisor with an explanation.

3. Human resources ensures the increase is within organization guidelines for increases and approves the increase by signing the form and submitting it to payroll. If not approved, HR meets with the department manager to review and explain why it was not approved.

4. Payroll notifies the supervisor of the date the increase will appear in the employee's pay.

5. The supervisor notifies the employee.

This procedure describes the sequence of activities, who does what, and the required form to use. The form can be revised, HR guidelines changed, budgets increased or decreased, and supervisors and managers transferred, but none of these normal occurrences affect the procedure as written. It is still applicable. However, if the HR salary increase guideline was more detailed, the procedure might have to be rewritten annually.

So, keep it clear, concise, and simple.

CONCLUSION

One item you need to consider is the actual physical format you will be using for your policies and procedures. As with most things in this book, there is no one correct format, and your organization (particularly if you are revising existing policies and procedures) may already have one.

The next chapter provides a format you can use or adjust to fit your needs. It is used with all the sample policies and procedures provided in this book and on the accompanying disk.

6

A Policy and Procedure Format

"Be not careless in deeds, nor confused in words, nor rambling in thought."

—Marcus Aurelius Antoninus

THERE ARE MANY FORMATS FOR PUBLISHED POLICIES and procedures. This book cannot address all of them, and in the final analysis, it is the content rather than the format that matters. So, for our purposes, we will use a fairly standard and straightforward format. Basically, it presents the policy and procedure in a numbered outline format.

The paragraph numbering provides a convenient reference when referring to specific elements of the policy and procedure. The outline format is one with which most people are familiar, and its structure quickly identifies major subjects and their components.

MAJOR ELEMENTS

The policy and procedure begins with a heading that provides basic nomenclature. The heading does not have a number. The other major elements and their numbers are:

1. Policy Statement

2. Scope

3. Accountability

4. Definitions
5. Forms
6. Procedure
7. References
8. Approvals

Heading

A typical heading includes the policy and procedure's title, a reference number, its effective date, and its edition or revision.

Title. The title is the general subject matter of the policy and procedure.

Number. Many organizations assign a reference number to each policy and procedure. Sometimes, it is just a consecutively assigned number for referral purposes, such as 100, 156, and 59. When there are several functions within the organization issuing policies and procedures, the reference number may reflect the function. For example, numbers in the 100 series could be HR policies and procedures; numbers in the 200 series, legal ones; and numbers in the 300 series, finance. Sometimes the numbers have an alpha prefix to indicate function (e.g., human resources—HR, legal—L, and finance—F). For our purposes, we will use a reference numbering system beginning with 100 and HR to indicate they are human resources policies and procedures.

If there are versions of the same policy and procedure that apply to separate locations or functions of the organization, the reference number may also reflect the appropriate location. One company color-codes its policies and procedures by location. Yellow paper is used for the corporate office. Blue paper is used for one of its two plants, and pink paper for the other.

The heading generally appears at the top of the first page of the policy and procedure. However, some organizations place the heading, or an abbreviated version of it, at the top of every page of a policy and procedure. In this book, the heading will only appear on the first pages.

The heading for a typical human resources policy and procedure covering attendance might appear as follows:

Title: Attendance   Number HR14
Effective Date: March 13, 2004   Edition: Third Revision

Policy

Since the policy statement explains the organization's purpose for the policy and procedure, it should be the first item. Again, using the attendance topic, the major element appears as follows:

1. POLICY

It is the policy of the organization for all employees to report for their scheduled work in a timely fashion unless unavailable due to a reason beyond their control.

The policy statement may have several elements. In this case, the outline numbering format is introduced, as follows:

1. POLICY

1.1 It is the policy of the organization for all employees to report for their scheduled work in a timely fashion unless unavailable due to a reason beyond their control.

1.2 It is the policy of the organization to limit the number of unapproved instances of employee lateness.

Scope

In other instances, the policy statement may have subelements, beginning with a definition of its scope. The scope identifies the employees and locations of the organization that are covered by the policy and procedure. In many organizations, almost all policies and procedures apply to all employees at all locations, but that is not always the case. Here are two different scope statements.

EXAMPLE A

2. SCOPE

This policy and procedure applies to all employees of the organization at all locations.

EXAMPLE B

2. SCOPE

> This policy and procedure applies to all full-time employees at the main office.

When a policy and procedure does not apply to every employee, the scope statement may include a reference to another policy and procedure. However, it is best not to write out the other policy and procedure in the reference item. Remember that the general rule is to write something only once. For example:

2. SCOPE

> This policy and procedure applies to all full-time employees at the main office. See policy and procedure HR124 for an applicable policy and procedure for part-time employees, and policy and procedure HR133 for employees at other locations.

Accountability

There are two basic types of accountability. The first is accountability for the implementation and administration of the policy and procedure. The second is accountability for performing as the policy and procedure requires. Accountability regarding attendance could be written as follows:

3. ACCOUNTABILITY

> 3.1 Employees
>
> 3.1.1 Employees are accountable for reporting to work by their scheduled starting time and remaining through their scheduled workday, unless unable to due to a reason beyond their control.
>
> 3.1.2 Employees are accountable for notifying the person to whom they report as soon as possible about their unavailability and the reason.
>
> 3.2 Managers and Supervisors
>
> 3.2.1 Managers and supervisors who have one or more employees reporting to them are accountable for maintaining a record of each employee's punctuality and absences.

3.2.2 If an employee exceeds the allowable number of tardiness and/or lateness absences, or is unavailable for work for an extended period, or fails to notify the manager or supervisor of the absence and reason for it, the manager and supervisor are accountable for taking the actions described in the following procedure.

Definitions

Any definitions unique to the policy and procedure and terms that require specific definitions should be included. For example:

4. DEFINITIONS

The following definitions apply to the interpretation and implementation of this policy and procedure:

4.1 *Absence*. An employee not being at work for an entire workday as scheduled.

4.2 *Tardiness*. An employee not being at the assigned workstation by the time scheduled.

4.3 *Scheduled Starting Time*. The time determined by the employees' supervisor at which employees are to be at their workstations ready to begin work.

Forms

Not all policies and procedures require forms. If that is the case, leave the item in but write "None." Where forms are required, indicate them by number or title. For example:

5. FORMS

5.1 Employee's Report of Absence

5.2 Employee Attendance Record

Procedure

In this section, the steps of implementation are detailed. In some cases, you may have a policy and procedure that covers several topics or procedures. Each topic becomes a subsection. For example, a policy and procedure covering length of service may only have a single procedure, but a policy and procedure covering attendance may have a subsection on absences, another on lateness, and one on scheduling work times.

References

Often a policy and procedure has a relationship with one or more other policies and procedures. For example, a policy and procedure covering selection of employees may require elements from a policy and procedure on equal employment practices. A policy and procedure on employee travel may require elements of a finance policy and procedure on payment for such expenses.

Using the attendance policy and procedure as our example, the reference section may appear as follows:

7. REFERENCES

    7.1 Positive Discipline Policy and Procedure

    7.2 Pay for Time-Off Policy and Procedure

Approvals

This final section records the approval of the policy and procedure as well as any revisions. Typically, it includes who approved it, when it was approved, the revision number, and the date of the edition the revision replaced. For example:

Approved by:	Approval Date:
Senior Management Committee	February 28, 2004
Revision: Three	Replaces: January 2, 2000

A SAMPLE POLICY AND PROCEDURE

This chapter concludes with an actual policy and procedure from a company using the format described. It is included to illustrate the subject and the format and implementation system for a company's HR policies and procedures.

CONCLUSION

Now that you have identified the policies and procedures that require development or revision (as covered in Part One), and have a format for writing them (covered in Part Two), the next chapter begins the section on the development of the most common HR policies and procedures. Each subsequent chapter will explain the development of a single subject (e.g., from employee selection to compensation, benefits, grievance resolution, and termination, among others).

HUMAN RESOURCES POLICY AND PROCEDURE

Subject: Human Resources Policies and Procedures	Number HR100
Effective Date: October 1, 2004	Edition: Three

1. POLICY

The Organization provides consistent, specific, and clear communication of its human resources (HR) policies and procedures through use of a standard format for their development writing, approval, and publication.

2. SCOPE

The format herein described applies to all of the Organization's HR policies and procedures.

3. ACCOUNTABILITY

3.1 The Senior Vice President of Operations and the Human Resources Manager are accountable for initiating, writing, and publishing all approved HR policies and procedures.

3.2 The Senior Management Committee is accountable for approving all HR policies and procedures.

3.3 The Human Resources Manager is accountable for maintaining files of all policies and procedures, and updating and distributing them as necessary.

3.4 All managers are accountable for ensuring the terms of the HR policies and procedures are correctly implemented in their areas of accountability.

4. DEFINITIONS

4.1 *Policy*—The Organization's intent.

4.2 *Procedure*—The method for implementing the Organization's intent.

4.3 *Human Resources Mission and Role*—The mission and role of the Organization's HR function is to obtain and maintain qualified employees for the Organization; administer all employee-related activities; ensure all legal requirements regarding employees are met; ensure the fair and equal treatment of all employees; and provide advice and counsel to the Organization management regarding all employee issues and concerns.

5. FORMS

Human resources policies and procedures are published in an approved format.

6. PROCEDURE

6.1 Human Resources shall regularly review local, state, and federal laws; requirements of the Organization's operations; developments in the HR area; Organization benefits; and the expressed needs of operating managers and make recommendations to the Senior Management Committee for any new HR policies and procedures and/or revisions to existing HR policies and procedures.

6.2 Upon the approval of the Senior Management Committee, Human Resources shall draft new HR policies and procedures and/or revisions to existing HR policies and procedures.

6.2.1 Final drafts of new and revised HR policies and procedures require the approval of the Senior Management Committee and appropriate operating managers.

6.2.2 Once approved, the new and revised HR policies and procedures shall be published and distributed to all holders of HR policies and procedures binders.

6.2.3 Each manager and supervisor is to be issued a complete HR policies and procedures binder by the Human Resources department, and these binders are to be updated as required by the issuance of new and revised HR policies and procedures.

6.3 When necessary, the Human Resources Manager conducts orientation and training for managers in the new and revised HR policies and procedures.

6.4 Annually, the Human Resources Manager shall review HR policies and procedures to ensure they are current, meet all legal requirements, and reflect the needs of the Organization.

7. REFERENCES

None

8. APPROVALS

Approved by:
   Senior Management Committee
Revision: Original

Approval Date:
   September 15, 2004
Replaces: None

Key Human Resources Policies and Procedures

Common Elements

"Even in slight things the experience of the new is rarely without some stirring of foreboding."
—ERIC HOFFER

THE CHAPTERS IN PART THREE OF THIS BOOK, starting with this one, deal with the most common human resources policies and procedures. Each chapter will introduce a subject and provide you with the type of questions you need to answer in order to ensure your organization's policy and procedure is complete and expresses its desires.

Each chapter includes a review of the subject. Then appropriate questions are asked in each area of the policy and procedure format. Your answers to those questions should supply you with the basic information you need to create the policy and procedure. In some cases, your answers may send you on another information-gathering quest.

Keep in mind that this book does not attempt to recommend what your organization's policies and procedures should be. It is a book to assist you in writing a policy and procedure for whatever practice your organization has selected.

Also, although the chapters that follow are written as if you are developing a new policy and procedure, the same questions apply to existing policies and procedures. Your answers to them will assist in identifying the specifics of any needed revisions.

SUBJECT REVIEW

The subject review describes the basic elements included—the major topic and any subtopics. In subsequent chapters, the subject review of each topic will also take a look at some of the common practices and uses of the subject. Actually, before you and your senior management attempt to begin work on a policy and procedure, it is important to ensure that you are dealing with common understandings. Otherwise, you can spend a great deal of time creating something that is not required.

> An Oklahoma company's senior vice president requested the human resources manager to develop a policy and procedure regarding flexible work hours. The HR manager conducted several meetings with operating managers to obtain their ideas and conducted research into what other companies in the area were doing.
>
> The manager then wrote a policy and procedure that described how employees could create flexible work schedules and presented the finished version to the vice president for review.
>
> The vice president returned the draft with the comment, "This is not what I wanted. I want our employees to understand we do not offer flexible work schedules."

QUESTIONS

The questions for a few elements of policies and procedures—such as Accountability, Forms, and Scope—are pretty much the same for all subjects.

Heading

The key element of the heading is the title. You should select a descriptive title that conveys the major subject of the policy and procedure. You want to make it easy for someone to locate the correct subject.

For example, if you are developing a policy and procedure covering reductions in workforce, call it that. Using euphemisms such as rightsizing, workforce adjustment, personnel balancing, downsizing, and reengineering do not add clarity. In fact, they often give the appearances of attempting to hide the true subject.

Select a title that best describes the policy and procedure subject. If you combine more than one subject in the same policy and procedure, then use both subjects as a title—for example, Internal and External Selection. You could also use Selection as a title to encompass both subjects. On the other hand, if you elect to have a separate policy and procedure for each selection practice, you might title each with the name of the activity, such as Job Posting.

You may find that some of these questions for developing the most appropriate heading have to wait until the policy and procedure is approved. Even so, they are offered here to remind you that these questions need to be considered.

- ❑ What is the appropriate title for this policy and procedure within your organization?
- ❑ If you are using a policy and procedure numbering system, what number are you assigning to this policy and procedure?
- ❑ By what date do you want this policy and procedure to become effective?

Scope

Here the basic question is always, "Who is covered by this policy and procedure?" Don't assume it is all employees. You always need to ask this question and consider other locations, functions, and types of employees.

An Indiana company issued a policy and procedure that included the statements: "Customer support employees are to be at work by 8:30 A.M., Monday through Friday," and "This policy and procedure applies to all employees and locations of the company."

The policy and procedure was distributed to all four of the company's customer support offices, but it was interpreted four different ways.

One office interpreted it as requiring all employees to be at their workstations ready to receive calls by 8:39 A.M. One office told its employees they must log in to their terminals for work by that time (the rationale being that it takes about five minutes after logging in before calls can be received).

The third office told its employees they were required to be in the work area by 8:30 A.M., and the fourth office told its employees they were to "punch in" (a time clock was used) by 8:30 A.M.

The point of this example is that the same policies and procedures should not be ambiguous. They should not be open to interpretation. You must be clear—clearly state to which areas and employees of the organization the policy and procedure applies. You need to consider functional areas, departments, divisions, geographic locations, and types of employees. Key questions are:

- ❑ Does this policy and procedure apply to all areas of the organization?
- ❑ If this policy and procedure does not apply to all areas of the organization, which ones are excluded and why?
- ❑ If there are areas not covered by this policy and procedure, will there be separate policies and procedures for those areas?
- ❑ Does this policy and procedure apply to all employees of the organization?
- ❑ If this policy and procedure does not apply to all employees of the organization, who is excluded and why?
- ❑ If there are employees not covered by this policy and procedure, will there be separate policies and procedures for them?

Here are a few sample scope statements that were written after considering all these factors:

> "This policy and procedure applies to all departments, locations, and employees of the organization."
>
> "This policy applies to all areas of the organization, but it contains separate procedures for its implementation at some (named) locations."
>
> "This policy and procedure applies to all employees of the organization."
>
> "This policy and procedure applies to all employees of the organization, except those covered by a union agreement."

Accountability

Questions are aimed at clarifying and identifying who is accountable for implementing, administering, and following the procedure. The key questions are:

❏ Who is accountable for ensuring that this policy is followed and the procedures correctly implemented?

❏ What accountability do operating managers have regarding the implementation of this policy and procedure?

❏ Does human resources have an identified accountability for this policy and procedure?

Here are some examples of accountability statements for employee selection. They are not mutually exclusive, so more than one statement can be used in the same policy and procedure:

"Human resources (HR) is accountable for obtaining candidates for all approved open positions and ensuring that selection procedures are followed."

"The supervisor of an open position is accountable for identifying candidates' qualifications and participating in the final selection."

"The manager of an area with an open position is accountable for approving and obtaining candidates for that position."

Definitions

In *Alice in Wonderland* and *Through the Looking Glass,* the author, Lewis Carroll, has Alice engage in a conversation with Humpty-Dumpty, who states: "When I use a word, it means just what I choose it to mean— neither more or less." Unfortunately, that is many times the case. We all have our own definitions for some words—even many commonly used ones—but those definitions are not necessarily mutually understood.

Policies and procedures must explain any unusual definitions, unique definitions, and definitions that must be specified. If your industry, organization, or geographic region uses jargon or special terms, these need to be defined, even if they are thought to be commonly understood.

A New Jersey–based company purchased a small manufacturing plant in Great Britain. The company wanted the same policies and procedures to apply to all locations, so it sent a set of the existing ones to the British-based human resources department.

The policy and procedure covering selection criteria and reference checking referred to "private schools" and "public schools." Both the British HR department and the American HR department knew exactly what these terms meant. However, they have opposite meanings in the two countries.

Another example is the term *overtime*. Here are three possible definitions (actually there are many more):

1. All hours actually worked in excess of the employee's normal scheduled hours
2. All hours worked in excess of forty hours in a single calendar week
3. All hours worked in excess of forty hours worked or paid in a single calendar week

If you are writing a policy and procedure on overtime, you want to be sure everyone has a common understanding of what overtime means for your organization. You need to identify any keywords used in the policy and procedure and define them. Also, if there are any words or phases used that have crucial definitions for implementation of the policy and procedure, they must be defined. For example, what is a workweek? Is it Monday through the following Sunday? Is it Sunday through Saturday? Is it seven consecutive days? Definitions are often key in understanding and administering a policy and procedure. Here are some questions that you want to get answers to:

❏ What words or terms in this policy and procedure are crucial to its correct understanding and implementation?
❏ What are the organization's definitions of those words?
❏ Are these definitions consistent with how the words are used in other policies and procedures?

Forms

Here you need to determine if a form is required or would be helpful. If one is needed, discover if it exists, exists but requires modification, or has to be created. You also want to identify where such forms can be obtained.

Before being able to identify forms, it is probably necessary to write the procedure. In the process, you will discover where forms are required. Examples of typical forms are Employee Status Change and Employee Salary Adjustment. Then you can answer these questions:

❑ Are any forms required for implementing the procedure?
❑ Are any required forms in existence?
❑ Do any forms need to be revised?
❑ Are any new forms required?

Procedure

In this book, rather broad policies and procedures are used. For example, a policy and procedure on internal selection covers numerous subtopics, including:

❑ Job Posting
❑ Promotions
❑ Transfers
❑ Demotions
❑ Record Searches

Although all these subjects are in the same policy and procedure, each one requires a separate procedure, so there will be a series of questions for each.

Some organizations prefer to have each topic represented by a separate policy and procedure. They separate policies and procedures for job posting, promotions, transfers, demotions, and record searches. There is no one correct way. You need to use the approach that best fits the realities of your organization.

In each of the remaining chapters in Part Three, some deviations from the policy and procedure will be described. However, there are many possibilities and they will vary by organizations. Therefore, only initial thoughts and overall directions will be provided.

References and Approvals

In both these areas, the information required is very straightforward and depends on your organization. Questions to ask about cross-references to other policies and procedures are:

❏ Are there any other existing or planned policies and procedures that relate to this one (such as external selection, equal treatment, and hiring)?

❏ Do any additional policies and procedures need to be created as a result of this one?

Some organizations have the people approving a policy and procedure actually sign the master copy. Whether or not you make that your practice, the two main questions to clarify the approval section are:

❏ Who approves this policy and procedure?

❏ On what date was the policy and procedure approved?

CONCLUSION

So, with this description of how the subsequent chapters dealing with individual subjects are structured, it's time to deal with the specific development of your organization's HR policies and procedures. Each of the next fourteen chapters (Chapters 8 through 21) deals with one specific subject and asks the questions related to that subject. The first subject, and the focus of Chapter 8, is internal selection.

8

Internal Selection

"You're in the front door, kid. What you do on this side of it is up to you."

—A. J. CAROTHERS

POSITIONS WITHIN AN ORGANIZATION ARE FILLED in one of two ways: either internally, drawing from existing employees, or externally, by recruiting people from outside the organization. This chapter deals with filling positions with existing employees and the various processes for making such selections. Chapter 9 covers external selection.

Some organizations combine these selection approaches into one policy and procedure. In this book, these two selection approaches are treated as separate policies and procedures. Examples of this separate approach are included at the end of this chapter and Chapter 9.

SUBJECT REVIEW

The word *selection* implies making a conscious choice from more than one alternative. In the case of internal selection, that means choosing an employee from a number of qualified employees to fill a position within the organization. This requires practices to determine when positions are filled from within the organization and how qualified employees are located.

An internal selection policy and procedure deals with how positions to be filled are identified, who can authorize their filling, how internal candidates are obtained, and how selections are made. It includes specific procedures for job posting programs and employee file searches. It also stipulates when internal selection is to be used over external selection, and any limitations on internal candidates being considered.

Internal selection is an activity that is perceived as one of major importance by employees since it describes the organization's approach to providing opportunities for advancement. The availability of such opportunities has direct bearing on their work, careers, future, and compensation.

POLICY CONSIDERATIONS

Because of the importance of this subject to employees, the policy statement should be carefully considered and worded. Employees want to know when they are eligible for other positions in the organization and what the procedure is for obtaining one.

> A candy manufacturer in Pennsylvania has a very low turnover of employees. It is perceived to be an excellent employer and there is always a waiting list of people to be hired.
>
> The company believes it can always find a qualified person from within for any open position, but its policy is to fill only 75 percent of openings from within. The reason is that the company believes to remain successful, it must continually bring in new people with different experiences and different ideas.

As another example:

> A large after-market automobile parts manufacturer in Detroit has a policy of developing its management personnel so that there are three possible candidates for promotion to a job at any one time. This company believes that its employees who know the policy work harder to ensure they are the ones in line for promotion when the opportunity arrives.

These examples are not offered as correct or incorrect policies, but as realities. Both companies have made a conscious decision about how employees will be selected and have published it as a policy. Unfortunately, not every organization is as careful in presenting its policy:

A Connecticut HMO states it policy regarding internal selection is: "To consider all qualified candidates prior to attempting to fill a position from outside the company."

The truth is that the company rarely considers internal candidates, but somehow it does not recognize that its employees long ago discovered the true policy.

Here are questions to answer that should assist in developing a policy statement that reflects what your organization wishes to accomplish with internal selection:

❑ When does your organization want to consider internal job candidates?

❑ When does your organization want to consider external candidates?

❑ Does your organization want to consider both internal and external candidates at the same time?

❑ Does your organization want to give preference to internal candidates or external candidates, or neither?

❑ Are employees within a department that has an open position considered first or given preference?

❑ Are existing employees required to have the same qualifications for an open position as external candidates?

Whatever your organization's true intent—that is, its true policy—is what should be published. Here are some possible policy statements:

"To promote from within whenever internal qualified candidates are available."

"To provide an opportunity for qualified employees to be considered for all open positions."

"To consider all qualified internal candidates before obtaining external ones."

"To give first consideration for an open position within a department to qualified employees in the same department, then to qualified employees elsewhere within the organization, and then to external candidates."

"To allow employees to apply for open positions simultaneously with external candidates."

Definitions

Here are three terms that may require definitions. These definitions are not necessarily the ones you should use, but they provide insight into how one organization defines them:

Demotion. An employee moving from a job to one of lower classification is demoted.

Promotion. An employee moving from a job to one of higher classification is promoted.

Transfer. An employee moving from a job to one of similar classification is considered a transfer.

PROCEDURES

Now you need to describe the basic procedures for fulfilling the selection policy. If a variety of methods is used, each will have to be detailed. When you answer the questions regarding implementation procedures, identify the who, what, and when for each answer.

Questions are provided for the following procedures:

- ❒ Identification of a Position to Be Filled
- ❒ Selection from Within a Department
- ❒ Employee Notification of Open Positions
- ❒ Job Posting
- ❒ File Search
- ❒ Promotion, Demotion, and Transfer

Identification of a Position to Be Filled

Identifying a position within the organization that requires filling is the action that initiates the selection process. A position to be filled can be the result of the incumbent leaving the job so that a replacement is required, or it can be a newly created position. Whatever the reason, a commitment of resources, including compensation and benefits, is needed to obtain that person. Therefore, it is important to identify who can authorize the selection process. Here are some considerations:

Supervisor of the Position to Be Filled. Sometimes this position has the authority to initiate the selection process. Other times, this position initiates a request to be approved by some other position.

Manager of the Supervisor of the Position to Be Filled. In some organizations, this position is given the authority for initiating a selection requisition, but in others, the manager is assigned the authority for approving a request initiated by the supervisor of the open position.

Senior Management Position in the Area. Some organizations require the top management position of a functional area or location to also approve any addition to the workforce. This keeps senior management informed of what is occurring within the area.

Human Resources. Some organizations require HR approval of any selection request. Generally, this occurs in organizations in which human resources is accountable for ensuring certain requirements have been met, or where HR is accountable for implementing or monitoring some type of employee plan.

Finance. In some organizations, someone from finance is required to countersign a selection request because finance has budget oversight or control accountabilities.

Which process is correct? The answer depends on your organization and its assignments of accountabilities. As with all policies and procedures, it is important to consider all possibilities but select the approach that best meets your organization's requirements. Here are some questions to answer:

- ❐ How is an open position identified for filling?
- ❐ Who has the authority to request a position to be filled?
- ❐ Who has authority to approve the filling of a position?
- ❐ Who identifies the qualifications a position requires?
- ❐ Who determines from where internal candidates are obtained?
- ❐ Who determines if external candidates are to be considered simultaneously?

❐ Who determines if preference is given to candidates from one source?

❐ Who obtains candidates?

❐ Who interviews candidates?

❐ Who makes the selection decision?

Many organizations require the request to be in writing, and most seem to require a specific form to be used in requesting and authorizing an employee selection. Generally, the form includes:

Initiating person

Approving person(s)

Title of position

To whom position reports

Requirements for position

Compensation of position

Position description (optional)

Standards of performance for position (optional)

Selection from Within a Department

Just as promotions are important to all employees in an organization, they are perceived as even more important to employees within the department. Often employees within a department feel they deserve consideration for any open position. Some organizations attempt to fill an open position from within the department or functional area before considering other sources of candidates.

Again, the rules need to be clearly described so there are no surprises and no unfounded expectations when an opportunity occurs. Consider these key questions:

❐ Are department employees considered before candidates are obtained from other sources?

❐ How are candidates from within a department identified?

❐ Are all employees within a department eligible for consideration?

❐ How do department employees apply for an open position?

❐ What specific requirements, if any, are there for department employees to be considered (e.g., attendance, length of time in current job, promotions only, current performance)?

Employee Notification of Open Positions

If internal candidates are to be considered for a position, there needs to be a process for making employees aware of available positions. There are numerous options—from general information bulletin boards to employee newsletters, special bulletin boards, e-mail announcements, and internal Web sites.

Sometimes there is a progression of notifications. For example, first department employees are notified. Next, location employees are notified, and finally all employees are notified. When this approach is used, there may be different methods of notification for different employee groups. Also, there may be restrictions on what available positions are communicated to certain groups of employees. For example, one company communicates all open positions within a functional area to all employees in that same functional area, but only announces open supervisor and manager positions to other areas. Key questions are:

❏ Which employee groups are notified of which open positions?

❏ How are employees notified of open positions?

❏ Who notifies employees of open positions?

❏ What do the notifications include (e.g., position qualifications, employee requirements, compensation, position classification, department name, name of supervisor that position reports to)?

❏ How do employees apply?

❏ How are employees notified of results?

Job Posting

An often-used procedure for finding internal candidates is the job posting. It can be covered in the internal selection policy and procedure or in one of its own.

Job posting is a formalized process of announcing available positions and their requirements to employees. It includes a method for applying for a position and receiving notification of results. Often there are dedicated job posting boards with accompanying applications located throughout work areas, and positions are posted for a specific period in a standard format. Key questions are:

❐ Which jobs are posted?

❐ Who determines which jobs are posted?

❐ How are posted jobs communicated to employees?

❐ How long are jobs posted?

❐ Are external candidates simultaneously being considered?

❐ Who can apply?

❐ What special requirements are there for applicants? (For example, employees must meet performance standards, be in their current position a minimum amount of time, have no disciplinary problems, and cannot apply for a similar position within a specified amount of time. Some organizations limit applicants to those applying for a promotion and not a transfer or demotion.)

❐ Who posts jobs and maintains the posting?

❐ Who receives and evaluates applications?

❐ How do employees apply?

❐ How is selection made?

❐ How are employees notified of results?

File Search

All organizations have some type of files for their employees. At minimum, they contain the factual record of the employee's history with the organization and any required personal information. Sometimes the files may contain additional information that may provide another source for identifying and locating job candidates.

Even small organizations find it impossible to know all current information about their employees without some type of formal system. Actually, PC software makes it relatively easy to search for employees who have the required qualifications, and the program retrieves their names. For such a system to be effective, however, employee records must contain the appropriate information, and they must be updated regularly. Many organizations have their employees complete a personnel inventory when they are hired. Then it is returned to them for review and updating, usually on an annual basis, at the time of their anniversary with the organization.

A small New York City firm (less than 100 employees) received a letter from the widow of one of its largest customers. The letter was written in a form of Arabic. They were about to call the Arab nation consulate when someone suggested an employee file search.

The search discovered two employees who could read Arabic. Management had no idea of this internal asset, even though the company did considerable business in the Middle East.

When employee files are searched for qualified job candidates, the key questions to consider are.

☐ For what positions are employee files reviewed?

☐ Who conducts the review?

☐ How are employee files maintained and updated?

☐ Are employees regularly preidentified for other positions (e.g., through replacement charts and management planning documents)?

☐ Is there a system for searching employee files and identifying employee qualifications?

☐ How are employees identified by a file search made aware of their consideration for an available position?

Promotion, Demotion, and Transfer

Promotions are generally perceived as a positive benefit by employees. Promotional opportunities that are filled from outside the organization are generally viewed negatively, unless there are no internal qualified candidates. However, it may not always be possible to promote from within instead of recruiting from the outside, so the organization should clearly describe the rules regarding promotional opportunities.

The definition of promotion is important. Generally, it is moving to another job that is evaluated higher than the current one. However, sometimes other factors create the perception of promotion. Location, office size, expense accounts, clothing allowances, and work hours usually reflect on an employee's standing in the company.

There are some promotions that are not perceived favorably by all employees. For example, moving from a job that pays overtime to one with higher base pay but no overtime is one such case. Moving to a higher-paying job that is on an undesirable work schedule is another.

Many organizations make the following statement part of their promotion policy:

Any employee receiving a promotion will receive a salary increase.

Demotion is the reverse of promotion—a move to a lower-rated job. Many organizations do not reduce compensation, but freeze the employee's current rate if it is higher than what the new job pays.

Transfers are lateral moves, and the same factors that affect perceptions of promotions and demotions need to be considered:

❑ How does employee eligibility differ for these three types of selection?

❑ How do selection procedures differ for these three types of moves?

❑ If there is a union, how are moves from union to nonunion jobs made? (It is assumed a union contract covers internal moves within union jobs.)

❑ If there is a union, how are moves from nonunion to union jobs made?

❑ Does a promotion always include a salary or wage increase?

❑ Does a demotion include a salary or wage reduction?

❑ How are nonvoluntary promotions, transfers, and demotions handled?

❑ Can employees apply for all three types of status change?

ELECTRONIC JOB NOTIFICATION

With the increasing use of electronic communication and employee PC availability, many organizations now use internal Internet (i.e., intranet) systems or services to post jobs and notify employees of job opportunities within the company. If this is a reality at your organization, be sure to include electronic job notification in all procedures relating to internal selection.

A SAMPLE POLICY AND PROCEDURE

At the end of this chapter is an example of one organization's internal selection policy and procedure. It is not provided for you to copy, but rather to illustrate one organization's approach within the guidelines provided in this book. The policy and procedure, like all examples in this book, is from a real organization (though they are not all from the same organization). It has been somewhat simplified, with specific references to the organization removed.

HUMAN RESOURCES INTERNAL SELECTION POLICY AND PROCEDURE

1. POLICY

It is the policy of the Organization to fill positions by drawing from internal candidates possessing the desired qualifications, and to promote from within whenever possible.

2. SCOPE

This policy and procedure applies to all departments and employees of the Organization.

3. ACCOUNTABILITY

3.1 All managers are accountable for identifying the staffing needs of their department and the qualifications for each position within their department.

3.2 Human Resources is solely accountable for obtaining qualified candidates for all open positions and providing all necessary forms to implement this policy and procedure.

4. DEFINITIONS

4.1 *Transfer*—Moving an existing employee to a new position, department, or location at the same level within the Organization.

4.2 *Promotion*—Moving an existing employee to a new position, department, or location at a higher level within the Organization.

4.3 *Demotion*—Moving an existing employee to a new position, department, or location at a lower level within the Organization.

5. FORMS

5.1 Employee Requisition

5.2 Job Available Notice

6. PROCEDURE

6.1 Identifying Open Position and Obtaining Candidates

6.1.1 When a position becomes available, the supervisor to whom that position reports will first decide whether to fill the position from within or from outside the Organization, based on the position's requirements. This decision is to be reviewed with and approved by the person to whom the manager reports.

6.1.2 If the position is to be filled from within the Organization, the supervisor of the open position first considers employees within the department and/or a reorganization of the department's work.

6.1.3 In the event a qualified candidate is not available within the department, the supervisor consults with the person to whom he/she reports to determine if there is a qualified person within the division.

6.1.4 If no employees within the department and division are qualified for the position, and if the work cannot be reorganized, the supervisor and the supervisor's manager decide whether to post the position within the Organization and/or obtain candidates from outside the Organization.

6.1.5 The supervisor completes an Employee Requisition, has it approved and signed by the manager to whom he/she reports, and submits it to Human Resources, along with a request for job posting and/or external candidates.

6.1.6 Human Resources first conducts a search of employee files to determine if there is an already-identified candidate for the job.

6.1.7 Procedures if there are no identified internal candidates:

6.1.7.1 If the job is to be posted, Human Resources completes a Job Available Notice and posts it, as per the Job Posting procedure (6.2 below).

6.1.7.2 If external candidates are to be sought, Human Resources implements the External Selection Policy and Procedure.

6.2 Job Posting

Job posting is used to notify existing employees of a position's availability and obtain qualified internal candidates of it.

6.2.1 Human Resources posts the Job Available Notice at all job posting locations, stating a description of the position with salary grade, required qualifications, and the date by which applications must be received. If external candidates will also be considered, it is stated on the Notice.

6.2.1.1 The Notice for the position is posted by Human Resources on the employee information bulletin board(s) or on separate job posting bulletin board(s) maintained by Human Resources.

6.2.2 Any eligible and qualified employee may apply for a posted position by completing an application supplied by Human Resources. However, applications will only be considered for the position if the employees:

6.2.2.1 Provide evidence that they possess the required qualifications.

6.2.2.2 Have been in their current position at least six (6) months.

6.2.2.3 Have no current Performance Improvement notifications.

6.2.2.4 Have not been excessively absent or late during the past twelve (12) months.

6.2.2.5 Have received at least a Good rating on their last performance appraisal.

6.2.2.6 Have been an employee of the Organization for at least one (1) year.

6.2.2.7 Have not applied for more than three (3) posted positions within the last twelve (12) months.

6.2.3 Human Resources will notify an employee within one (1) week of receiving an application if the employee does not meet the above requirements. Such notice will state which requirement(s) was not met, and that the employee will not be considered for the position unless the employee can provide information to support her/his qualifications within one (1) week.

6.2.4 Applications from employees who apply for the position and possess the required qualifications are forwarded, after the closing date for applying, to the supervisor of the position.

6.2.5 The supervisor of the position interviews all qualified applying employees and makes a decision regarding each one.

6.2.5.1 In the event there are two (2) or more employees with identical qualifications, the supervisor is encouraged to use length of service with the Organization as a tie-breaker.

6.2.6 When the selection has been made, Human Resources notifies the selected candidate and any nonselected but considered candidates.

6.2.7 Human Resources coordinates the date of the employee transfer/promotion.

6.2.8 The supervisor initiates the Employee Status Change form and submits the form to the employee's current supervisor.

6.2.9 The employee's current supervisor approves the Employee Status Change form and returns it to the new position's supervisor, who then submits it to her/his manager.

6.2.10 The manager ensures it is within budget, approves it, and submits it to Human Resources.

6.2.11 Human Resources approves the Employee Status Change form if it is within guidelines and submits it to Payroll.

6.2.12 Payroll notifies the supervisor of the effective date.

7. REFERENCES

7.1 External Selection Policy and Procedure

8. APPROVALS

External Selection

"I believe in the adage: Hire people smarter than you and get out of their way."

—HOWARD SCHULTZ

CHAPTER 8 DEALT WITH ONE METHOD of filling job positions—from existing employees. This chapter deals with a second method—from outside the organization. Although these are presented as two different policies and procedures, they have many similar requirements and are often implemented simultaneously.

SUBJECT REVIEW

A policy and procedure covering external selection deals with some of the same elements as the one for internal selection: Who authorizes positions to be filled? How are candidates obtained? What methods are used for determining candidate qualifications? How are selections made? If this information duplicates the internal selection procedure, you can consider referring to the other procedure rather than having the procedural steps written in two places.

The external selection procedure concentrates on methods and sources for identifying external candidates. It also stipulates when external (as opposed to internal) selection is used and explains any limitations on the recruitment of external candidates.

Definitions

Often external selection policies and procedures include the following definitions:

Search Firm. An external organization contracted to obtain qualified candidates and used mainly for executive and professional positions. Generally, the search firm's fee is paid whether or not a candidate is hired.

Employment Agency. An external organization furnishing qualified candidates and used mainly for nonexempt, administrative, first-level management, and entry positions. Generally, no fee is paid unless a candidate is hired.

Hiring. Adding a new employee to the organization.

POLICY CONSIDERATIONS

Like internal selection, this subject is important to employees, so the policy statement needs to reflect that level of interest. The statement should relate to internal selection. Unfortunately, that is not always the reality:

A Maine financial services company ran a "blind newspaper ad" for salespeople. A blind ad uses a post office box number and includes no identification of the company. The company was seeking people experienced in its business. It received very few inquiries from qualified people.

At a trade show, the human resources director met a qualified sales representative from a competitive company who indicated he wanted to change jobs. The HR director asked if he had seen the ad. The salesman said he had, so the HR director asked why he had not inquired about the position.

The salesman said, "It sounded like it might be with my company, and I didn't want them to know I was looking."

Subsequently, the company changed its advertising. Now, when there is a position available, the company notifies its employees and encourages any qualified employees to apply. Simultaneously, it seeks external candidates. The company still uses blind ads, but now the ads always include the statement: "Our employees know of this ad."

Here are questions to answer that should assist in developing a policy statement that reflects what your organization wishes to accomplish with external selection:

❑ When does your organization want to consider external candidates for a position?

❑ When are both internal and external candidates considered at the same time?

❑ What preference is given to either internal candidates or external candidates?

❑ What external sources does your organization use for assistance in finding candidates?

Whatever is your organization's true intent—its true policy—is what should be published. Here are some possible policy statements:

"To promote from within whenever internal qualified candidates are available, and if no qualified internal candidates are available, to obtain external candidates."

"To consider both internal and external candidates for open positions and select the one best meeting the position's requirements."

PROCEDURES

You need to identify the various processes of external selection by answering applicable questions and then laying out the steps for their implementation. The key procedural areas to consider are:

❑ Identification of Positions to Be Filled

❑ Use of External Sources of Candidates

❑ Selection Process

❑ Tests and Reference Checks

❑ Unsolicited Resumes and Applications

❑ Employee Referrals

Identification of Positions to Be Filled

This is basically the same procedure as described in the previous chapter on internal selection. Identifying a position to be filled is the action that initiates the selection process, so the same considerations and questions apply (see Chapter 8), regardless of where the candidates for the open position are obtained.

Use of External Sources of Candidates

Once a requisition has been properly submitted, finding candidates is the next step. Sometimes internal job candidates are considered first. Sometimes only external candidates are considered, and sometimes it is a combination. However, someone needs to have the authority for obtaining candidates.

What is important is not to assign the same authority to more than one person. Doing otherwise can create confusion and duplication of efforts.

An Alabama wire manufacturer allowed both the supervisor of an open position and the human resources manager to find job candidates. Since both had slightly different perceptions and priorities about the position and its requirements, a rather embarrassing situation developed. The same person was approached by both people about the job. However, each one described the job differently. The candidate, who was very qualified, decided not to apply. He said, "If they have that much confusion about the job requirements, imagine what it would be like to work there."

Generally, the responsibility for obtaining job candidates is assigned to one person or function—usually human resources, if there is such a function. If not, it is usually assigned to the manager or supervisor of the position to be filled.

If the person submitting the requisition believes there is someone in the department of the vacant position qualified to fill it, this candidate is often given first preference. Some organizations assign the responsibility of obtaining qualified candidates to an outside organization, such as an employment agency or search firm, and for some trade jobs, the local union selects people.

There are numerous sources of external candidates. Which ones your organization uses most likely depends on your geographic location and your industry. Another consideration is the type of positions you are trying to fill. Different sources provide different types of candidates. Sources to consider are:

- ❐ Newspaper Advertising
- ❐ Trade Publication Advertising
- ❐ Unsolicited Applications and Resumes
- ❐ Private Employment Agencies
- ❐ State Employment Agencies
- ❐ Search Firms
- ❐ Colleges and Associations
- ❐ Web Sites

Each has its own advantages and disadvantages. Some are free services and others require a payment. If these sources are considered, the organization needs to make a decision about what it will pay. Here are the questions to consider in developing this procedure:

- ❐ Are resumes and applications that have already been received from external candidates reviewed before seeking external assistance?
- ❐ What external sources are used for what types of positions?
- ❐ Who can authorize the use of an external source?
- ❐ Who deals with external sources?
- ❐ Who determines which external sources to use?
- ❐ Who pays for external source charges?
- ❐ What specifications are given to external sources?

Selection Process

The selection process for external candidates usually consists of more steps than are required for internal selection. The organization already has a great deal of personal and performance information on existing employees. With external candidates, the organization has very little information, so it must have a procedure in place to obtain what it needs to make a decision that's good for the candidate and the organization. Key questions are:

- ❏   How are applications and resumes of external candidates evaluated?
- ❏   How are interviews conducted?
- ❏   What reference checks and/or tests are used?
- ❏   How are candidates notified of results?
- ❏   How is compensation determined and an offer made?
- ❏   How is a selected candidate for the position notified?

Tests and Reference Checks

Tests and reference checks are often used as methods for obtaining information to assist with a hiring decision. Both of these activities can provide useful information, but if not handled professionally, they can produce unreliable or faulty information and potentially violate numerous federal and state laws.

A Wisconsin manufacturer of copper fittings used a short written test in its selection process. Candidates had to obtain a certain minimum score to be considered. The test only required twelve minutes to complete, and it was administered by the assistant to the HR manager.

One day the HR manager was walking in the hallway. He observed the assistant outside the testing room door with a timer in her hand. As he approached, the timer rang. Then the assistant counted to a hundred. After her count, the assistant went into the testing room.

Later that day, the HR manager asked the assistant why she was counting to a hundred. She replied, "I really liked that candidate. Anytime I think a candidate would be good for our company, I give them extra time on the test."

Four types of preemployment tests are covered by legislation: drug testing, physical examinations, polygraphs, and psychological/performance tests. In some instances, they may be used, but in others they are prohibited. If your organization uses any of these testing methods, you should be confident you are using them correctly and legally. Be sure your labor attorney has reviewed this practice. If it has not been reviewed and one or more of these tests are being used, be sure to provide your attorney with answers to the following questions:

❑ Who is required to take the test?

❑ What is the basis for requiring the test?

❑ What evidence does the organization have to support use of the test?

❑ Was the test professionally developed?

❑ Is the test conducted by a professional who has been properly trained?

❑ Are candidates told of their test results?

❑ What are the procedures for retaining test results?

❑ For which candidates are reference checks conducted?

❑ Who conducts reference checks?

❑ Are reference checks limited to certain areas? If so, which areas?

❑ Are candidates asked for permission to conduct reference checks?

❑ How is reference check information maintained?

❑ Have your managers and supervisors been advised of what to say when called for reference checks?

Unsolicited Resumes and Applications

You may receive resumes and applications as a result of your external search efforts. But you may also receive unsolicited resumes and applications, and sometimes these represent people qualified for current open positions. Sometime they may be qualified for positions not currently available, and other times they may not have any of the qualifications your organization seeks.

Having a procedure to properly handle these unsolicited resumes and applications has many benefits. One is that you may discover the perfect candidate for a position. Another is that there are legal implications for not handling them properly.

A Washington chemical company never bothered to read unsolicited resumes. They were discarded. Yet, for "public relations" purposes, a letter was sent to each applicant, thanking them and stating, "We currently do not have a position available that meets your qualifications. However, if one should open in the near future, you will be considered a candidate for it."

When a position opened for a specialized biochemist, the company placed the job with a search firm for candidates. The search firm approached a biochemist at a local laboratory. The chemist was very qualified for the job, but he had submitted a resume to that company just two months earlier and had received its standard letter.

When he mentioned this fact to the search firm, the firm elected not to submit him as a candidate. Another person was hired. The biochemist filed a lawsuit against the company based on the letter he had received. The company claimed no contest and settled out of court.

The biochemist later said, "It was not about the money, and it was not about someone else getting the job. It was about being lied to."

Whatever your practice is for accepting resumes and applications, evaluating them, providing a response, or keeping them and referring to them, it should be described in this policy and procedure. Questions to consider are:

❐ What is done when a resume and application is received?

❐ What type of evaluation is made?

❐ What type of response is sent?

❐ How are the resumes and applications recorded and maintained?

❐ How long are resumes and applications kept?

❐ What procedures are used for reviewing resumes and applications in the event of an open position?

Employee Referrals

Many organizations encourage employees to recommend candidates for positions. Usually some type of cash award is paid to an employee who recommends a candidate who is eventually hired. However, for such a policy to be successful, there are a number of important considerations.

First is timing. Some organizations only allow recommendations for specific job openings. Others allow recommendations at any time. Whatever the case, the recommendations must be recorded by date received, and then maintained for a specified period of time.

Prohibited from making such recommendations—or at least prohibited from being awarded anything—are employees such as the supervisor of the position, executives, and HR professionals. Some organizations also prohibit employees from recommending relatives.

There also needs to be a method for handling situations where the same person is recommended by two or more employees, or is recommended by some other source, such as a search firm. In addition, a company must define what "hired" means. Consideration has to be given to how long hires stay with the organization and how well their performance is.

Finally, there is the question of how great the award should be for a referral. Some organizations pay a flat amount. Others pay different amounts for different positions, and some pay a percentage of starting compensation. Along with the amount, the company must decide when it is paid.

The questions raised by employee referrals are:

❒ For what positions can employees recommend others?

❒ Who is allowed to make recommendations?

❒ How long are recommendations maintained?

❒ How are duplicate recommendations resolved?

❒ What type of award is paid?

❒ What are the conditions for receiving an award?

❒ When is the award paid?

❒ What is the procedure for making a recommendation?

Miscellaneous Issues

In addition, there are also a number of related items to consider. Many laws require that certain notices be posted concerning employment. For example, the federal Wage and Hour Law requires that employers post information pertaining to the minimum wage. There are similar requirements to display notices about state workers compensation benefits. In these cases:

❑ What are the procedures and accountabilities for maintaining and posting required notices?

❑ What are the procedures for the actual hiring process (e.g., placing the new employee on the payroll, orienting the new employee to conditions of employment, and obtaining required legal documents)?

❑ What are the procedures for handling responses to ads and "walk in" applicants?

A SAMPLE POLICY AND PROCEDURE

This chapter concludes with an example of one organization's external selection policy and procedure. In this case, it happens to be from the same organization whose internal selection policy and procedure was presented in Chapter 8. Again, it is not provided as an example of what your organization's policy and procedure should be. Rather, it is a model for writing a policy and procedure in the format suggested in this book, after answering all key questions.

HUMAN RESOURCES EXTERNAL SELECTION POLICY AND PROCEDURE

1. POLICY

It is the policy of the Organization to select employees from candidates possessing the required qualifications for a position. When qualified internal candidates are not available, external candidates are considered.

2. SCOPE

This policy and procedure applies to all departments and employees of the Organization.

3. ACCOUNTABILITY

3.1 All managers are accountable for identifying the staffing needs of their departments and the qualifications for each position within their departments.

3.2 Human Resources is solely accountable for obtaining qualified candidates for all open positions, conducting reference checks, negotiating compensation and start date, processing new employees, and providing all necessary forms to implement this policy and procedure.

3.3 The Supervisor of the position, Department Manager, and Human Resources are jointly accountable for making the selection decision.

4. DEFINITIONS

4.1 *Search Firm*—An external organization contracted to obtain qualified candidates and used mainly for executive and professional positions. Generally, the fee is paid whether or not a candidate is hired.

4.2 *Employment Agency*—An external organization furnishing qualified candidates and used mainly for nonexempt, administrative, first-level management, and entry positions. Generally, no fee is paid unless a candidate is hired.

5. FORMS

5.1 Employee Requisition

5.2 Employee Recommendation

5.3 Application for Employment

5.4 Emergency Information Sheet

5.5 Federal Form I-9

5.6 Federal Form W-4

5.7 Employee Handbook

5.8 Benefit Enrollment Forms and Manuals

5.9 Reference Authorization and Release

6. PROCEDURE

6.1 When a position becomes available, the supervisor to whom that po-sition reports and his/her manager decide whether to obtain external can-didates (see Internal Selection Policy and Procedure).

6.2 If external candidates are to be considered for the position, the super-visor completes an Employee Requisition, has it approved and signed by the manager to whom he/she reports, and submits it to Human Re-sources, along with a request for external candidates.

6.3 Human Resources obtains qualified candidates and refers them to the supervisor submitting the requisition.

6.4 Human Resources may use whatever sources it views as appropriate for obtaining external candidates, such as, but not limited to, employee recommendations (see 6.11 below), applications and resumes on file, new applications and resumes, newspaper advertising, school references, job fairs, professional references, employment agencies, and search firms.

6.5 The Human Resources manager has the sole authority for selecting candidates to be considered, scheduling interviews, checking references, and obtaining a completed Application for Employment and a signed Ref-erence Authorization and Release.

6.5.1 Human Resources submits applications and/or resumes of can-didates meeting qualifications to the supervisor of the position for re-view.

6.5.2 If approved by the supervisor, Human Resource schedules inter-views for a candidate.

6.6 The selection decision is made by the supervisor from the candidates provided by Human Resources, with the approval of the supervisor's man-ager.

6.6.1 Human Resources negotiates starting compensation and dates with the selected candidate and prepares and sends a written offer of employment (see 7.2 Compensation Policy and Procedure).

6.6.2 When the employment offer is accepted by the selected candi-date, Human Resources notifies all other candidates for the position. If the selected candidate declines the offer, the external selection process is continued.

6.7 During the first hours of employment, Human Resources has the employee complete all required forms: Emergency Information Sheet, Federal Form I-9, Federal Form W-4, and any other required forms.

6.8 When all forms are completed, Human Resources will explain all appropriate conditions of employment and then escort the new employee to the supervisor to whom she/he will report.

6.9 Between sixty (60) and seventy-five (75) days after the date of employment, Human Resources will meet with the employee to explain the health and dental benefits programs. Prior to the ninetieth (90th) day of employment, the employee will be required to accept or decline (in writing) the benefits programs.

6.10 Record Keeping
Human Resources is accountable for maintaining the following records and files:

6.10.1 Applicant Log listing all applicants, from whatever sources, by date of application.

6.10.2 A file of completed applications and resumes.

6.10.2.1 Applications and resumes are filed by type of position for which they were made or are qualified.

6.10.2.2 Applications and resumes in each category are maintained by date received.

6.10.2.3 Applications and resumes are retained for at least twelve (12) months.

6.10.2.4 After twelve (12) months, they are discarded.

6.10.3 Bulletin Board
Human Resources maintains a bulletin board at each location where candidates and applications are received. The bulletin boards include a posting of all required local, state, and federal employment notices.

6.11 Employee Referrals
A system for existing employees to recommend external candidates for positions within the organization.

6.11.1 Human Resources may notify all employees of open positions by bulletin board notices.

6.11.2 Any employee may recommend a nonemployee for any posted position by submitting to Human Resources a completed Employee Recommendation form, accompanied by an Application for Employment completed by the individual being recommended.

6.11.3 Human Resources retains all Employee Recommendation forms in a separate file for six (6) months from date of receipt.

6.11.4 If the recommended individual is hired, the recommending employee will receive a reward after the newly hired employee has completed six (6) months of service with the organization.

6.11.5 In the event two (2) or more employees recommend the same individual, the employee making the recommendation first will be paid any award, and the other recommending employees will be so notified.

6.11.6 Awards are:

6.11.6.1 $**** for commissioned sales positions.

6.11.6.2 $**** for all positions other than commissioned sales positions.

6.11.7 No awards will be paid if:

6.11.7.1 The individual applied to the Organization within the past six (6) months and prior to the receipt of the Employee Recommendation form.

6.11.7.2 The individual was suggested to the Organization by a search firm or employment agency within the past six (6) months and prior to the receipt of the Employee Recommendation form.

6.11.7.3 There is a completed Application for Employment on file that was received prior to the receipt of the Employee Recommendation form.

6.11.7.4 The individual is hired more than six (6) months after the Employee Recommendation form is received.

6.11.7.5 The employee making the referral is no longer employed by the Organization at the time the award is scheduled for payment.

6.11.7.6 The recommended individual is terminated for any reason prior to one hundred eighty (180) days of service.

6.11.7.7 The referring employee is in the Human Resources department; is an officer or senior manager of the Organization; is a relative of the referred individual (sibling, divorced former spouse, parent, child, grandparent, grandchild, spouse, father-in-law, mother-in-law, brother-in-law, sister-in-law, son-in-law, or daughter-in-law); or is the supervisor or manager of the position.

7. REFERENCES

7.1 Internal Selection Policy and Procedure

7.2 Compensation Policy and Procedure

10

Compensation

"Good work must, in the long run, receive good reward or it will cease to be good work."

—CHARLES HANDY

COMPENSATION, AS THE TERM IS USED IN THIS CHAPTER, refers to the money paid to employees for their work. It recognizes that there are numerous compensation systems in use, but it also recognizes there are certain common elements that can be used to construct your compensation policy and procedure.

SUBJECT REVIEW

The variety of compensation methods occurs not only between types of organizations but within a single organization. The most familiar methods are salary, hourly wages, piecework, and commissions. However, over the past few decades new approaches have emerged to meet changing needs. Many of these new approaches link compensation directly to performance (as a salesperson's commission traditionally has done). Other systems defer payment for compensation to a later date—usually a date with more favorable tax implications for the employee—or pay a "sign on" bonus to attract new employees.

In addition to the many compensation methods, within each one are numerous permutations. For example, commissions to salespeople may be based on gross sales or net sales. They may vary with product or service sold, or decline over time. They may be based on sales less advances, a minimum guarantee, a base salary plus commission, or a sliding scale— and these are but a portion of the possible methods in practice.

Compensation also often includes other payment factors—for example, shift differential pay, bonuses, gain-sharing, lump-sum payments, awards, increases, and cost-of-living adjustments, etc. The list goes on and on.

In spite of all these individuals approaches, they all have some elements in common, and those elements serve as the basis for a policy and procedure. Then, within that structure, the individual details can be described. In many cases, an organization that uses several approaches may create a separate policy and procedure for each approach.

Definitions

Generally, the key definitions for a policy and procedure on compensation have to do with the terms used. Terms such as "hourly," "salary," "wage," "production," and "gross sales" can have very specific meanings. Definitions may also be required for the operating elements of the procedure, such as "community," "similar jobs," and "survey of positions." In developing a compensation policy and procedure, you need to identify such terms and include definitions for them.

POLICY CONSIDERATIONS

Often policy statements for compensation do not actually describe an organization's philosophy or objective. For example, offering "a fair day's pay for a fair day's work" may sound good to investors, but it hardly describes what the organization's approach is.

Here are two policy statements from organizations that, whether or not you agree with them, do give specific direction:

"To pay employees 80 percent of the average rate for similar jobs in our community and provide a performance bonus payment that can bring total compensation up to 150 percent of the rate for the same jobs."

"To pay employees 10 percent above the average rates for similar jobs in our industry."

Developing a policy statement for compensation may be more time-consuming than other subjects. However, a clear statement makes the development of a procedure much easier and is of considerable assistance in helping employees understand the rationale behind their amount and method of compensation.

PROCEDURES

The questions that follow need to be answered for each type of compensation method your organization uses. In some cases, a question may not apply. In others, you may have to create your own question. Overall, though, these questions should guide you in writing a policy and procedure. They are grouped, by topic, as follows:

❏ Evaluating Job Worth

❏ Determining Method of Compensation

❏ Establishing Rate of Compensation

❏ Adjusting Compensation

❏ Related Compensation

Evaluating Job Worth

Actually, this task refers both to determining the competitive worth of a job in the marketplace and the internal worth of the job within the organization. For example, an accounting clerk's position can be compared to other accounting clerks in the community and industry (assuming similar responsibilities) and an average rate determined. However, the accounting clerk also has an internal value when compared to other positions within the organization.

External worth can be determined by conducting a community or industry survey of similar positions. Some compensation methods include an arrangement for annual surveys of organizations using the same approach, and some professional associations offer salary surveys for their industries or communities. Key questions to consider are:

❏ What method does your organization use to determine external job worth?

❑ How often is external job worth determined (i.e., updated)?

❑ Who is accountable for determining job worth?

❑ How are the results of determining external job worth communicated to employees?

Similarly, there are many different methods for determining internal worth. Some evaluation techniques assign numerical values to job positions. There are forced-ranking techniques that develop a list of jobs classified by their value to the organization, and there are methods that rely solely on external competitive wages. When developing a policy and procedure on this subject, questions to ask are:

❑ What method does your organization use to determine internal job worth?

❑ What conditions require a reevaluation of the internal worth of a job?

❑ Who is accountable for determining internal job worth?

❑ How are the results of determining internal job worth communicated to employees?

Determining Compensation Method

As mentioned previously, there are numerous methods of compensation. If you have a clear organizational policy statement for compensation, the method used should support the aims of that policy.

A direct marketing firm paid its salespeople a commission that increased with volume, but no commission was paid after they reached 110 percent of their sales target for the year. The firm believed that if it tried for greater sales volume, it would be difficult for the sales force to deliver at the desired quality level.

The best salesperson usually attained her 110 percent goal by March each year. For the balance of the year, she worked two days a week just visiting existing clients. "There is no reason for me to make additional sales until the next year," she confided.

It is also possible for a single job to be compensated by more than one method. For example, restaurant waitpeople are usually paid a base hourly wage plus all or a percentage of tips. Therefore, the key questions are:

- ❏ What methods of compensation does your organization use?
- ❏ What jobs are assigned each method of compensation?
- ❏ What are the guidelines for each method of compensation?
- ❏ What are the implementation steps for each method?

Establishing Rate of Compensation

Once the worth of a job is determined and the method of compensation determined, a rate of pay needs to be attached. It can be an hourly amount, a daily amount, a weekly amount, a monthly amount, or an annual amount. It can be stated as a percentage, such as in sales, or as a rate per piece produced or per project completed. Key questions are:

- ❏ How are rates of job compensation established?
- ❏ How are job compensation rates communicated to employees?
- ❏ What are the procedures for job rate increases?
- ❏ What are the procedures for individual employee pay increases?
- ❏ When (or how frequently) are job rates revisited?
- ❏ What procedures are in place for dealing with an employee's pay that is more or less than a job's rate?

This last question refers to situations in which the employee may have to be paid more or less than the worth and rate for the job. Employees demoted to a job paying less than the one they previously held may have a rate higher than their new job's assigned rate. A reevaluation of a job may lower its rate to below that being paid to an incumbent. A difficult position to fill may require paying more than the job's rate in order to obtain someone. All of these are not unusual situations. Your policy and procedure should provide for them.

Adjusting Compensation

Job evaluations, competitive rates, and individual performance may all require adjustments to compensation rates. Inflation, organizational performance, and availability of specific skills can also have an impact. How your organization makes any necessary adjustments should be described in the policy and procedure after answering these questions:

❏ What procedures are in place for reviewing factors that may necessitate compensation adjustments?

❏ If individual employee performance increases are given, what are the implementation and approval steps?

❏ If general increases are given to all employees, what are the implementation and approval steps?

❏ What procedures are used to determine when compensation adjustments are required?

Sign-On Bonus

In recent years, offering a sign-on bonus to attract new employees has been used more and more. Initially, these employees were those with specifically desired skills or those in hard-to-find professions. During the 1990s, when employment was difficult to gain, sign-on bonuses were used by some organizations for all types of employees.

A sign-on bonus is a lump sum payment made to a new employee for joining the organization. Usually it is a single payment, although some organizations make it in two payments: one at the time of hire, and one at a specific time period later (often one year) if the employee is still with the organization.

Questions to consider here are:

❏ When is sign-on bonus used?

❏ How is the amount of a sign-on bonus determined?

❏ Who recommends and who approves a sign-on bonus?

❏ How is the sign-on bonus paid?

❏ Are there any stipulations attached to the sign-on bonus?

Related Compensation

Related compensation includes bonuses, gain-sharing, profit-sharing, shift differential pay, overtime compensation, lump-sum payments, deferred compensation, and geographic adjustments or allowances. Actually, there are other related forms of compensation, some of which are unique to local areas or industries, such as punctuality bonuses and discretionary anytime awards. Key questions are:

❐ What type of related compensation does your organization offer?

❐ What are the established procedures for determining and paying related compensation?

How compensation is actually paid needs to be covered as well. Organizations can mail checks, distribute checks, pay cash, and make direct bank deposits. The compensation policy and procedure should make clear if different payment methods are used for different jobs. Also, the pay period and payday need to be described. The key questions are:

❐ What actual pay methods are used for what jobs?

❐ What options do employees have for selecting their method of pay?

❐ What are the pay periods for what jobs?

❐ What are the pay dates for what jobs?

A SAMPLE POLICY AND PROCEDURE

The balance of this chapter consists of two sample policies and procedures from the same company. The first example covers compensation for all employees, except those in sales, and describes payment of overtime (Chapter 12 on Terms of Employment details overtime procedures). The second example is a policy and procedure for commission payment to salespeople.

HUMAN RESOURCES COMPENSATION POLICY AND PROCEDURE

1. POLICY

The Organization maintains a compensation program that is equitable to employees; competitive in the market; and assists the Organization in attracting and maintaining the type of employees necessary to meet its goals and conduct its operations.

1.1 Every position is evaluated to determine both its relative internal worth and external worth based on a written position description.

1.2 A formula is used for converting position evaluations to salary ranges.

1.3 Salary surveys are periodically conducted to ensure salary ranges remain competitive and the results are communicated to all employees.

1.4 Individual employee performance is annually reviewed and salary adjustments are made based on salary surveys, economic conditions, position in range, and individual performance.

2. SCOPE

This policy and procedure applies to all positions within the Organization except commission sales positions and senior management positions.

3. ACCOUNTABILITY

3.1 Human Resources and the Senior Management Committee are accountable for reviewing and approving all salary ranges, changes to salary ranges, and annual salary increase guidelines.

3.2 Human Resources is accountable for maintaining all position evaluation and salary-range information; maintaining individual employee salary history; conducting salary surveys; and recommending annual salary increase guidelines.

3.3 Human Resources is accountable for annually notifying each supervisor of the current salary of all employees in the supervisor's area of accountability; the individual and general salary increase guidelines; and the due date and salary range for each employee reporting to the manager.

3.4 Individual supervisors are accountable for annually reviewing the performance of every employee reporting to them (see Performance Evaluation Policy and Procedure) and recommending a salary adjustment or nonadjustment on a form provided by Human Resources.

3.5 Every supervisor is accountable for ensuring that all salary adjustments are made within the terms of this policy and procedure and annually published guidelines.

3.6 Human Resources is accountable for reviewing all salary adjustments to ensure they are within guidelines.

4. DEFINITIONS

4.1 *Base Pay* is the amount employees are paid for their normally scheduled work, exclusive of any commission, contracted amount, draw, loan, shift differential, lump-sum payments, bonuses, advance payments, and overtime.

4.2 *Pay Period* is every two (2) weeks on Friday for that week and the previous week.

5. FORMS

5.1 Payroll Change Notice

6. PROCEDURE

6.1 Position Description

Every position is to have a written position description approved by the position's supervisor, the person to whom the supervisor reports, and Human Resources. All position descriptions are to be in a format supplied by Human Resources.

6.2 Position Evaluation

Every position is evaluated by a Position Evaluation Committee using a point comparison system supplied by Human Resources. This process assigns a numerical value to each position.

6.2.1 The chairperson of the Position Evaluation Committee is the Human Resources manager.

6.2.2 The other five members of the Position Evaluation Committee are senior managers appointed by the senior vice president of operations.

6.3 Salary Ranges

6.3.1 Human Resources converts each numerical position evaluation into a salary range by use of a formula approved by the Senior Management Committee.

6.3.1.1 The midpoint of each salary range shall represent the position's external competitive worth; that is, the rate at which a fully qualified and experienced person is compensated within the metropolitan area of the Organization's location.

6.3.1.2 The minimum of each salary range shall be sixty-five percent (65%) of the range's midpoint.

6.3.1.3 The maximum of each salary range shall be two hundred percent (200%) of the range's minimum.

6.3.2 Human Resources, at least every two (2) years, shall conduct or participate in or purchase salary surveys for similar positions in the metropolitan area of the Organization's location. The results of those surveys shall be used to adjust the formula and/or individual salary ranges.

6.3.3 No employees are to be paid less than ten percent (10%) below the salary range for their position. In such an instance, the position's supervisor shall bring the individual's qualifications and salary up to at least the minimum within six (6) months.

6.3.4 No employees are to be paid more than ten percent (10%) above the salary range for their position. In such an instance, there are to be no salary increases until the employee's salary again falls within the range for the position.

6.3.5 Employees below the maximum cannot receive an increase that takes them more than ten percent (10%) over the range maximum. Any increase taking an employee above the maximum, but within ten percent (10%) of the maximum, requires the approval of the senior vice president of operations.

6.3.6 Once an employee's salary is above the maximum, there are normally no salary increases until the employee's salary again falls within the range for the position.

6.3.6.1 Employees paid above the maximum may be recommended for a lump sum equal to half a normal increase based on performance.

6.3.6.2 Such recommendation is made by the employee's direct supervisor and requires the approval of the person to whom the supervisor reports and the senior vice president of operations.

6.3.6.3 Such increases may be recommended at the employee's normal salary review dates.

6.3.6.4 Such increases may only be given once every three (3) years.

6.3.7 Individual salaries below the salary range minimum for a position require the approval of Human Resources and the Senior Management Committee.

6.4 Hiring Salaries

6.4.1 Hiring salaries are based on an individual's qualifications and experience and are generally to be within the lower half of the salary range for the position.

6.4.2 Specific hiring salaries are recommended by the position's supervisor and approved by the person to whom he/she reports.

6.4.3 Specific hiring salaries are reviewed by the Human Resources manager to ensure they are within the terms of this policy and procedure and to determine the impact they may have on existing employees in similar positions.

6.4.4 In unusual situations in which a person selected for a position does not possess the basic qualifications for the position, the individual may be hired as a Trainee and offered a salary up to ten percent (10%) below the minimum for the position. In such an instance, the position's supervisor is to bring the individual's qualifications and salary up to at least the minimum within six (6) months.

6.4.5 Hiring salaries above the midpoint require the prior approval of the Human Resources manager and the senior vice president of operations.

6.4.6 Sign-on bonuses require the approval of the position's supervisor, manager, Human Resources manager, and senior vice president of operations.

6.5 Promotional Increases

6.5.1 An employee is promoted when moved to another position with a higher evaluation salary range.

6.5.2 Every employee who is promoted receives a salary increase in addition to any performance increase.

6.5.3 Promotion increases are recommended by the new position's supervisor and approved by the person to whom the supervisor reports and the Human Resources manager.

6.5.4 A promoted employee's new salary is to be within the salary range for the new position unless the individual is considered not to possess all of the basic qualifications for the position. In such an instance, the individual may be offered a salary up to ten percent (10%) below the minimum for the position, and the position's supervisor is to bring the individual's qualifications and salary up to at least the minimum within six (6) months.

6.5.5 Promotion increases are to be at least five percent (5%) of current base salary, provided such an increase places the employee within the new position's salary range and agrees with all other requirements of this policy and procedure.

6.6 Annual Salary Review

Each year every employee's salary is reviewed by the employee's supervisor with respect to performance and position in the salary range.

6.6.1 Salary reviews occur on each employee's anniversary date.

6.6.1.1 An employee's anniversary date is the employee's date of hire, last promotion, or last transfer, whichever is most recent.

6.6.2 Each year Human Resources prepares guidelines for employee salary reviews. After approval by the Senior Management Committee, they are distributed to all supervisors who conduct salary reviews, along with salary ranges for positions reporting to them.

6.6.2.1 Salary review guidelines are presented in a table that relates position in range with job performance.

6.6.2.2 Salary guidelines are communicated by Human Resources to supervisors for individual employees, along with salary backgrounds, sixty (60) days in advance of the employee's anniversary date.

6.6.3 All supervisors review the salary of each employee reporting to them and submit to the person to whom they report a recommendation regarding salary for the employees.

6.6.3.1 If the recommendation is approved by the person to whom the supervisor reports, it is then submitted to Human Resources.

6.6.3.2 Human Resources reviews the recommendation.

6.6.3.2.1 If it does not meet guidelines, it is returned to the submitting manager.

6.6.3.2.2 If it meets guidelines, Human Resources approves it and submits it to Payroll.

6.6.3.3 Once an approved recommendation has been received by Payroll, Payroll notifies the supervisor of the receipt and the effective date for the increase.

6.6.4 Annual Reviews and Promotional Increases

6.6.4.1 If an employee is promoted or transferred within three (3) months of receiving an annual salary review, there is no increase other than a promotion increase.

6.6.4.2 If an employee is promoted or transferred more than three (3) months after receiving an annual salary review, the current supervisor reviews the employee's performance since the last salary review and, using the previous salary review guidelines, gives the employee any appropriate prorated salary adjustment. Such an increase is in addition to any promotional increase (see paragraph 9).

6.7 Overtime

Employees are compensated for working more than their scheduled hours (see Terms of Employment Policy and Procedure).

6.7.1 Nonexempt employees are paid time and one half for all work performed within a workweek (Monday through Sunday) in excess of forty (40) hours. The forty (40) hours of work can consist of actual time worked and any paid-for time off and paid holidays.

6.7.2 Exempt employees who earn less than $***** a year in base salary and are requested by the Organization to work significantly more than their regularly scheduled hours may be paid a bonus if approved by the senior vice president of operations.

6.7.2.1 A bonus is recommended to the senior vice president of operations by the manager of the employee and must include the approval of the division senior manager.

6.7.2.2 Such a bonus recommendation for an employee is to be made no more frequently than once every ninety (90) days.

6.8 Pay Basis

6.8.1 Nonexempt employees are paid based on their signed, submitted, and approved time sheets.

6.8.2 Exempt employees are paid based on a normally scheduled workweek, unless otherwise notified in writing by the appropriate manager.

6.8.3 Overtime and any other pay adjustments for the second week of a pay period will be paid in the next pay period.

7. REFERENCES

7.1 External Selection Policy and Procedure

7.2 Terms of Employment Policy and Procedure

HUMAN RESOURCES COMMISSION COMPENSATION POLICY AND PROCEDURE

1. POLICY

The Organization provides a commission compensation program for sales employees and their managers that encourages sales performance and is equitable, competitive in the market, and assists the Organization in attracting and maintaining the type of employees necessary to meet its goals and conduct its operations.

2. SCOPE

This policy and procedure applies to all sales and sales management positions that have been identified as eligible for commission compensation.

3. ACCOUNTABILITY

3.1 The Human Resources manager, senior vice president of operations, and senior manager of a sales department and/or division are accountable for reviewing and approving all commission compensation programs and eligible employees.

3.2 Human Resources is accountable for maintaining all position evaluation and salary-range information; maintaining individual employee salary history; conducting salary surveys; and recommending annual salary increase guidelines.

4. DEFINITIONS

4.1 *Draw*—A predetermined amount against commissions paid to the employee on the Organization's regular paydays.

4.2 *Salary*—A predetermined amount paid to the employee on the Organization's regular paydays.

4.3 *Base Compensation*—Either an employee's draw or salary.

4.4 *Advance*—An amount paid in advance of receipt of payment on which a commission is based.

4.5 *Commission*—A percent of income received by the company from an individual's or team's sales.

4.6 *Closing*—Signing of a contract and receipt of all required documents to complete a sale.

4.7 *Gross Revenue*—The actual amount received from a sale.

4.8 *Commission Calculation Date*—Either the date of closing or the date payment is received.

4.9 *Bonus*—An amount based on individual and/or team sales revenue volume.

5. FORMS

5.1 Payroll Change Notice

5.2 Commission Calculation

6. COMMISSIONS PROCEDURE

6.1 Positions eligible for compensation consisting of a salary or draw and commission and/or bonus are determined by the senior manager of the employee's division with the approval of the senior vice president of operations.

6.2 Salary and draw grades are created by the senior managers in the sales division, the senior vice president of operations, and the Human Resources manager.

6.2.1 Each eligible position is assigned a salary grade or draw.

6.2.2 All employees in the same eligible positions are assigned the same salary or draw.

6.2.3 Human Resources maintains the salary/draw grades and list of eligible employees.

6.3 Human Resources periodically surveys compensation for similar positions in the area and recommends any changes to the existing salary/draw grades.

6.4 Employees in positions assigned salaries may receive annual salary increases if approved by the senior manager of the division or department, the senior vice president of operations, and the Human Resources manager.

6.5 Employees in positions assigned draws are not eligible for draw increases.

6.6 Commission, Advances, and Bonuses

6.6.1 The amount of commission, advance, and/or bonus for each position and the payment dates are determined by the senior manager of the division with the approval of the senior vice president of operations.

6.6.2 The Organization reserves the right to change amounts and payment terms at any time by providing at least ninety (90) days advance notice to employees.

6.6.3 All commission and bonus payments are made on the next regular scheduled payday following approval of payment.

6.6.4 Any outstanding draws and advance amounts are deducted from commission and bonus payments.

7. REFERENCE

7.1 Compensation Policy and Procedure

CHAPTER 11

Benefits

"(My Dad) didn't have health insurance or benefits, and I saw the debilitating effect that had on him. I decided if I was ever in a position to make a contribution to others in that way, I would."

—HOWARD SCHULTZ

BENEFITS ARE OFTEN REFERRED TO as noncash compensation. Generally, they are services provided by the organization that employees would have to pay for if acquired on their own. Often the organization purchases these services for less per employee than an individual could. Sometimes they are services that cannot be purchased individually, and sometimes the organizations merely obtains them for less and prorates the entire cost among employees.

Some organizations classify government-mandated activities as benefits, such as unemployment insurance, workers compensation insurance, and the employer's half of Social Security. Others do not. Actually, what is described as employee benefits differs considerably among organizations.

For our purposes, we have classified benefits as time away from work, mandated benefits, insurance, retirement benefits, and specials.

TIME AWAY FROM WORK

Vacation

Family Leave

Personal Days

Sickness

MANDATORY BENEFITS

Jury Duty

Military Leave

Workers Compensation

One-Half Social Security

Disability

Unemployment

INSURANCE BENEFITS

Health

Dental

Vision

Prescription Drugs

Long-Term Care

Life

Accidental Death and Dismemberment

Short-Term Disability

Long-Term Disability

Travel

RETIREMENT BENEFITS

Noncontributory Pension Plans

Contributory Pension Plans

Retirement Savings Plans

Nonfunded Retirement Plans

Deferred Income Retirement Plans

SPECIAL BENEFITS

Company Products and Services Discounts

Clothing Allowance/Uniforms

Personal Safety Equipment

Tuition Reimbursement

Day Care Center

Saving Bond Deduction

Health Account

Meal Discounts

Free Coffee

There are many more benefits that could be added to the list, and there are many variations within each benefit. In addition, benefits such as insurance are also often available in full or part for the employees' dependents. Obviously, it is almost impossible to cover so many benefits and so many variations in one policy and procedure.

All of the retirement and insurance benefits have separate documents covering them, and mandated items have government documents. It is not necessary to repeat that information in a policy and procedure, but having said that, there are some organizations that do.

This chapter deals with a policy and procedure to administer benefits. Insurance, retirement, and mandatory benefit documents are referenced but remain outside the policy and procedure. Also, time away from work is treated as a separate policy and procedure, and some benefits such as tuition reimbursement are treated in other policies and procedures as well. There is no one correct approach. You should select an approach to benefits that best meets your organization's culture and administrative requirements.

DEFINITIONS

Often, benefit administration policies and procedures include definitions of dependents, although in some cases these definitions remain in the governing documents, such as the master insurance policies and contracts. Sometimes the definitions differ by benefit. Key questions are:

❒ Who are considered eligible dependents for benefits?

❒ Are the same dependents eligible for all benefits?

❒ Are nontraditional relationships considered dependents?

PROCEDURES

Concentrating on administrative procedures, the key points to cover are:

- ❐ Eligibility
- ❐ Effective Dates
- ❐ Adjustments
- ❐ Vesting
- ❐ Contributions
- ❐ Reporting
- ❐ Cafeteria Benefits
- ❐ Terminating Employment

Eligibility

When is an employee eligible for benefits? What type of employee is eligible for benefits? When do dependents become eligible for benefits? Which dependents are eligible for benefits? These key questions have to be asked for each type of benefit.

Some answers are mandatory. For example, unemployment insurance and workers compensation are required for all employees and begin at their times of hire. However, eligibility for life insurance and health insurance coverage could begin after a probationary period is completed, immediately on hiring, the first of the month after hiring, or on any other date, as long as the procedure is consistently applied to all eligible employees.

Many organizations group the eligibility dates for all elective coverages. Many organizations limit elective benefits to full-time employees. However, in order to treat all employees the same, this requires part-time employees to work less than 1,040 hours in a year. That is approximately one half the typical full-time schedule. If an employee classified as part-time works more hours, the employee is full-time and then receives benefits.

Among the questions you need to answer for each benefit are:

- ❐ What types of employees are eligible for this benefit?
- ❐ What dependents are eligible for this benefit?
- ❐ When does eligibility for this benefit occur?
- ❐ How is the employee notified of eligibility for this benefit?

❏ Are retirees eligible for the benefit?

❏ Are employees on leave eligible for this benefit?

Effective Dates

Often the effective date is the same as the eligibility date. However, in some benefits there is a difference. For example, eligibility may refer to when an employee can enroll in the benefit, but once enrolled, the benefit becomes effective sometime later. For example, insurance coverage may become effective the first of the month following enrollment. Again, you need to answer these questions for each benefit:

❏ What is the effective date for this benefit?

❏ Is there a waiting period for any portion of the benefit?

❏ Are there differences in the effective dates for the employee and dependents?

Adjustments

An employee's status often changes after originally enrolling in a benefit. For example, a marriage may add a dependent, the employee may change a beneficiary, or the employee's name may change. These are all changes that require immediate adjustments. Other changes don't.

For example, an employee may want to change the level of coverage or change a contribution. The employee may want to enroll in a benefit previously declined. These types of elective changes are often limited to specific times of the year, often called enrollment or re-enrollment periods.

Again, your answers to these questions should be for each benefit:

❏ What changes can an employee initiate to benefits?

❏ When can employee changes be made?

❏ When do employee-initiated changes take place?

❏ How do employees initiate benefit changes?

❏ Is there a specific re-enrollment period?

❏ How are employees notified of any re-enrollment period?

Vesting

Some benefits, such as 401(k) plans and noncontributory pension plans, include a cash contribution from the organization. The main question is when does the employee have a right to all or part of that contribution. When does the employee have a vested interest in it?

Vesting times vary with benefits and range all the way from immediately (for some organization's cash contributions to retirement plans) to after ten years of uninterrupted full-time service. Vesting requirements also may differ within the same organization by benefits. These questions need to be answered for each benefit:

☐   Are there vesting privileges associated with this benefit?
☐   What are the vesting times?
☐   Is the vesting complete or partial?
☐   How is service defined?
☐   How are employees leaving the organization and then returning treated with respect to vesting?

Contributions

Benefits are paid for in three ways, which can differ by benefit within the same organization. Some are fully paid by the employee. For example, an organization may provide health insurance coverage for employees, but require employees to pay for dependent health coverage.

Some benefits are paid fully by the organization. This is always true of mandated benefits, such as the employer's portion of Social Security and workers compensation coverage.

Sometimes the cost of benefits is shared. Examples include personal, nonrequired safety equipment paid for partially by the employee and the organization, and employee and organization contributions to a retirement plan.

Ask these questions for all benefits:

☐   Who pays the cost of this benefit?
☐   How are employee contributions to the benefit made?
☐   What authorization procedure is used for payroll deductions?

Reporting

Benefits represent a large cost to most organizations. A recent survey of nonmandatory benefits indicated the average was between 24 percent and

35 percent of actual payroll. However, the definition of what qualified as a benefit was inconsistent in the survey.

Organizations generally want employees to realize that their benefits represent a significant cost. In addition, they need to notify employees about any vesting interests and about how any money an employee contributes to benefits is being used. This communication generally takes some form of a report to employees—usually an annual report. In addition, organizations often survey similar organizations, those in the same industry and in the same community. These benefit surveys are then published and distributed to employees.

The key questions to ask are:

❐ Are the costs of benefits calculated and reported to employees?

❐ When and how are reports made?

❐ Are benefit surveys conducted? If so, when and how and with whom are they conducted?

❐ Are benefit survey results communicated to employees? If so, how and when?

Cafeteria Benefits

Organizations have discovered that benefits have different value to different employees. For example, a young employee just beginning her career usually does not see a pension plan as a needed benefit. Instead, health insurance and time-off may be of greater importance. An older employee may feel just the opposite.

When benefits were a relatively small cost of an organization's operations, it was relatively easy to provide all benefits to all employees. However, many organizations feel they need to control benefit costs, so they are attempting to meet employee benefit needs in a less costly manner. This has led to one approach known as cafeteria benefits.

In the basic cafeteria benefits plan, the organization awards to each employee a certain amount of money to be spent as the employee desires on benefits. Then the benefits are listed with an individual cost. The employee informs the organization how the assigned money is to be spent.

The plans differ depending on how much money each employee is assigned; whether the employee can spend additional money on benefits; and what benefits are included. Obviously, mandated benefits have to be provided. Some organizations also require all employees to maintain benefits such as life and health insurance, so these are not offered as options.

Cafeteria plans are opened for enrollment and adjustments at various times. Also, the amount of money assigned to each employee is regularly reviewed and communicated. Key questions are:

❑ How are employees informed of the amount of money assigned to them?

❑ How often is the amount assigned to employees received and/or adjusted?

❑ What benefits are included in the cafeteria plan?

❑ Are there any limitations to the cafeteria plan benefits?

❑ When may changes be made by employees to their individual plans?

❑ When are enrollment periods offered?

❑ May employees make additional contributions to the purchase of benefits?

The preceding questions are ones to answer to assist in writing this policy and procedure, but they are not meant to provide enough detailed information for establishing a cafeteria benefits plan. For that, you need to obtain professional advice from someone who knows your organization's details and operations.

Terminating Employment

What happens to an employee's benefits when the employee leaves employment? Vesting explains some benefits. Legislation deals with others such as heath coverage. Your policy and procedure needs to recognize and reflect these requirements. However, some benefits are not that clear. In addition, you may have different practices depending on the reason an employee terminates employment. Key questions are:

❑ How are terminating employees notified of the status of their benefits?

❑ What is a terminating employee's benefit eligibility?

❑ In situations where employees return to the company, is there any coordination with previous benefits?

A SAMPLE POLICY AND PROCEDURE

Two policies and procedures are given at the end of this chapter as models for writing in the format suggested in this book. The first covers benefits administration in a company. The second example, which is taken from another company, deals with a cafeteria benefits plan.

HUMAN RESOURCES BENEFITS POLICY AND PROCEDURE

1. **POLICY**

   The Organization offers an employee benefits program that is equitable to employees; competitive in the market; and assists the Organization in attracting and maintaining the type of employees necessary to meet its goals and conduct its operations.

2. **SCOPE**

   This policy and procedure applies to all employees within the Organization.

3. **ACCOUNTABILITY**

   Human Resources is accountable for developing and administering all employee benefits programs.

4. **DEFINITIONS**

   4.1 *Short-Term Disability*—Coverage for time away from work due to a nonwork-incurred disability (injury or illness) from the eighth continuous day of disability through the 180th day.

   4.2 *Long-Term Disability*—Coverage for time away from work due to a nonwork-incurred disability (injury or illness) from the 181st day until the employee's return to work or retirement, whichever comes first.

   4.3 *Dependents*—Spouse, children under eighteen years of age or who are full-time students, and a state-recognized legal partner.

   4.4 Time away from work for holidays, illness, vacations, and other reasons, and tuition reimbursement, are covered in separate policies and procedures.

5. **FORMS**

   Human Resources maintains a supply of all enrollment forms and descriptive materials regarding employee benefits.

6. **BENEFITS PROCEDURE**

   6.1 Required
   The Organization provides all employee benefits that are required by federal and state law, such as workers compensation, Social Security, and unemployment coverages.

   6.2 Additional Benefits
   In addition, the Organization provides:

6.2.1 Health, dental, long-term disability, short-term disability, life, travel, vision, and accidental death and dismemberment insurances. Human Resources has descriptive materials regarding the coverages available to employees, but the terms and conditions stated in the master insurance policies govern these benefits.

6.2.2 Retirement 401(k) plan. Human Resources has descriptive materials regarding the coverages available to employees, but the terms and conditions stated in the master policies govern these benefits.

6.3 Eligibility

6.3.1 Regular full-time employees and their dependents are eligible for all coverages the first of the month after their date of employment. Eligibility for insurances is described in the master insurance policies for each coverage.

6.4 Enrollment

6.4.1 At the time of employment, Human Resources describes all benefits and provides an opportunity for employees to enroll or decline coverage for themselves and dependents.

6.4.2 Any time there is a change in an employee's dependent status, such as a birth, marriage, divorce, or death, the employee may make the appropriate change to the benefit enrollment by contacting Human Resources within two (2) weeks of the change.

6.4.3 Optional changes in enrollment can only be made at regular scheduled re-enrollment times offered twice a year.

6.5 Communication of Benefits

6.5.1 Human Resources offers a monthly meeting at which the details of all benefits are described, literature is distributed, and employee questions are answered.

6.5.1.1 New employees are scheduled to attend the first such benefit meeting following their dates of employment.

6.5.1.2 All other employees eligible for employment can make arrangements with Human Resources to attend such a meeting.

6.6 Benefits Review

6.6.1 The Human Resources manager reviews at least every two (2) years all the benefits being offered by the Organization to ensure they are competitive with other organizations in the community and are meeting the needs of employees.

6.6.2 The results of the benefits review are communicated to all employees by Human Resources.

7. REFERENCES

7.1 Terms of Employment Policy and Procedure

7.2 Time Away from Work Policy and Procedure

7.3 Education and Training Policy and Procedure

HUMAN RESOURCES CAFETERIA BENEFITS PLAN POLICY AND PROCEDURE

1. POLICY

The Organization provides a full range of benefits for its employees and a flexible system to meet their individual needs.

2. SCOPE

The terms of this policy and procedure apply to all employees of the Organization.

3. ACCOUNTABILITY

3.1 Human Resources is accountable for providing a complete selection of competitive benefits for employees in a "cafeteria" approach.

4. DEFINITIONS

4.1 *Cafeteria Benefits Plan*—A system that allows employees to select the benefits that best meet their individual needs.

4.2 *Dependents*—For insurance benefit purposes, a spouse, children under eighteen years of age, and full-time students.

5. FORMS

5.1 Cafeteria Benefits Enrollment

6. PROCEDURE

6.1 During November of each calendar year, Human Resources will distribute to each employee a Cafeteria Benefits Enrollment form that includes:

6.1.1 An amount of money assigned to each employee to use for selecting benefits.

6.1.2 Identification and descriptions of any required benefits, such as health insurance (unless the employee can provide evidence of already having similar coverage).

6.1.3 A list and description of available benefits with their individual costs.

6.1.4 A statement of any additional amounts of money an employee may contribute to benefit purchases.

6.2 During November, after or at the same time as the distribution of Cafeteria Benefits Enrollment forms, Human Resources holds meetings for all employees to describe benefits in the cafeteria plan and answer questions.

6.2.1 Descriptions of all benefits will be summarized in literature that is available at the employee's request from Human Resources.

6.3 Each employee must elect the benefits desired by completing the Cafeteria Benefits Enrollment form and submitting it to Human Resources before December 31.

6.3.1 Employees not submitting the completed enrollment form by December 31 will be considered to have the same benefits selections as they had the previous year.

6.3.2 New employees are required to make their selections at the time of employment.

6.4 Benefits selections shall become effective the first scheduled workday in January that the employee is at work.

6.5 Benefits selected by the employee shall remain in effect for the calendar year, and the only revisions allowed during the calendar year are as the result of status changes such as the birth of a child, marriage, divorce, and death

6.6 Benefits included in the cafeteria approach are:

6.6.1 Life Insurance

6.6.2 Accidental Death and Dismemberment Insurance

6.6.3 Employee Health Insurance

6.6.4 Dependent Health Insurance

6.6.5 Employee Dental Insurance

6.6.6 Dependent Dental Insurance

6.6.7 Employee Vision Insurance

6.6.8 Dependent Vision Insurance

6.6.9 Employee Prescription Drug Insurance

6.6.10 Dependent Prescription Drug Insurance

6.6.11 Vacation

6.6.12 Personal Days

6.7 Benefits not included in the cafeteria plan are:

6.7.1 Tuition Reimbursement

6.7.2 Leaves of Absence

6.7.3 Mandatory Time-Off (whether paid or unpaid)

6.7.4 Scheduled Holidays

6.8 Eligibility

6.8.1 All full-time employees are eligible.

7. REFERENCES

7.1 Time Away from Work Policy and Procedure

CHAPTER 12

Terms of Employment

"If standards are not formulated systematically at the top, they will be formulated haphazardly and impulsively in the field."

—JOHN C. BIEGLER

CERTAIN HUMAN RESOURCES SUBJECTS CAN BE TREATED as separate policies and procedures or combined into a few. This chapter deals with several topics and presents them in a single policy and procedure.

SUBJECT REVIEW

This policy and procedure covers all of the specific terms of employment, except those that have been presented as separate policies and procedures. It includes types of employment, work schedules, rules and regulations, length of service (i.e., seniority), and employment at will. However, you can add other subjects not otherwise covered or remove subjects and treat them separately.

POLICY CONSIDERATIONS

Generally, terms of employment policies aim to do two things:

❒ Provide maximum flexibility to employees and the organization by offering various types of employment status

❒ Provide consistent terms of employment that ensure all employees are treated equally and fairly

Questions for you to consider are:

- ☐ What should this policy and procedure cover?
- ☐ What is the organization's overall policy regarding terms of employment?

Definitions

To a large extent, this subject requires a policy and procedure made up of definitions and descriptions. The major ones are:

TYPES OF EMPLOYMENT

Regular Full-Time. Employees scheduled to work twenty or more hours per week on a regular and continuing basis.

Regular Part-Time. Employees scheduled to work less than twenty hours per week on a regular, continuous basis.

Temporary. Employees hired to work either full-time or part-time for less than 1,020 hours in a twelve-month period.

Contract. Employees who have a signed agreement with the organization that describes their terms of employment.

Nonexempt. Employees who are covered by the federal Wage and Hour Law with respect to overtime payment and reporting of time worked.

Exempt. Employees who are exempt from coverage by the federal Wage and Hour Law with respect to overtime payment and reporting of time worked.

WORK SCHEDULES

Standard Workweek. The standard workweek is forty hours for regular full-time employees.

Scheduled Hours of Work. Each employee is assigned a work schedule.

Standard Workday. The standard workday is eight hours, exclusive of meal periods.

Overtime. All work performed on holidays and beyond an employee's scheduled weekly hours of work qualifies as overtime.

ORGANIZATIONAL DEFINITIONS

Supervisor. The employee to whom other employees directly report.

Manager. An employee who manages a function and is not a senior manager.

Senior Manager. An employee who manages a department or division.

Management. Includes all supervisors, managers, and senior managers.

Division. A major organizational unit headed by a senior manager.

Department. An organizational unit of a division, headed by a manager who reports directly to the division's senior manager.

Length of Service (Seniority). The total amount of continuous time a person has been employed by the organization. (Department, shift, and job length of service can also be calculated.)

PROCEDURES

The following terms of employment are considered for this policy and procedure:

- ❑ Types of Employment
- ❑ Scheduled Work Hours
- ❑ Overtime
- ❑ Time Reporting
- ❑ Length of Service
- ❑ Employment at Will
- ❑ Employee Conduct
- ❑ Solicitations
- ❑ Dress Code
- ❑ Drug- and Smoke-Free Work Environments

Types of Employment

The types of employment and organizational definitions provided earlier in this chapter need to be more fully described. For example, regular full-time employment was previously defined as employees scheduled to work twenty or more hours per week on a regular and continuing basis.

However, this definition may need to be expanded to clarify its status in the organization and the terms affecting it. For example:

Regular Full-Time. Employees scheduled to work twenty or more hours per week on a regular and continuing basis and who are eligible for all employee benefits.

The earlier definition of a nonexempt employee was someone covered by the federal Wage and Hour Law with respect to overtime payment and reporting of time worked. This definition could be expanded as follows:

Nonexempt. Employees who are covered by the federal Wage and Hour Law with respect to overtime payment and reporting of time worked. This status is determined for each position by the human resources manager based on the requirements of the federal Wage and Hour Act.

So, for each type of employment and each definition, consider the following questions:

❒ What other conditions and descriptions need to be included?
❒ Does the definition correctly and fully describe the type of employment?

Scheduled Work Hours

In some situations, the meaning of scheduled work hours is very straightforward. There is a single starting and finishing time for all employees. A standard meal break and, at times, rest breaks are included. The procedure could read as follows:

Standard Workweek. The standard workweek is forty hours, exclusive of meal periods and breaks, and begins on Monday at 12:01 A.M. and ends on the following Sunday at 12:00 midnight.

Standard Workday. The standard workday is eight hours, exclusive of meal periods, and begins at 12:01 A.M. and ends at 12:00 midnight the same day.

Meal Period. Meal period is not paid time. It must be at least thirty continuous minutes in length and at a time approved by the employee's supervisor. Meal periods are to be taken as near the middle of the employee's workday as possible.

Breaks. Each employee is entitled to a fifteen-minute break during each half of the employee's scheduled full workday, at times approved by the employee's supervisor.

Schedule. An employee's supervisor determines a specific work schedule for each employee. Employees are expected to be at their workstations, ready to work, at the beginning of their scheduled work time and not to leave, except for breaks, meal periods, and operational reasons until the conclusion of their scheduled work time.

Emergency Closing. The decision to close the office due to inclement weather or any other type of emergency may only be made by a senior manager. If such a decision is made prior to the start of the workday, an attempt will be made to notify all affected employees. Unless notified, employees are expected to report for work at their normal scheduled time.

This is a relatively easy description. However, nowadays there are many other types of work schedules to consider. There are employees who work away from the office, including salespeople and those assigned to other locations. Some organizations allow flexible hours in which employees are expected to work the required number of hours, but the actual times and days are optional. Some employees may perform all or part of their work at home, and some employees are scheduled to meet certain objectives, regardless of the time involved.

Consequently, when you write this procedure you need to make sure you have considered all possible work schedules within your organization. Also, you must recognize that these variations affect time reporting, overtime payment, employee availability, and supervision. Answer questions such as:

❐ What types of employment do we offer?

❐ What are the requirements for each type of employment?

❐ What type of work schedules do we offer?

❐ What are the requirements for each type of work schedule, in terms of time reporting, performance, and compensation?

Overtime

The U.S. Wage and Hour Law requires nonexempt employees to be paid for all hours worked in excess of forty per week. It does not require overtime pay for certain professional and management positions, and it provides a strict test to determine what positions are exempt. From the law's point of view, all your employees can be nonexempt, but you have to be able to prove any employee's exempt status. Sounds simple, but as always, the devil is in the details.

Here are the questions you need to be able to answer:

❑ Is overtime paid for just over forty hours a week actually worked or a combination of hours worked and hours paid (such as sick days, holidays, and vacations days)?

❑ Is overtime paid for work performed on holidays?

❑ On what element of pay is overtime calculated—regular time, shift differential, commission, or piecework?

❑ Can an employee trade time-off without pay for time worked in excess of scheduled time on another day during the same week or pay period?

A secretary to the operations supervisor at a Nebraska company was scheduled to work from 8 A.M. to 5 P.M. with an hour for lunch. Her husband worked at another company nearby, but he was scheduled to report for work at 7:30 A.M. Since it was convenient for him to drive her to work, she arrived each morning at about 7:15 A.M. She remained until her scheduled finishing time.

When she arrived each morning she read the paper and then began work about 7:30. She never submitted a request for overtime payment. When her boss arrived each morning he saw her at work and sometimes commented, "You must love your job to give it all that extra time."

Another employee filed a complaint that was being investigated by a representative of the Department of Labor. In the course of the investigation, several employees were selected at random to be interviewed. The secretary was one. During the interview, she explained how much she liked her job and the company. She told the investigator that was why she was willing to work three to four hours a week overtime without pay.

Eventually, the company received a substantial fine and the secretary was awarded back overtime pay for the previous four years. The ruling was that the company (i.e., supervisor) knew she was working overtime and did not pay her or tell her to stop.

Exempt employees' overtime must also be addressed. An operations supervisor may be scheduled to work the same overtime as employees, but receives no overtime pay because the supervisory position is exempt. Organizations sometimes pay supervisors overtime or straight time for their work. If the overtime is not continuous, organizations offer exempt people compensatory time-off, so a supervisor working an occasional Saturday overtime is allowed to take a normally scheduled day off in exchange. Key questions to answer are:

❏ What type of overtime procedure exists for exempt employees?

❏ Is exempt overtime paid for just over forty hours a week actually worked or a combination of hours worked and hours paid (such as sick days, holidays, and vacation days)?

❏ Is exempt overtime paid or work performed on holidays?

❏ On what type of pay is exempt overtime based—regular time, shift differential, commission, or piecework?

❏ Can an employee trade time-off for time worked in excess of scheduled time on another day during the same week or pay period?

Time Reporting

Directly related to overtime and scheduled work hours (and also covered by the Wage and Hour Law) is the reporting of time by employees. For nonexempt employees, time reporting is a must. Time sheets or time cards indicating actual hours worked and time away from work, signed by the employee and approved by the employee's supervisor, are required.

Although time sheets are not required by the Wage and Hour Law for exempt personnel, many organizations require them nonetheless. They are used for recording the exempt employee's time at work and time away from work, including vacation taken and any other days off (and the reason for the time-off). Time sheets serve as a record when organizations pay exempt overtime or give compensatory time. Key questions are:

❑ When and how are time sheets and/or cards prepared and submitted?

❑ What employees are accountable for what type of time reporting?

Length of Service

Length of service, or seniority, has many uses in a typical organization. How long someone has been employed by an organization can affect the employee's vacation, retirement, or pension benefits and shift and job assignments. Seniority is sometimes taken into consideration during layoffs and reductions in force. Like overtime, length of service may seem a very straightforward issue, but there are many exceptions to consider.

❑ If an employee leaves the organization and later returns, how are the two lengths of service treated?

❑ Are there different definitions of length of service for different purposes (e.g., vacation is based on length of service as of January 1, but retirement benefits are based on actual length of service)?

❑ If a part-time and/or temporary employee becomes a regular full-time employee, how are the two lengths of service treated?

❑ How is the length of service affected when an employee is away from the organization on military, jury duty, personal, or medical leave?

❑ If another company is acquired or divisions are merged, how are the two lengths of service treated?

Employment at Will

If your organization subscribes to an "employment at will" policy or any other overall employment policy, it should be described as part of the terms of employment. Some organizations do not have any overall policy; others adjust their overall employment policy by state. Some states have laws that may require such changes. The key questions to ask are:

❑ What is your organization's overall employment policy?

❑ Does your organization's overall employment policy apply to all employees and locations within the organization?

Employment of Relatives

Many organizations have a policy regarding employment of relatives. Some prohibit it. Some allow it if the employees do not work together or do not have an employee/supervisor relationship. Whatever the policy, a definition of what is construed as a relative is required, and if there is a limitation, what happens when there is a status change. For example, if two employees marry, they go from a nonrelationship category to a relationship category.

Here, questions to answer are:

- ☐ Who is considered a relative for this policy and procedure?
- ☐ What are the limitations on employment of relatives?
- ☐ How are any relationship changes that occur after employment handled?

Employee Conduct and Related Issues

In some policies and procedures, the organization's rules and regulations regarding employee behavior need to be stated. Some organizations include employee conduct in their policy and procedure on performance improvement, grievances, or disciplinary actions. There may also be rules and regulations related to enforcing a dress code, prohibiting solicitations on work premises, and creating drug-free and smoke-free work environments.

Normally, these are overall rules and regulations that affect a major division or location. Department rules and regulations are generally referenced but made a separate activity. At times, certain rules are described under a separate heading or in other policies and procedures. For example, maintaining a smoke-free environment could be in a safety and health policy and procedure.

The three most important points regarding rules and regulations is that they must be complete, they must meet legal requirements (and not conflict with legal requirements), and they must be administered fairly and equally.

An Oregon auto-parts distributor discovered that one of its employees was distributing religious literature in the lunchroom during the lunch break. It warned him twice. When he persisted, the company discharged him. Subsequently, the company published a new rule: "Employees may not distribute any literature on company property during work hours without the company's prior obtained permission."

The discharged employee claimed he had been discharged for violating a rule that did not exist. He also cited that at the same time he was distributing his literature, another employee was distributing literature encouraging voting in the upcoming city election, and no action was taken against that employee.

The company made a settlement with the former employee, but initiated a training program for its management on the need to have complete and consistent rules and regulations and to enforce them equally and fairly.

When writing a policy and procedure for employee conduct and related issues, the key questions are:

- ❐ What are the organization rules and regulations for employee conduct?
- ❐ What differences are there in the organization's rules and regulations by state, location, and division?
- ❐ Do the rules and regulations conform to federal and state requirements?
- ❐ What enforcement procedure is there?
- ❐ Are enforcement procedures designed to treat all employees the same?
- ❐ Have supervisors and managers been trained in how to implement the organization's rules and regulations?

A SAMPLE POLICY AND PROCEDURE

A sample Terms of Employment policy and procedure concludes this chapter. It covers all the subjects discussed in this chapter.

As mentioned at the outset, this policy and procedure can be used as a kind of catch-all where you can also add other subjects not otherwise covered in another or a separate policy and procedure. The hiring of employees' relatives is an example of one such subject. In the sample document that follows, this subject is treated as a specific term of employment and is given its own section.

HUMAN RESOURCES TERMS OF EMPLOYMENT POLICY AND PROCEDURE

1. POLICY

Maximum flexibility is provided to employees and the Organization by offering various types of employment status and consistent terms of employment that ensure all employees are treated fairly and equally.

2. SCOPE

The terms of employment of this policy and procedure apply to all departments and employees of the Organization.

3. ACCOUNTABILITY

3.1 Every manager is accountable for ensuring that the terms and types of employment described in this policy and procedure are administered fairly, equally, and consistently.

3.2 Human Resources is accountable for maintaining a record of each employee's employment status and type of employment and ensuring companywide compliance with all terms of employment.

4. DEFINITIONS

4.1 *Types of Employment*—The following classifications are used to describe an employee's status:

4.1.1 *Full-Time*—Employees who are regularly scheduled to work forty (40) hours a week or more.

4.1.2 *Part-Time*—Employees who are regularly scheduled to work less than forty (40) hours a week.

4.1.3 *Regularly Scheduled*—Employees, both full-time and part-time, who are scheduled to work the same number of hours each week.

4.1.4 *Temporary*—Employees who are employed for less than ninety (90) continuous days in a calendar year.

4.1.5 *Contract*—Employees who have a signed agreement with the Organization that describes their terms of employment.

4.1.6 *Nonexempt*—Employees who are covered by the federal Wage and Hour Law with respect to overtime payment and reporting of time worked. This status is determined for each position by the Human Resources manager based on the requirements of the federal Wage and Hour Law.

4.1.7 *Exempt*—Employees are exempted from coverage by the federal Wage and Hour Law with respect to overtime payment and reporting of time worked. This status is determined for each position by the Human Resources manager.

4.1.8 *Supervisor*—The employee to whom other employees directly report.

4.1.9 *Managers*—Employees who manage a function and are not senior managers.

4.1.10 *Senior Managers*—Employees who manage a department or division.

4.1.11 *Management*—Includes all supervisors, managers, and senior managers. The word *manager* is sometimes used to describe all employees in management.

4.1.12 *Division*—A major organizational unit of the Organization headed by a senior manager who reports directly to the CEO.

4.1.13 *Department*—An organizational unit of a division, headed by a manager who reports directly to the division's senior manager.

4.2 Types of Work Schedules

4.2.1 *Standard Workweek*—The standard workweek is forty (40) hours, exclusive of meal periods and breaks, and begins on Monday at 12:01 A.M. and ends on Sunday at 12:00 midnight.

4.2.2 *Standard Workday*—The standard workday is eight (8) hours, exclusive of meal periods, and begins at 12:01 A.M. and ends at 12:00 midnight the same day.

4.2.3 *Meal Period*—Meal period is not paid time. If a meal period is taken, it must be at least thirty (30) minutes and at a time approved by the employee's supervisor.

4.2.4 *Schedule*—An employee's supervisor is accountable for determining an employee's specific work schedule. Employees are expected to be at their desks, ready to work, at the beginning of their scheduled work time and not to leave until the conclusion of their scheduled work time.

5. FORMS

Human Resources will prepare and furnish any necessary forms to ensure the implementation of this policy and procedure.

6. PROCEDURE

6.1 Time Reporting

6.1.1 Nonexempt Employee Time Reporting—Each nonexempt employee is required to complete a Weekly Time Sheet at the end of each workweek.

6.1.1.1 An employee's time sheet must show actual hours worked and any time at meal periods; time away from work for any reason, such as vacation and personal time; and individual starting and ending times. It must be signed by the employee and submitted to the employee's supervisor.

6.1.1.2 The supervisor must sign the Weekly Time Sheet to indicate approval and then submit it to Payroll no later than 5:00 P.M. on the Monday of a payroll week.

6.1.2 Exempt Employee Reporting—Each exempt employee is required to complete a Weekly Report at the end of each workweek indicating days worked and days away from work.

6.1.2.1 The report is submitted to the employee's supervisor, who approves it and submits it to Payroll no later than 5:00 P.M. on the Monday of a payroll week.

6.2 Overtime is time worked in excess of the employee's scheduled time.

6.2.1 Nonexempt Overtime—Nonexempt employees will be paid time and one-half for all hours worked during a single workweek in excess of forty (40) hours. Included in hours worked for calculating overtime is any paid time-off and paid holidays.

6.2.2 Compensatory Time—With a supervisor's prior approval, a nonexempt employee may work compensatory time to make up for any paid time away from work, but compensatory time is to be worked during the same week as the time away from work.

6.3 Emergency Closing—The decision to close the office due to inclement weather or any other type of emergency may only be made by the senior vice president of operations.

6.3.1 If such a decision is made prior to the start of the workday, an attempt will be made to notify all affected employees.

6.3.2 Unless notified, employees are expected to report for work at their normal scheduled starting time on any scheduled workday.

6.3.3 If the closing occurs after the employee is at work, the employee will be paid for the actual time worked that day with a minimum of four (4) hours pay.

6.4 Length of Service

An employee's length of service is the continuous, uninterrupted service with the Organization.

6.4.1 Employees joining the Organization from an acquired company or other divisions of the Organization will be credited with their continuous, uninterrupted service with the acquired company and/or division, provided there was no elapsed time between leaving the acquired company or division and joining the Organization.

6.4.2 Any approved absence, whether paid or not, will not affect an employee's length of service, provided the employee returns to work as the approved absence requires.

6.4.3 Employees whose employment with the Organization is terminated for any reason and who are then rehired are considered as having continuous, uninterrupted service if they are re-employed within sixty (60) days of their termination.

6.5 Employment at Will

Each employee serves at the pleasure or will of the Organization. Employment of any employee may be terminated by the Organization or employee at any time (unless otherwise covered by the terms and conditions of a specific employment agreement with the employee).

6.5.1 Any statements regarding discharge, promotion, or other aspect of employment shall be interpreted consistent with an employment-at-will relationship between the Organization and its employees, regardless of whether such statements are in written form or transmitted orally to employees.

6.5.2 The policy of at-will employment shall be applied consistently for all employees without regard to their position, length of service, and standards of performance.

6.5.3 The policy of at-will employment may only be varied by written agreement between the Organization and an employee and signed by an officer of the Organization.

6.5.4 As a part of the initial selection and hiring procedure, Human Resources will obtain from each employee a signed statement confirming the employee's understanding of and agreement to the employment-at-will policy.

6.6 Code of Business Conduct

Human Resources will obtain at time of hire, and update each calendar year, a Code of Business Conduct statement signed by the employee indicating the employee's understanding and agreement with the Organization's Code of Business Conduct (see Code of Business Conduct policy and procedure).

6.7 Employment of Relatives

6.7.1 Employees related to another employee (a sibling, divorced former spouse, parent, child, grandparent, grandchild, spouse, father-in-law, mother-in-law, brother-in-law, or sister-in-law) may not hold a position within the Organization where there is a reporting relationship between them.

6.7.2 This prohibition applies to employees in different departments when one employee's work depends on or impacts the work of the other, or the employees are in the same department.

6.7.3 If, at the time this policy is implemented or at a later time, a transfer, adoption, or marriage results in a violation of this policy, one of the employees must transfer positions within six (6) months of the violation or the employment of one (1) or both employees will be terminated.

6.7.4 In the event just one (1) employee is to be terminated, the employee with the shortest length of service will have his/her employment terminated.

6.8 Employee Conduct

6.8.1 All employees of the Organization are expected to conduct themselves at all times in a manner appropriate to the operation and goals of the Organization. Employees should avoid any type of action or statement that would reflect adversely on the Organization.

6.8.2 Employees are required to use discretion in any discussion of the Organization's business and records, but this does not limit an employee from reporting any violation of local, state, and federal laws.

6.8.3 Any information received by an employee in a confidential manner must be maintained in confidence, and any violation of the terms of this paragraph warrants the immediate termination of an employee's employment.

6.8.4 The following are examples of some, but not all, violations of Organization standards that may result in an employee becoming liable for disciplinary action and/or discharge:

6.8.4.1 Willfully falsifying Organization records of any type.

6.8.4.2 Abusing, destroying, or defacing Organization property or equipment, or the property or equipment of others on the Organization's premises.

6.8.4.3 Stealing property belonging to the Organization, fellow employees, or others on the Organization's premises.

6.8.4.4 Fighting, agitating a fight, threatening, attempting to do bodily harm or injury, or inflicting injury to another person on Organization property.

6.8.4.5 Bringing onto Organization property, or using while on Organization property, intoxicants, liquor, beer, wine, or illegal narcotics or other controlled substances (narcotics or controlled substances prescribed by a doctor or dentist to be taken at work require the prior approval of the Human Resources manager).

6.8.4.6 Reporting for work under the influence of intoxicants, liquor, beer, wine, or illegal narcotics or other controlled substances (narcotics or controlled substances prescribed by a doctor or dentist to be taken at work require the prior approval of the Human Resources manager).

6.8.4.7 Carrying or having on Organization premises firearms, explosives, switchblades, flammable liquids and substances, any other dangerous or illegal weapons, or any devices or substances considered unsafe by senior management.

6.8.4.8 Excessive, unexcused tardiness or absenteeism (see 7.1 Attendance Policy and Procedure).

6.8.4.9 Engaging in disruptive behavior that causes disharmony in the workplace.

6.8.4.10 Willfully and/or consistently disobeying any safety rule, health rule, or other Organization policy or rule.

6.8.4.11 Willfully and/or consistently disobeying any posted rule.

6.8.4.12 Impeding the performance of other employees.

6.8.4.13 Refusing to perform assigned work.

6.8.4.14 Any other actions by employees not detailed in this policy and procedure but which are contrary to the good of the Organization and/or its employees may also be subject to disciplinary action that may result in discharge.

6.9 Solicitation and Distribution

6.9.1 Employees are not permitted to solicit for any purpose during their working time or the working time of those being solicited. Examples of solicitation are: selling memberships or subscriptions for any public or private enterprises; gifts; purchase of products; and office pools.

6.9.2 Employees may not distribute any petition or notices or other printed material among employees during working time.

6.9.3 Employees may not distribute any literature, pamphlets, or other material in a work area.

6.9.4 Persons not employed by the Organization are forbidden from coming onto the property of the Organization without permission to solicit or distribute any material, and employees knowing of such activity are to report it immediately to their supervisor or the Human Resources manager.

6.9.5 Employees may not use working time or Organization property to prepare petitions, notices, or other printed material for distribution within the Organization or for other purposes.

6.10 Dress Code

6.10.1 The Organization considers its offices to be locations in which professional activities are conducted, so dress styles that contribute to the Organization's operations and goals are required.

6.10.2 Dress styles that are inconsistent with these operations and goals should be avoided.

6.10.3 Employees are required to dress in appropriate fashion for their assignment and contact with the public.

6.10.4 Employees' supervisors will advise employees on the type of dress required for their job.

6.11 Smoke-Free Environment

6.11.1 The Organization maintains a smoke-free environment, so the smoking of cigars, cigarettes, pipes, or any other lighted product is prohibited on Organization premises.

6.11.2 Chewing tobacco and using snuff are also prohibited.

6.11.3 Any employee wishing to smoke must do so outside of the building.

6.12 Drug-Free Environment

6.12.1 The Organization maintains a drug-free environment.

6.12.2 Controlled or illegal substances and their use are prohibited on the Organization's property (narcotics or controlled substances prescribed by a doctor or dentist to be taken at work require the prior approval of the Human Resources manager).

6.12.3 Candidates for a position with the Organization are subject to passing a preemployment drug test.

7. REFERENCES

7.1 Attendance Policy and Procedure

7.2 Compensation Policy and Procedure

CHAPTER 13

Equal and Fair Treatment

"If one worker's rights are abused, then I can no longer claim to be doing my best."
—BRUCE J. KLATSKY

ONE OF THE MAJOR OBJECTIVES of a set of human resources policies and procedures is to ensure the fair and equal treatment of all employees. Therefore, a procedure for preventing discrimination in the workplace comes as no surprise. However, this particular subject has other implications since there are numerous laws and regulations passed in the last three decades that address discrimination with respect to certain classifications of employees.

Similar laws deal with sexual harassment. Some organizations treat these two subjects as separate ones and issue a policy and procedure for both. In this book, the subjects of discrimination and sexual harassment are combined in one policy and procedure.

DEFINITIONS

Discrimination. Making employment decisions based on a person's gender, race, religion, national origin, age, veterans status, marital status, or disability. Discrimination is prohibited under the law.

Sexual Harassment. Unwelcome or unwanted conduct (verbal or physical) of a sexual nature. More precisely, sexual harassment is when submission to or rejection of this conduct by an employee is used as a factor affecting hiring, evaluation, promotion, or other aspect of employment, or when the conduct substantially interferes with an individual's employment or creates an intimidating, hostile, or offensive work environment.

197

(Examples of such behaviors should be available from your human resources department.)

Protected Class of Employees. Employees covered by the appropriate
laws and regulations.

EEO. Equal employment opportunity, which is a federal law (under Title
VII of the Civil Rights Act).

SUBJECT REVIEW

Fair and equal treatment for all employees needs to be considered when
developing all conditions of employment. Ideally, such an approach will
ensure that there is no decision regarding employees that's based on anything other than work performance.

Unfortunately, that was not always the case in all organizations. As a
result, a number of laws were enacted to address the issue with respect
to certain employees. In broad terms, these laws deal with prohibiting
discrimination based on gender, race, nationality, age, religion, physical
disability, marital status, and veterans status.

These federal laws and resulting regulations require certain actions by
the employer pertaining to, for example, the posting of notices, required
training, allowable records, specific wording in advertisements for employees, allowable questions in the hiring process, physical accessibility of
the workplace, reference checks, and equipment modifications. In many
states, the state laws describe additional requirements. Other laws address
sexual harassment in the workplace.

POLICY CONSIDERATIONS

A policy statement should reinforce the purpose of such laws and simultaneously ensure that all employees are treated fairly and equally without
discrimination based on nonwork-related conditions. Here are policy
statements from different organizations:

Example 1. Policy is to treat all employees fairly and equally; to not discriminate in making decisions regarding conditions of employment based
on race, sex, age, veterans status, nationality, religion, marital status, and
disability; to ensure all employees are not subject to harassment, sexual or

otherwise; and to provide an appropriate method for employees to address any violations of this policy.

Example 2. All decisions regarding employees will be made based on their performance and not on unrelated factors such as race, sex, age, veterans status, nationality, religion, marital status, and disability.

Example 3. Every employee is entitled to work without being subjected to any type of unwanted sexual harassment, so the organization has established procedures to ensure such harassment does not occur and to provide methods for an employee to report any violations of those procedures.

Example 4. The organization fully supports all legislation and regulations regarding discrimination and sexual harassment and has created procedures to ensure these requirements are met or exceeded.

Questions to consider are:

❒ Does the organization's policy meet the minimum legal requirements?

❒ Does the organization's policy exceed the minimum legal requirements?

❒ Does the organization's policy deal with areas not covered by legislation and regulations?

❒ Has the organization's labor attorney approved the organization's policy statement?

❒ Does the organization wish to treat nondiscrimination and sexual harassment together or with separate policies?

PROCEDURES

The procedure should cover the major elements required to implement the organization's fair and equal treatment policy and fulfill all legal requirements. Those elements are administration and communication, training, problem resolution, and auditing.

Administration and Communication

The laws governing this area require the use of certain wording in help-wanted ads, the posting of notices, the communication of policy, and record keeping. The methods to implement these requirements, and the identification of who performs these assignments and when, also need to be described. Questions that will assist you are:

☐ What notices are required, and who ensures they are posted and current?

☐ What wording is required when placing a help-wanted advertisement, and who ensures the appropriate wording is included?

☐ What type of communication of the organization's policies is made to all employees?

☐ What steps are taken to ensure all employees know of the organization's policies?

☐ What records are kept, and by whom, to ensure appropriate implementation information is available?

Training

A state's top court recently ruled that having a nondiscrimination policy, posting a confirming notice, and distributing a written copy of the policy to all employees was not adequate to ensure nondiscrimination. The court suggested that the organization should train all employees. There should be training for nonmanagement employees, who need to know and understand the policy and be acquainted with the organization's procedure for correcting violations of it, and management/supervisor training to ensure that management decisions were nondiscriminatory. Both training sessions should conclude with the participants signing statements confirming the objectives of the training.

The court indicated its approach was an action the organization should take immediately, but that similar actions would be required in the future. New employees and new supervisors required the same training, and existing employees and supervisors required regular reinforcement and review sessions.

The court's ruling was an effort to ensure that the nondiscrimination policies of the organization were adhered to and made a part of the organization's normal operations. Even if the laws did not include significant penalties for failure to abide by their terms, following the laws is just good business practice.

A Virginia manufacturer with approximately 1,000 employees received a court order to develop a different system for selecting supervisors. Although the employee population was 40 percent female and 30 percent African-American, only 5 percent of the supervisors were female and/or African-American.

The company created a new supervisor selection program, and within a year the percent of female and African-American supervisors had increased to 15 percent and was still growing. The new system selected supervisors based on their abilities rather than consideration of gender and race, so the quality of supervisors went up. The results were more efficient and productive operations.

At the time of the court decision, the company's president complained that the court had no business telling a private company how to conduct its operations. Yet, two years later, the same president hailed the court's decision as the best thing that had happened to the company in twenty years.

Here are some questions regarding the development of your nondiscrimination portion of the procedure:

- ❏ What type of nondiscrimination training is provided managers and supervisors?
- ❏ What type of training is provided all employees?
- ❏ What type of manager and supervisor follow-up training is provided?
- ❏ What type of employee follow-up training is provided?
- ❏ What type of reinforcement of training is provided on the job?
- ❏ What type of training is provided to assist all employees in accepting diversity?

Employees also require training about what constitutes sexual harassment, so they can understand its problems and consequences.

For years, a New Hampshire delivery company was composed of all-male truck drivers. In the 1990s, the company began to hire female drivers. This decision made available a larger population of potential employees.

The female drivers, individually, performed as well or better than some of the males. As a group, they performed better than the males, but their turnover as employees was very high. An investigation by an external consultant revealed the problem.

Over the years, the driver culture had become one in which males were comfortable. Their rest area had numerous female calendar photos on the walls and the lunch tables were strewn with girlie magazines. "It was like a locker room," one driver said. "A great deal of horseplay and kidding—much of it sexually based."

The company decided to conduct training sessions for the drivers and their supervisors. Initially, the male drivers said, "Hey, they [females] are welcome to join us, but they have to accept the existing conditions." The consultant reported the attitude was not anti-women. The male drivers just did not recognize why the women did not adjust.

Actually, the training was a success. Once the male drivers began to understand the perspective of their female counterparts and changed their ways, soon female drivers began to stay. The company did better, and all employees received better performance bonuses.

Sexual harassment also deals with the relationships on the job. It prohibits unwanted sexual advances and attention, so these types of actions also need to be a part of any training. The questions are similar to those asked about nondiscrimination:

- ❒ What type of training on sexual harassment is provided managers and supervisors?
- ❒ What type of training is provided all employees?
- ❒ What type of manager and supervisor follow-up training is provided?
- ❒ What type of employee follow-up training is provided?
- ❒ What type of reinforcement of training is provided on the job?

Problem Resolution

A grievance procedure of some type is required for complaints in both areas. Some organizations are able to adjust their traditional grievance procedure to meet this requirement. Others incorporate a separate grievance procedure for addressing sexual harassment and discrimination issues; others use a separate procedure for each issue.

Important to a grievance procedure is the assurance of protection for the employee. Any employee filing such a discrimination or sexual harassment grievance needs to know that no retaliatory action will be taken as a result. The need to ensure initial confidentiality is one reason organizations often create separate grievance procedures.

There is also the possibility that a nonemployee may file a complaint against the organization. This could be a former employee or a candidate for employment.

A New Mexico retail store discharged a ten-year employee, telling him the job was being eliminated. However, two months later the company hired a new employee for the same position. The new employee was less qualified than the former one. The new employee was twenty-five years old. The former employee was fifty-six years old.

The former employee filed an age discrimination charge and won.

An Indiana company was seeking a new salesperson. One of the candidates was a female. During her interview, the sales manager asked her: "Are you married? If you are, might that interfere with the required travel? For the same reason, are you planning to have children?"

The woman had excellent credentials, but the job was filled with another candidate. The woman filed a claim stating she was discriminated against because she was a woman. She cited the two questions as evidence. She won.

When preparing a grievance procedure for resolving problems, then, your organization must consider methods for dealing with both employee complaints and possible nonemployee complaints. Key questions are:

❒ What grievance procedure do you have for discrimination complaints?

❒ What protection is there for an employee filing a sexual harassment complaint?

❑ What protection is there for an employee filing a discrimination complaint?

❑ What type of procedure do you have for handling nonemployee complaints?

❑ What type of procedure do you have for handling complaints of former employees?

Auditing

An organization needs to have in place a process for continually ensuring all procedures are being implemented correctly and that they are effective in eliminating any sexual harassment and discriminatory behaviors. This process involves record reviews, grievance reviews, and surveys of operations. Ask these questions:

❑ What procedures does the organization follow to ensure its nondiscrimination policies and procedures are being correctly implemented?

❑ What procedures does the organization follow to ensure its sexual harassment policies and procedures are being correctly implemented?

❑ Who conducts such audits, and when are they conducted?

❑ What type of independent audits are conducted?

❑ What type of record reviews are conducted?

❑ What type of audit is conducted of the results of the grievance procedure?

❑ What type of external audits are made of your organization?

A SAMPLE POLICY AND PROCEDURE

In the sample document that's presented at the end of this chapter, both subjects—discrimination and sexual harassment—are covered together in one policy and procedure.

HUMAN RESOURCES EQUAL AND FAIR TREATMENT POLICY AND PROCEDURE

1. POLICY

1.1 It is the policy of the Organization to be nondiscriminatory in all matters regarding the selection, hiring, termination, promotion, transfer, work assignment, scheduling, and compensation of employees, and any or all other conditions of employment.

2. SCOPE

This policy and procedure applies to all employees of the Organization.

3. ACCOUNTABILITY

3.1 All managers are accountable for ensuring the terms and intent of this policy and procedure are met at all times.

3.2 Human Resources is accountable for ensuring all employees understand the terms of this policy and procedure.

3.3 Human Resources is accountable for ensuring all selection processes are conducted within this policy and procedure.

4. DEFINITIONS

4.1 Discrimination is prohibited in making decisions of employment if based on gender, race, religion, national origin, age, veterans status, marital status, and disability.

4.2 Sexual harassment is defined as unwelcome or unwanted conduct of a sexual nature (verbal or physical) when:

4.2.1 Submission to or rejection of this conduct by an employee is used as a factor affecting hiring, evaluation, promotion, or other aspect of employment.

4.2.2 This conduct substantially interferes with an individual's employment or creates an intimidating, hostile, or offensive work environment (examples of such behavior are available from Human Resources).

5. FORMS

None

6. PROCEDURE

6.1 Nondiscrimination

6.1.1 No decisions regarding employees will be influenced by race, sex, color, religion, national origin, age, disability, veterans status, marital status, or any other unlawful basis.

6.1.2 The Organization seeks to provide a collegial work environment in which all individuals are treated with respect and dignity.

6.1.3 Any employees violating this policy are subject to the Performance Improvement Procedure or immediate discharge, depending on the type and degree of violation.

6.1.4 Any employees knowing of a violation of this policy by any other employee are expected to report such violation immediately to their supervisor, Human Resources, the senior vice president of operations, or the general counsel of the Organization.

 6.1.4.1 Any such complaint will be promptly investigated.

 6.1.4.2 The complaint and its investigation will be kept confidential to the maximum extent possible.

 6.1.4.3 Upon completion of the investigation, the complainant and, if appropriate, the alleged violator will be notified of the results of the investigation and any action to be taken by the Organization.

6.1.5 If a party to a complaint disagrees with its resolution, the party may file a written disagreement with Human Resources, the senior vice president of operations, or general counsel of the Organization.

6.1.6 In the event a complaint is found to be false or malicious, the complainant will be subject to the Performance Improvement Procedure.

6.1.7 The Organization will not in any way retaliate against an employee who makes a valid complaint of a violation.

6.1.8 A more detailed description of the handling of such complaints is available from Human Resources.

6.2 Sexual Harassment

6.2.1 Each employee has the right to work in a professional atmosphere that promotes equal opportunities and prohibits discriminatory practices, including sexual harassment.

6.2.2 No employee will be permitted to harass, intimidate, or subject any other employee to a hostile work environment because of that employee's race, sex, color, religion, national origin, age, disability, veterans status, marital status, or any other unlawful basis.

6.2.3 Any employees violating this policy are subject to the Performance Improvement Procedure or immediate discharge, depending on the type and degree of violation.

6.2.4 Any employees knowing of a violation of this policy by an employee are expected to report such violation immediately to their supervisor, the Human Resources manager, the senior vice president of operations, or the general counsel of the Organization.

6.2.4.1 Any such complaint will be promptly investigated.

6.2.4.2 The complaint and its investigation will be kept confidential to the maximum extent possible. However, the Organization cannot guarantee that a complaint of sexual harassment will be able to be kept confidential in all cases.

6.2.4.3 Upon completion of the investigation, the complainant and the alleged violator will be notified of the results of the investigation and any action to be taken by the Organization.

6.2.4.4 If a party to a complaint disagrees with its resolution, the party may file a written disagreement with the senior vice president of operations or the general counsel of the Organization.

6.2.4.5 In the event a complaint is found to be false or malicious, the complainant will be subject to the Performance Improvement Procedure.

6.2.5 The Organization will not in any way retaliate against an employee who makes a valid complaint of a violation.

6.2.6 A more detailed description of the handling of such complaints is available from Human Resources.

6.3 Every nonmanagement employee will attend an annual meeting at which the terms and conditions of this policy and procedure will be reviewed and explained.

6.3.1 At the conclusion of the meeting, employees will sign a statement to indicate their understanding and agreement with the policy and procedure.

6.4 Every management employee will attend an annual meeting at which the terms and conditions of this policy and procedure will be reviewed and explained.

6.4.1 The meeting will include descriptions of acceptable and unacceptable behavior.

6.4.2 At the conclusion of the meeting, management employees will sign a statement to indicate their understanding and agreement with the policy and procedure.

CHAPTER 14

Time Away from Work

"Beware the employee who never takes a day off."

—JOHN RUTTENBERG

IN MOST ORGANIZATIONS, there are many types of time away from work. Personal days, family leave, illnesses, vacations, and holidays are the most common. Some organizations handle each with a separate procedure. Others group them together in a single procedure.

SUBJECT REVIEW

From the employee's and the organization's point of view, time away from work can be placed into two general categories: paid and unpaid time. Then the main issue becomes how one qualifies for each.

Definitions

Although there are varying definitions for various days away from work, your policy and procedure needs to define the ones used by your organization. The following definitions are used by one organization:

Holidays. Individual days recognized by the organization and for which the organization is normally closed and/or most employees are not scheduled to work. Holidays may or may not agree with those recognized by the government.

Vacations. A number of days an employee may use, annually, to be away from work for periods of time.

Illness or Sick Days. Days away from work due to illness or injury that is not work-incurred.

Personal Days. Days the employee may elect to use for personal business.

Family Leave. A period of time when an employee is away from work to care for a family member—a child, spouse, and/or parent.

Leaves of Absence. A requested period of time away from work, in excess of seven days, for medical, personal, educational, military, family, or other reasons.

POLICY CONSIDERATIONS

Organizations sometimes have different policies for each of the six types of time away from work just described, which means six different policy statements. Other organizations attempt to have a single policy covering all. When organizations have different policies for each type of time away from work, they generally have a different policy and procedure for each.

Generally, organizations pay for a specified amount of time away from work for holidays and vacation. Some pay for a specified amount of time away from work for sick days and personal days. Some organizations even pay for certain leaves of absence. The following are a few sample policy statements, each from a different organization, so there is no coordination between them:

> "The organization provides employees with eight holidays per year: New Year's Day, Memorial Day, July Fourth, Labor Day, Thanksgiving, Christmas Day, and two days to be determined each year by management."

> "The organization believes all employees benefit from an annual vacation, so it provides vacation time based on length of service and requires each employee to use the time provided."

> "The organization believes employees too ill to work should remain away until well and provides a number of paid sick days each year for that purpose."

> "The organization recognizes employees have occasional personal need to be away from work and provides each employee with a number of unpaid days annually for that purpose."

"The organization provides employees unpaid leaves of absence for varying purposes requiring time away from work in excess of ten continuous days."

Organizations that combine the various forms of time away from work in a single policy and procedure generally treat them similarly. That is, there is a common procedural or beneficial element in them; they are somehow coordinated; and all days off are drawn from a bank of days. The following is a policy statement from an organization that provides employees an annual bank of days to use as they wish:

"The organization provides its employees a flexible and consistent procedure for time away from work."

PROCEDURES

Let's examine each type of time-off separately. Since each has considerations of its own, questions will be grouped by the subheadings of:

- ❏ Holidays
- ❏ Vacations
- ❏ Illness
- ❏ Personal
- ❏ Family Leave
- ❏ Leaves of Absence
- ❏ Miscellaneous (e.g., jury duty, voting, military service, religious days, death in family)

Holidays

The number of recognized holidays varies by industry and region of the country. The ones most often recognized are Christmas, New Year's Day, and the Fourth of July. The next most often recognized are Labor Day and Memorial Day. Then come such days as Veterans Day, the day before Christmas, the day before New Year's, Martin Luther King Day, Good Friday, and Presidents' Day. Some organizations treat their employees' birthdays and/or anniversary dates with the organization as holidays. Proponents of this policy say it spreads time away from work throughout the year and gives employees an additional holiday while not requiring the organization to close for that day. Part of the decision is normally made based on the practices of the community and the industry.

Organizations with a large population of employees of one nationality or religion may also include days specific to this group, such as Yom Kippur. Organizations that do not recognize these types of days as holidays often provide a way for employees observing them to take them as a holiday, such as giving all employees personal days to use as they wish.

Key questions to answer are:

❑ What holidays does your organization recognize?

❑ Are a set number of holidays recognized?

❑ Are there local holidays recognized by some or all locations?

❑ How are religious days that are not considered holidays handled for those who wish to observe them?

Holiday Pay

Not all organizations that recognize holidays close on those days, or provide employees those days off, or pay employees for the holidays.

Some organizations, particularly those that operate seven days a week, often only compensate employees for holidays that fall on their scheduled straight time workdays. Some do not provide time-off for holidays and instead pay employees, in addition to their regular pay, for holidays. Some organizations pay employees their regular base pay but not any additions, such as shift differentials.

Some organizations pay part-time employees for holidays that fall within their scheduled work time. That pay is usually equal to what the employee would have been paid had the employee worked that day as scheduled. For example, if a part-time employee normally is scheduled to work four hours every Tuesday and a holiday falls on Tuesday, the employee receives four hours of pay. However, if the part-time employee is not normally scheduled to work on Friday, and a holiday falls on Friday, the part-time employee receives no holiday pay.

Two issues with respect to holiday pay have to do with the employee's type of compensation and work performed on a holiday. First, how is the employee who receives some type of performance compensation paid for the holiday? And second, how is an employee paid if the employee works on the holiday?

Generally, employees are paid what they would normally receive if they worked that day. In the case of employees paid by commission or piecework, some formula needs to be established to determine their holiday pay. Typical for a piecework employee is the following formula:

> Holiday pay for piecework employees will be the average daily earning for the employee's five previous workdays.

Some organizations use a similar average calculation for commission-paid employees. However, some do not pay commission employees for holidays.

In almost all cases, holiday pay is normal straight time pay, so what happens if an employee worked on the holiday? Some organizations pay time and one-half. Others pay double time, and some pay only straight time. Other organizations allow the employee to trade the holiday worked for another day off.

What happens if a holiday occurs during the vacation period? That depends on your policy. If each employee is awarded certain holidays, it is generally considered a holiday and not a vacation day. However, if holidays are only paid when an employee is scheduled to work, it may go unrecognized.

Many organizations do not offer holiday pay unless the employee is at work the scheduled workday immediately preceding and following the holiday.

Here are some questions to consider regarding holiday pay:

❒ Which holidays are recognized?
❒ Do employees receive holiday pay?
❒ What eligibility requirements are there for receiving holiday pay?
❒ How is pay for work on a holiday handled?

Vacations

Vacations have many variations in how they are provided and paid. Some organizations require the employee to earn vacation. For example:

An employee earns one day of vacation for each full month worked in a calendar year. The earned vacation can be taken the following year.

Some other organizations award vacation time to employees using a different formula. Here's an example:

An employee is awarded vacation time on January 1 to be taken that year. The amount of vacation time awarded is based on the employee's length of service as of January 1. Time awarded is calculated as follows:

Number of Full Years of Service	Vacation Time Awarded
Less than half a year	5 days
Half a year through 10 years	10 days
11 through 15 years	15 days
16 years or more	20 days

Some organizations offer extra days after the employee completes a certain number of years of service. For example, in one organization, employees with fifteen or more years of service may have two months for vacation once every five years.

Some organizations reduce allowed or awarded vacation time if an employee is not at work for the full year. For example, if an employee is off work for several months due to an illness, the organization might reduce available vacation that year by a specific number of days.

Some organizations treat vacation as vacation pay and not necessarily as time-off. In these organizations, employees may be allowed to take their vacation pay in addition to their regular pay and take no time-off.

Some organizations allow employees to take their vacation time in whatever increments they wish. For example, an employee may take every Friday as vacation in the summer months. Other organizations require a vacation to be taken at one time in its entirety, and there are all the possible variations in between.

Some organizations allow employees to carry over unused vacation until the next year (or a part of the next year). Some require employees to take their vacation or lose it. Some require employees to take their vacation unless requested by management to remain at work and then offer some type of compensating arrangements. And some organizations have a vacation shutdown and require all employees to take their vacation at that time.

A vacation shutdown eliminates the problem of balancing the requests of employees for vacation time. Often these requests are for the same dates, so a procedure is needed to determine which employee has first choice of a date. Some organizations award a date to the first person requesting it. Others award it to the employee with the longest length of service, but most organizations maintain a policy similar to the following:

> The organization requires an adequate workforce at all times, so vacation requests will be granted based on the needs of a department to fulfill its performance objectives.

In industries such as retail that have specific high-volume times—the Friday after Thanksgiving and the day after Christmas, for example—employees may not be allowed to take any vacation time.

What happens to unused vacation time when an employee leaves the organization? If it was earned the previous year to be taken in the current year, it should be paid. If it is awarded, should it be paid? Organizations differ in their answers. Some pay it, some don't.

A Utah financial services company awarded vacation to its employees, but had a policy of not paying terminating employees for unused vacation. However, the company changed its policy when it discovered that employees desiring to leave the company would take vacation and then, at the end of the vacation, resign.

Here are vacation questions to consider:

- ❏ How is vacation earned/awarded?
- ❏ What are the steps for requesting vacation?
- ❏ What are the requirements for taking vacation?
- ❏ What happens to unused vacation?
- ❏ What eligibility requirements are there for receiving vacation?
- ❏ How is pay for work on a holiday handled?

❏   How are requests for the same vacation time resolved?

❏   How is vacation pay determined?

Illness

Organizations have many different approaches to time-off due to illness. Some of the considerations are similar to those for vacations. Some organizations award so many days a year for illness. Others have employees earn sick days based on their length of service. Some limit the number of days that can be accumulated; others allow unlimited accumulation.

> A man who worked for the post office was awarded a certain number of sick days each year, but he was rarely ill. The sick days accumulated. In the 1960s, he was eligible to retire, but by using his total sick days, he actually stopped reporting to work three months before his official retirement date.

Some organizations do not pay employees when they take time-off due to illness. Some organizations pay the employee all or part of unused annual sick days. Others do not. Some organizations won't pay for the first one, two, or three days off due to illness, while others pay from the first day. Most organizations have a limit on the number of days for which they will pay. Quite often, this limit is coordinated with short-term disability benefits. Some require a physician's note when an employee is out sick in excess of three days. When establishing a policy and procedure for sick days, the key questions to ask are:

❏   What type of time-off due to illness does the organization allow?

❏   What type of pay is there for time-off due to illness?

❏   What are the eligibility requirements for time-off due to illness and for receiving pay?

❏   What happens to unused days?

❏   How is the organization's policy and procedure coordinated with leaves of absence and disability benefits?

Personal

Personal days are just that. They are days an employee can use for what-ever purpose the employee desires. Some organizations allow them. Others do not. Some pay for a certain number of personal days each year. Others allow the days, but do not pay for them.

For personal days, the same questions that were asked for time-off due to illness can be used:

❒ What type of time-off for personal reasons does the organization allow?

❒ What type of pay is there for personal time-off?

❒ What are the eligibility requirements for personal time-off and/or pay?

❒ What happens to unused personal days?

❒ How is the organization's policy and procedure coordinated with leaves of absence and disability benefits?

Family Leave

The Family and Medical Leave Act requires some employers to allow employees to take time-off for family needs, such as to care for a newborn child, an ill parent, or an ill spouse or child. The act does not require the employer to pay the employee. (You should consult with an attorney for other policy implications.)

Leaves of Absence

Leaves of absence are for lengthy time away from work. The approved length of time-off varies by organization and reason for the leave. Some leaves of absence are also governed by law. The most common reasons are:

❒ Military Service (long term)

❒ Birth of a Child

❒ Short-Term Illness

❒ Long-Term Illness or Disability

❑ Educational

❑ Government Service/Appointment

❑ Jury Duty (long term)

In all cases, a leave is granted so the affected employees are not removed from the payroll, even though they are probably not being paid. The benefits can be that employees continue to accumulate length of service and, in some organizations, are eligible for continuation of benefits such as health insurance and retirement credits.

The first question to answer is: What leaves of absence does the organization offer? Next, answer the following questions for each type of leave of absence:

❑ What is the length of the leave of absence?

❑ What are the eligibility requirements for the leave of absence?

❑ How do employees make application for the leave of absence?

❑ Is the leave of absence coordinated with other time-off provisions?

❑ Must the granted leave of absence be renewed?

❑ What are the eligibility requirements for returning from a leave of absence?

❑ Is an employee on the leave of absence eligible for benefits? If so, which benefits?

Miscellaneous

There are a number of other reasons employees may be away from work and those also have to be covered in your policies and procedures. A few are:

❑ Jury Duty (short term)

❑ Voting Day

❑ Military Service (short term)

❑ Religious Holidays

❑ Death in Family

Jury Duty

Time-off is mandatory, but in most instances, pay is not. Some organizations will attempt to have an employee excused from jury duty. Others will not. Some pay the employee while on jury duty but require the employee to submit any jury duty pay to the organization. Others do not. Some pay the employee and allow the employee to keep any jury duty pay. Some require an employee to report for work on days not selected for duty.

Voting Day

Some organizations give a day off (often for national elections) and/or a half-day (for local and state elections). Others give employees an hour or two off at the beginning or end of the workday.

Military Service

Employees in the reserves or National Guard have their jobs protected by law. Some organizations continue their normal pay while on service for up to a specific number of days or weeks. Others keep the employee on the rolls without pay, but allow participation in benefits. Others place the employees on a military leave of absence. When national emergencies and war require employees to serve extended periods of time, there are sometimes specific laws or regulations (see Chapter 3) to cover the situations. You must ensure that your policies and procedures covering both short- and long-term military service are in compliance with federal and state requirements.

Religious Days

Some organizations allow time-off with pay for employees to observe religious holidays. Others consider it personal time and follow whatever their procedure is for personal days.

Death in Family

The definition of family may encompass a father, mother, child (adopted, natural, step, or foster), father-in-law, mother-in-law, sister, brother, brother-in-law, aunt, uncle, cousin, grandparent, grandparent-in-law, or another, such as a close friend.

How many days are allowed? Some companies allow three days; others increase the number to five for immediate family. Some require that all the days be consecutive scheduled workdays. Some allow additional time-off if travel over 100 miles is required.

Some organizations pay for a certain number of days. Some do not. Some require evidence of death in the form of a death certificate, for example.

Time-Off as a Benefit

Time-off, particularly paid time-off, is often classified as an employee benefit. Organizations offering cafeteria-type benefits plans often include sick days, personal days, and vacation days as a time away from work benefit. Employees are then allowed to use their assigned monetary amount for benefits toward purchase of days. This approach is covered in Chapter 11 on benefits.

Time Away from Work Banks

Some organizations, instead of dealing with all the separate time away from work issues, set up a "bank of days" from which employees can take different types of time-off. The concept is somewhat similar to the cafeteria-type benefits approach in that it offers flexibility. Each employee is assigned a certain number of days each year (sometimes earned, sometimes based on length of service). Employees may then use these days as they wish. Generally, they may be used for vacation, illness, and personal days. Holidays, leaves of absences, and mandatory time-off are not part of the time-off bank. Also, rules still apply for obtaining vacation time.

SAMPLE POLICIES AND PROCEDURES

Two policies and procedures follow. One deals separately with each type of time away from work. The other describes a time away from work bank. These examples are from two different organizations.

HUMAN RESOURCES TIME AWAY FROM WORK POLICY AND PROCEDURE

1. POLICY

The Organization provides its employees a flexible and consistent procedure for time away from work.

2. SCOPE

This policy and procedure applies to all employees of the Organization.

3. ACCOUNTABILITY

3.1 All managers are accountable for ensuring the employees reporting to them receive and correctly use their time away from work as provided in this policy and procedure.

3.2 Human Resources is accountable for providing reports to managers of the current status of their employees' time away from work.

3.3 All managers are accountable for ensuring that accurate records of their employee's time away from work are maintained, and that all time away from work is reported to Payroll the week in which it occurs.

4. DEFINITIONS

4.1 *Holiday*—Individual days recognized by the organization and for which the organization is normally closed and/or most employees are not scheduled to work. Holidays may or may not agree with those recognized by the government.

4.2 *Vacation*—Annually, a number of days an employee may use to be away from work for periods of time.

4.3 *Illness or Sick Days*—Days away from work due to illness or injury that is not work-incurred.

4.4 *Personal Days*—Days the employee may elect to use for personal business.

4.5 *Family Leave*—A period of time an employee is away from work to care for a family member—a child, spouse, and/or parent.

4.6 *Leaves of Absence*—A requested period of time away from work, in excess of seven days, for medical, personal, educational, military, family, or other reasons.

4.7 Employee's family is defined as the employee's child, parent, spouse, sibling, grandparent, spouse's parent, and spouse's sibling.

5. FORMS

5.1 Weekly Time Sheet

5.2 Absentee Report

5.3 Vacation Request

6. PROCEDURE

6.1 Voting Day

The Organization encourages good citizenship among its employees and, accordingly, allows employees to arrive up to one (1) hour late or leave up to one (1) hour early, without loss of pay, for voting purposes on a national, state, or local election day.

6.2 Holidays

The Organization provides a minimum of eight (8) paid holidays each year:

6.2.1 New Year's Day

6.2.2 Memorial Day

6.2.3 Independence Day

6.2.4 Labor Day

6.2.5 Thanksgiving

6.2.6 Christmas Day

6.2.7 Two (2) days are annually determined by management.

6.2.8 Holiday schedules for the following calendar year will be communicated to all employees by November 30.

6.2.9 The Organization may elect to provide additional partial or full days as paid or unpaid holidays during a year.

6.2.10 If a holiday falls on a nonscheduled workday (Saturday or Sunday), the Organization may elect to celebrate the holiday on either the day immediately preceding or following a regularly scheduled workday.

6.2.11 Employees regularly scheduled to work less than a full workweek will receive holiday pay equal to the number of hours they would have been scheduled to work on the holiday had they worked.

6.2.12 Employees required to work on a holiday will receive both their regular pay and the holiday pay for that day, or may request compensatory time within the rules for such time.

6.3 Jury Duty

The Organization encourages good citizenship among its employees and, accordingly, continues an employee's regular base pay for any time the employee spends on jury duty.

6.3.1 The employee is expected to be at work unless actually serving on a jury or being required to be in attendance at the courthouse for jury selection.

6.3.2 Employees notified prior to noon on any jury duty day that they will not be required to serve on a jury or remain at the courthouse that day are expected to return to work.

6.3.3 Employees regularly scheduled to work less than a full workweek will receive pay equal to the number of hours they would have been scheduled to work during the time they are on jury duty.

6.3.4 In order to be paid for the time spent on jury duty, employees are required to submit to Human Resources the appropriate jury duty confirmation form supplied by the court.

6.4 Reserve or National Guard Service

6.4.1 Any employee required to serve up to two (2) weeks at annual reserve or National Guard training shall be considered to be on temporary military leave of absence without pay during such period, provided that a copy of the official orders are submitted along with such request for leave.

6.4.2 Employees may elect to use all or part of their vacation for part or all of their reserve or National Guard training.

6.4.3 Employees are expected to notify their manager of their annual reserve or National Guard training dates as early as possible. In no case shall such notification for annual military training be less than one (1) month in advance of the actual dates.

6.5 Death in the Family

6.5.1 An employee may have up to five (5) consecutive days off with pay due to the death of a member of the employee's family living in the employee's house.

6.5.2 An employee may have up to three (3) consecutive days off with pay due to the death of a member of the employee's family not living in the employee's house.

6.5.3 Death in the family pay is an employee's base pay.

6.5.3.1 Employees regularly scheduled to work less than a full workweek will receive pay equal to the number of hours they would have been scheduled to work during the approved time they are away for a death in the family.

6.6 Vacation

All permanent regularly scheduled employees receive vacation time-off each year with pay according to their length of service.

6.6.1 The amount of eligible vacation in a calendar year is based on the number of full years of service the employee will have completed during that calendar year:

Number of Full Years of Service	Eligible Vacation Time-Off with Pay
1 through 5 years	10 days
6 through 10 years	15 days
11 years or more	21 days

6.6.1.1 During their first calendar year of employment, employees will receive five (5) vacation days with pay once they have been employed for at least six (6) months. Employees hired after July 1 will not receive any vacation with pay that year.

6.6.2 Vacation pay is an employee's base pay.

6.6.2.1 Employees regularly scheduled to work less than a full workweek will receive pay for vacation equal to the average number of hours they work in a week. Average number of hours is calculated by averaging their hours worked per week the preceding year.

6.6.3 Vacation time with pay not used in a calendar year is lost.

6.6.3.1 New employees may take any vacation with pay due their first calendar year of employment during the first quarter of their second calendar year of employment.

6.6.4 An employee may not receive vacation pay in lieu of taking the vacation time-off.

6.6.5 Vacation time is requested by an employee using the Vacation Request form provided by Human Resources and submitting the completed form to the employee's manager.

6.6.5.1 If approved, the employee may take the days off.

6.6.5.2 The Organization requires an adequate workforce to be available during scheduled working hours. If an employee's request for vacation time-off interferes with Organization or department requirements, the manager may deny the employee's request. In such an instance, the employee will have to request other dates.

6.6.6 If more employees request the same vacation dates and the manager cannot allow all to be away at the same time, the manager will meet with each employee involved in an attempt to arrive at a mutually acceptable schedule.

6.6.6.1 If these meetings do not produce an acceptable schedule, the manager will approve the requests based on first received being first approved.

6.6.6.2 If the requests were received at the same time, length of service will be used for approving the requests—greatest length of service being first approved.

6.6.7 Employees separating from the Organization as voluntary terminations in good standing with proper notice (at least two [2] weeks) will receive pay for their unused vacation.

6.6.7.1 Employees who have not worked at least twelve (12) months as of date of termination will receive no pay for unused vacation.

6.6.8 Employees who have approved scheduled vacation for the last quarter of a year, but are requested by the Organization to work during that approved scheduled vacation time, may carry their unused vacation time over into the first quarter of the following year, provided it is approved by the appropriate division senior manager and senior vice president of operations.

6.7 Personal Time-Off

All permanent regularly scheduled employees are eligible for personal time-off with pay.

6.7.1 After three (3) months of service, all permanent regularly scheduled employees are eligible for up to two (2) days off with pay each calendar year for personal reasons.

6.7.2 Personal time-off with pay is an employee's base pay.

6.7.2.1 Employees regularly scheduled to work less than a full work-week will receive pay equal to the number of hours they would have been scheduled to work during the approved personal time-off.

6.7.3 Personal time-off not used in a calendar year is lost.

6.7.3.1 An employee may not receive personal time-off pay in lieu of taking personal time-off.

6.7.4 Personal time-off is requested by employees of their supervisor.

6.7.4.1 If approved, the employee may then take the approved days off.

6.7.4.2 Requests for personal time-off for valid religious purposes and for a serious illness in the employee's family (spouse, child, and parent) will always be approved.

6.7.4.3 Requests for personal time-off for other reasons will be approved based on the Organization requirements to have an adequate workforce available during scheduled working hours.

6.7.5 Employees separating from the Organization for any reason will not be paid for any unused personal time-off.

6.7.6 The smallest unit of time-off for personal reasons is four (4) hours.

6.8 Time-Off Due to Illness

All permanent regularly scheduled employees are eligible for paid time-off due to illness.

6.8.1 All permanent regularly scheduled employees, except during their first year of employment, are eligible for up to eight (8) days off with pay each calendar year due to illness.

6.8.2 During the calendar year in which they are hired:

6.8.2.1 Employees do not receive any paid time-off for illness during their first three (3) months of employment.

6.8.2.2 For any additional time worked, after the first three (3) months of employment that calendar year, they may take up to one (1) day during each three (3) month period.

6.8.2.3 Eligible days not taken in one (1) three (3) month period may be cumulated with other eligible days that first calendar year of employment.

6.9 Time-off pay for illness is an employee's base pay.

6.9.1 Employees regularly scheduled to work less than a full workweek receive pay equal to the number of hours they would have been scheduled to work during the personal time-off.

6.9.2 Time-off due to illness not used in a calendar year is lost. An employee may not receive time-off due to illness pay in lieu of taking time-off due to illness.

6.9.3 To be eligible for paid time-off due to illness, employees must report their illness each day during the first hour of their regularly scheduled work time, unless there is a valid reason for being unable to make such a report.

6.9.3.1 The report may be made by telephone to the employee's supervisor, the Human Resources manager, or the receptionist.

6.9.3.2 Messages left on voice mail are not considered as proper notification.

6.9.4 Employees away from work due to illness (whether paid or not) for more than three (3) consecutive days are required to furnish evidence of the illness, such as a doctor's or hospital's confirmation of treatment.

6.9.5 Employees absent for three (3) or more consecutive days without notifying the Organization will be considered voluntary terminations.

6.9.6 Employees who are frequently absent or late, or whose absence and lateness form a pattern, may be subject to the terms of the Attendance Policy and Procedure (see 7.2).

6.9.7 Employees separating from the Organization for any reason will not be paid for any unused time-off for illness.

6.9.8 The smallest unit of time-off due to illness is four (4) hours.

6.10 Leaves of Absence

Any time-off in excess of eligible time-off with pay as described in this policy and procedure must be requested as a leave of absence in writing by the employee and approved by the employee's supervisor and the Human Resources manager.

6.10.1 Employees will not be granted time-off without pay in excess of one (1) day unless they have already used all time-off with pay for which they are eligible.

6.10.2 Family and Medical Leaves of Absence

The Organization supports the objective of the federal Family and Medical Leave Act that assists employees in balancing the demands of the workplace with the needs of the family.

6.10.3 Under this policy, eligible employees are entitled to a total of twelve (12) weeks of unpaid leave of absence in a twelve (12) month period (measured backward from the date of an employee's use of any family and medical leave).

6.10.4 An employee's serious health condition may also make the employee eligible for short- and long-term disability benefits in concurrence with a family and/or medical leave of absence (see 7.3 Benefits

Policy and Procedure) and the short- and long-term disability insurance master policies governing details for these benefits.

6.10.5 To be eligible for a family or medical leave of absence, an employee must have been employed by the Organization for at least twelve (12) months and must have worked at least one thousand two hundred fifty (1,250) hours during the twelve (12) months immediately preceding commencement of the leave.

6.10.6 An eligible employee is entitled to a leave of absence for a serious health condition, the birth of the employee's child, the placement of a child with the employee for adoption or foster care, or to care for the employee's child, spouse, or parent who has a serious health condition.

6.10.7 For purposes of the family and medical leaves of absence, the following definitions shall apply:

6.10.7.1 *Health Care Provider*—A doctor of medicine or osteopathy who is authorized to practice medicine or surgery by the state in which the doctor practices, or any other person determined by the secretary of labor to be capable of providing health care services.

6.10.7.2 Others "capable of providing health care services" include only:

6.10.7.2.1 Podiatrists, dentists, clinical psychologists, optometrists, and chiropractors (limited to treatment consisting of manual manipulation of the spine to correct a subluxation as demonstrated by X-ray to exist) authorized to practice in the state and performing within the scope of their practice as defined under state law.

6.10.7.2.2 Nurse practitioners and nurse-midwives who are authorized to practice under state law and who are performing within the scope of their practice as defined under state law.

6.10.7.2.3 Christian Science practitioners listed with the First Church of Christ, Scientist in Boston, Massachusetts. Where an employee or family member is receiving treatment from a Christian Science practitioner, an employee may not object to any requirement from the Organization that the employee or family member submit to an examination (though not treatment) to obtain a second or third certification from a health care provider other than a Christian Science practitioner.

6.10.7.2.4 Any health care provider from whom the Organization will accept certification of the existence of a serious health condition.

6.10.7.2.5 Certain health care providers who practice in a country other than the United States.

6.10.7.3 *Serious Health Condition*—An illness, injury, impairment, or physical or mental condition that involves:

6.10.7.3.1 Period of incapacity or treatment.

6.10.7.3.2 Inpatient care in a hospital, hospice, or residential medical care facility.

6.10.7.3.3 A required absence from work, school, or other daily activities of more than three (3) calendar days that also involves continuing treatment or supervision of a health care provider.

6.10.7.3.4 Continuing treatment by or under the supervision of a health care provider for a chronic or long-term condition that is incurable or, if not treated, could result in a period of incapacity of more than three (3) calendar days.

6.10.7.3.5 Pregnancy or prenatal care.

6.10.7.3.6 Permanent or long-term care due to a condition for which treatment may not be effective.

6.10.7.3.7 Reduced or intermittent leave of absence schedule, which is defined as a leave, when medically necessary, that reduces the number of working hours per week or hours per day.

6.10.7.4 *Parent*—The biological parent of an employee or an individual who stood in place of a parent.

6.10.7.5 *Son or Daughter*—A biological, adopted, or foster child, stepchild, legal ward, or child of a person standing in place of a parent who is under eighteen (18) years of age, or eighteen (18) years of age or older and incapable of self-care because of physical or mental disability.

6.10.8 Leave Requirements

Eligible employees covered by other paid time-off (vacation, sick time, and personal time) will be required to take such paid time-off as part of the twelve (12) weeks of leave that the employee is entitled to under this policy, to the full extent permitted by regulations issued by the Department of Labor.

6.10.9 Advance Request for Leave

6.10.9.1 A minimum of thirty (30) days advance notice of a request for leave of absence is required where practical for the expected birth of a child or the planned medical treatment of a son, daughter, spouse, or parent with a serious health condition. If the date of birth or placement requires the leave of absence to begin in less than thirty (30) days, the employee shall provide such notice as is practical.

6.10.9.2 Employees requesting leaves of absence for planned medical treatment of a son, daughter, spouse, or parent should make a reasonable effort to schedule treatment so as not to disrupt their department's work schedules, consistent with the requirements of the health care provider.

6.10.9.3 Eligible employees anticipating the need to request unpaid leaves of absence should submit a written request to their supervisors accompanied by a Medical Certification of Physician or Practitioner. The supervisors will forward the requests to the senior vice president of operations for approval. The requests will then be forwarded to the Human Resources manager for further approval and processing. A copy of an approved request will be returned to the requesting employee.

6.10.9.4 If both spouses work for the Organization, they are limited to a total of twelve (12) weeks family leave in a twelve (12) month period between them for the birth or adoption of a child or for caring for a parent with a serious health condition.

6.10.9.4.1 If only a portion of an entitled leave of absence is used, then each employee is entitled to the additional time, up to twelve (12) weeks in a twelve (12) month period, for a spouse who is ill and unable to work or a child with a serious health condition.

6.10.10 Medical Certification

6.10.10.1 An employee's request for a leave of absence to care for a seriously ill spouse, child, or parent must be supported by a Medical Certification of Physician or Practitioner form issued by the appropriate health care provider. Leaves of absence may be denied until the required certification is provided.

6.10.10.2 The Organization reserves the right to require the employee to obtain the opinion of an Organization-approved second health care provider at the Organization's expense. If the first and second opinions differ, the Organization at its own expense may require the binding opinion of a third health care provider, approved jointly by the Organization and the employee.

6.10.11 Intermittent or Reduced Work Schedule

6.10.11.1 If a leave of absence is sought on an intermittent or reduced schedule because of an employee's serious illness or to care for a sick family member, the certification must contain additional declarations from the health care provider stating that intermittent or reduced schedule leave is medically necessary and the amount of time that will be needed.

6.10.11.2 Intermittent or reduced schedule leaves of absence may be taken when medically necessary for the serious illness of an employee or to care for the employee's eligible family member. An employee requesting an intermittent or reduced schedule may be temporarily transferred to an alternative position for which the employee is qualified with equivalent pay and benefits, and which better accommodates recurring periods of leave.

6.10.12 Restoration of Employment

6.10.12.1 As a condition of returning to work, the Organization requires employees on a leave of absence to notify their supervisor in writing, with a copy to Human Resources, on a biweekly basis, of the employee's status and intention to return to work.

6.10.12.2 An employee taking a leave of absence due to a serious health condition of an eligible family member must submit subsequent recertification of the medical condition to the Organization biweekly.

6.10.12.3 Employees returning to work from an unpaid leave of absence under this policy shall be restored to the same or equivalent position with equivalent benefits, pay, and all other terms and conditions of employment.

6.10.12.4 Employment restoration rights may be denied if an employee is within the highest ten percent (10%) of all Organization employees in compensation, performs the duties of a highly specialized nature that cannot be performed by other employees, sets policy on behalf of the Organization, or directs the activities of a major organizational segment of the Organization and is necessary to prevent "substantial and grievous economic injury to the Organization."

6.10.12.5 Failure to comply with any requirements listed in this policy and procedure may result in the denial of family or medical leave of absence, and leaves of absence in excess of that permitted under this policy and procedure will result in loss of protection under the Family and Medical Leave Act.

6.10.13 Military Leave

6.10.13.1 Employees serving in the reserve or National Guard who are activated will be placed on leave of absence and their position retained for their return.

6.10.13.2 The employee must provide the Organization with written documentation of such activation.

6.10.13.3 Employees activated for less than six (6) months must report back to work within two (2) weeks of the termination of their activity duty, and employees activated for six (6) months or more must report back to work within thirty (30) days of the termination of their activity duty. Employees not reporting back to work within the time required will be considered to have voluntary quit.

6.10.14 Maintenance of Adequate Workforce

The Organization requires an adequate workforce to be available during scheduled working hours. If an employee's request for a leave of absence, other than for those reasons described in this policy and procedure, interferes with Organization requirements, the Organization may deny the request.

7. REFERENCES

7.1 Terms of Employment Policy and Procedure

7.2 Attendance Policy and Procedure

7.3 Benefits Policy and Procedure

HUMAN RESOURCES TIME AWAY FROM WORK BANK

1. POLICY

The Organization provides employees with a flexible and individual procedure for time away from work.

2. SCOPE

The terms of this policy and procedure apply to all employees of the Organization.

3. ACCOUNTABILITY

3.1 All managers are accountable for implementing the terms of this policy and procedure.

3.2 Human Resources is accountable for annually calculating and communicating allocated days for time away from work.

3.3 Payroll is accountable for recording each employee's used time away from work.

4. DEFINITIONS

There are no unique definitions to terms used in this policy and procedure.

5. FORMS

5.1 Nonexempt Weekly Time Card

5.2 Exempt Weekly Time Sheet

5.3 Request for Time Away from Work

6. PROCEDURE

6.1 Holidays

6.1.2 The organization provides eight (8) scheduled holidays each year to all employees: New Year's Day, Memorial Day, Independence Day, Labor Day, Thanksgiving, Christmas Day, and two (2) days determined by the Organization each year.

6.1.2.1 Holiday schedules for the following calendar year will be communicated to all employees by November 30.

6.1.2.2 The Organization may elect to provide additional partial or full days as paid or unpaid holidays during a year.

6.1.2.3 If a holiday falls on a nonscheduled workday (Saturday or Sunday), the Organization may elect to celebrate the holiday on either the day immediately preceding or following a regularly scheduled workday.

6.1.2.4 Employees required to work on a holiday will receive both their regular pay and the holiday pay for that day, or may request compensatory time within the rules for such time.

6.1.3 Employees are paid holiday pay as per the Compensation Policy and Procedure (see 7.1).

6.1.4 Holidays are not considered part of an employee's allotted time away from workdays.

6.2 Mandatory Time Away from Work

6.2.1 Mandatory time away from work does dot require the use of an employee's allotted time away from work, but in some cases the employee may elect to do so.

6.3 Time Away from Work

6.3.1 An allocation of days is made to each employee each calendar year to be used at the employee's desecration for death in the family, illnesses of less than five (5) days, vacation, or personal reasons.

6.3.1.1 Time away from work due to illness and disabilities is covered by short- and long-term insurances and are not covered by allocated time away from workdays.

6.4 Annual Time Away from Work Allotment

6.4.1 At the beginning of each calendar year, every full-time employee receives an allotment of time that the employee may use for eligible paid time away from work.

6.4.2 The size of each employee's allotment is based on the employee's length of service as of the beginning of the calendar year.

6.4.3 For full-time employees with at least one (1) year's length of service as of January 1, the allotments are:

Length of Service	Nonexempt Allotment	Exempt Allotment
Less than six months	12 days	18 days
Six months to 5 years	21 days	26 days
5 to 10 years	26 days	31 days
10-plus years	31 days	36 days

6.4.4 The additional time allotted to exempt personnel is to compensate them for unpaid overtime work.

6.4.5 For newly hired employees, their time allotments the first two (2) years of their employment are based on the month in which employment was begun:

Month Hired	Nonexempt Employee		Exempt Employee	
	First Calendar Year of Employment	Second Calendar Year of Employment	First Calendar Year of Employment	Second Calendar Year of Employment
January	13 days	21 days	14 days	26 days
February	12 days	21 days	13 days	24 days
March	11 days	20 days	12 days	23 days
April	10 days	20 days	11 days	22 days
May	9 days	20 days	10 days	21 days
June	8 days	19 days	9 days	20 days
July	7 days	18 days	8 days	19 days
August	5 days	17 days	6 days	18 days
September	4 days	16 days	5 days	17 days
October	3 days	15 days	4 days	16 days
November	2 days	14 days	3 days	15 days
December	1 day	13 days	2 days	14 days

6.4.6 Regular scheduled permanent part-time employees will receive the same allotted number of days based on their length of service, but each allotted day shall be for the average number of hours they work.

6.4.6.1 The average number of hours worked is determined by dividing an employee's total hours worked during a year by the total number of days during which the hours were worked. Days during which overtime was paid are not included in calculating an average.

6.4.7 Time away from work allotments can be taken in units as small as two (2) hours.

6.4.8 To request a specific time away from work, the employee completes a Request for Time Away from Work form and submits it to the employee's supervisor.

6.4.8.1 No request for time away from work can be submitted prior to January 1 of the year in which the time is being requested, but an employee requesting time during the first quarter of the year may request it during the last quarter of the previous year.

6.4.8.2 The supervisor may approve or deny all requests.

6.4.8.3 It is recognized that an adequate workforce to meet the organization's performance objectives is required at all times, so requests for time away from work must be approved by the employee's supervisor.

6.4.8.4 In instances where more employees are requesting the same time away from work and to grant all requests will not allow the unit to perform as it should, the supervisor will discuss the situation with all employees and attempt to resolve it. All else failing, the employees' lengths of service will become the determining factor

6.4.8.5 The supervisor may also prohibit any time-off for specific days if that time-off would prohibit the unit from performing its required work.

6.4.8.6 Any employee taking time-off with pay will have that number of days deducted from the employee's time away from work bank.

6.4.8.7 If employees disagree with the supervisor's decision, they may use the grievance procedure (see Grievance Resolution Policy and Procedure).

6.4.8.8 Employees may elect not to use allotted days for reserve and National Guard annual service and receive no pay for that time away from work.

6.4.8.9 An employee may not use any combination of regular pay and time away from work allotment pay if it exceeds the employee's normal pay for the period.

6.4.8.10 Employees whose total allotment of days for a year is twelve (12) or more are required at least five (5) days of their allotted time be taken in five (5) continuous days.

6.4.8.11 All blocks of time (five or more days) must be requested by March 1 of each year.

6.4.9 If all allotted days are not used by the employee, all but five (5) are lost at year-end. The five (5) not lost can be carried over to the next year.

6.4.9.1 In no instance can more than five (5) days be carried over to the next year.

6.4.9.2 If for any reason management requests an employee not to use all or any part of the employee's allotted days, all remaining days can be carried over to the next year. This option may only be used once every three (3) years.

6.4.10 If the Organization closes on a normally scheduled workday or additional holiday(s) are granted, the employee will be paid for that day and it shall not be deducted from the employee's allotment.

6.4.11 Any employee terminating employment and giving at least one full pay period's notice will be paid for fifty percent (50%) of any remaining allotted days, but any employee not giving proper notice will not be paid for any unused days.

6.4.11.1 In the event the Organization terminates an employee's employment without at least one pay period's notice or payment of that amount in lieu of notice, the employee will receive full payment for all unused days.

6.4.11.2 Employees terminated for cause and employees not in good standing (see Termination Policy and Procedure) will not receive pay for any unused allotted days.

6.4.12 Employees requiring time-off for emergencies or illness are to notify their supervisor within their first hour of scheduled work.

6.4.13 Time away from work allotments may not be used to compensate for lateness of less than two (2) hours.

6.4.14 Employees promoted from nonexempt to exempt positions during a calendar year will receive additional allotment of days at the time of promotion equal to the difference between the eligible number of days for the employee's length of service.

6.4.14.1 Employees moving from exempt to nonexempt positions will retain their full exempt allotments for the year in which they change positions, but beginning the next year their allotment shall be the nonexempt employee allotment.

7. REFERENCES

7.1 Compensation Policy and Procedure

7.2 Grievance Resolution Policy and Procedure

7.3 Termination Policy and Procedure

CHAPTER 15

Attendance

"You must be present to win."   —Las Vegas Casino Sign

ALTHOUGH ORGANIZATIONS HAVE POLICIES AND PROCEDURES on time away from work for various reasons (e.g., personal time-off, vacations, and illness), and in many cases such time is paid, organizations also have a need to control absenteeism. Usually there is a separate policy and procedure for that purpose.

SUBJECT REVIEW

Absenteeism is basically an employee not reporting for scheduled work. Another way of looking at it is as unplanned time away from work. Absenteeism applies to both lateness and absence.

A policy and procedure on absenteeism usually deals with defining it, establishing limits, and describing results of excessive absenteeism.

Definitions

Both lateness and absences need to be defined. Here are two common definitions:

Lateness. Employees arriving at their workstations after the scheduled time to start work.

Absence. Employees not being at work during scheduled work time.

Some definitions differentiate between lateness or absences that are approved and not approved:

Approved. An employee's time away from work is approved if advance permission was obtained.

Not Approved. An employee's time away from work is not approved if no advance permission was obtained.

POLICY CONSIDERATIONS

Policy statements on attendance most often refer to the organization's need to have an adequate number of employees at work to fulfill its operating objectives during scheduled work hours.

A well-known food manufacturer struggled with the problem of the lateness of office employees—employees who traditionally did not sign in or punch a time clock. The company decided to request that all office employees (including executives) punch a time clock. The reward was a punctuality bonus of 10 percent of daily pay for each day the employee punched in and was on time. The company felt the time saved was worth the payment of a 10 percent bonus.

PROCEDURES

The key areas where procedures are needed are in establishing absenteeism limits and describing actions to take when limits are exceeded.

Absenteeism Limits

Quite often, two numbers are established as limits for both absences and tardiness. One is frequency of occurrences. How often is the employee late or absent—twice a month or four times a year? The other is a cumulative number—that is, how many total days or instances in a specific period the employee is absent from or late for work.

An organization may set as its limits eight absences in any one calendar year, with no more than two absences in any one month. Note these are absences and not length of absences. So, a three-day absence because the employee has the flu would count as a single absence and a total of three days absent.

Tardiness is similar. The limit per year for frequency might be twelve instances of lateness and an accumulative total of four hours in a year. Some organizations allow an employee to be tardy up to a certain amount of time (often one or two hours). After that, the employee is considered absent for the day.

A Georgia clothing manufacturer had all employees punch in using a time clock. The time cards were used to determine attendance as well as pay. However, the time clock recorded time in tenths of an hour, so it punched the card for 9:00 A.M. from 9:00 to 9:05, giving employees six minutes in which they could be late.

As mentioned previously, many organizations treat approved and unapproved absences differently. For example, if an employee requests to be late an hour the next day and the employee's supervisor agrees, then the employee would be late but it would not be counted against him. However, in other organizations, even approved absences can be counted against the employee.

Many times employees, particularly new ones, just stop coming to work. They may have found another job, or maybe they do not like the job they have in your organization. Whatever the reason, at some point you need to consider them voluntary quits. Often, an absence of three consecutive scheduled workdays is the threshold.

Here are some questions to answer:

❐ What are the limits (frequency and severity) for absences?

❐ What are the limits (frequency and severity) for tardiness?

❐ When is an employee considered a voluntary quit?

❐ What are the procedures for handling approved (advance request and notification) absences?

❐ Under what circumstances is time away from work not considered an absence?

Actions

Once absenteeism limits have been established, the next issue to consider is how to deal with infractions. Some organizations make infractions a part of their normal disciplinary procedure. (See Chapter 17 on Perform-ance Improvement for disciplinary policy and procedure.) Others treat infractions of the attendance policy as a separate issue. In either case, the thrust is usually the same: to correct the absenteeism. Key questions to ask are:

- ❒ What actions are taken when an employee approaches absenteeism limits?
- ❒ What actions are taken when an employee exceeds absenteeism limits?
- ❒ Do the actions taken when an employee is late or absent for regularly scheduled work also apply for scheduled overtime work?

A SAMPLE POLICY AND PROCEDURE

This chapter concludes with a typical policy and procedure for atten-dance. Again, it is not provided as an example of what your organization's policy and procedure should be. Rather, it is an example of a policy and procedure written in the format suggested in this book, after answering all of the previous questions.

HUMAN RESOURCES ATTENDANCE POLICY AND PROCEDURE

1. POLICY

The Organization's employees are expected to be present and ready for work during all of their scheduled work hours, and their attendance and punctuality will be considered in performance and salary reviews.

2. SCOPE

This policy and procedure applies to all employees of the Organization.

3. ACCOUNTABILITY

3.1 All managers are accountable for administering the terms of this policy and procedure with their employees, maintaining individual attendance and punctuality records for each employee, and ensuring that all Weekly Time Sheets are accurate and reflect actual hours worked.

3.2 Human Resources is accountable for regularly analyzing and reporting overall Organization attendance and punctuality information and monitoring the Organization to ensure equal administration of the terms herein.

4. DEFINITIONS

4.1 *Absence*—An absence occurs whenever employees do not report for work during their entire scheduled workday. This includes scheduled overtime days.

4.2 *Lateness*—Lateness is considered to have occurred when employees are not at their workstations ready to work at their scheduled starting time. This includes scheduled overtime.

4.3 The following are not considered absences if incurred as per the appropriate policy and procedure requirements:

4.3.1 Approved leaves of absence.

4.3.2 Jury duty.

4.3.3 Military leave.

4.3.4 Prior approved time-off for personal reasons.

4.3.5 Any Organization-approved absences or lateness such as caused by an emergency or weather conditions.

4.3.6 Paid-for time-off for a death in the family.

4.3.7 Paid-for and/or approved vacation.

4.3.8 Any time-off that is prior approved or requested is not considered in determining excessive absence and lateness.

5. FORMS

5.1 Weekly Time Sheets

6. PROCEDURE

6.1 Excessive Absence and Lateness

6.1.2 Employees absent on five (5) or more occasions and/or eight (8) or more days in any twenty-six (26) week period are considered to be excessively absent.

6.1.3 Employees who are late more than six (6) times in any twenty-six (26) week period are considered to be excessively late.

6.1.4 A manager may allow employees to work compensatory time (which must be within the same workweek for nonexempt employees) to make up for lateness or illness. However, the lateness or absence will still be used for calculating excessive absences and lateness unless the compensatory time was prior approved by the manager.

6.1.5 Employees who are excessively late or absent are subject to the Performance Improvement Procedure as described in that policy and procedure.

7. REFERENCE

7.1 Performance Improvement Policy and Procedure

7.2 Time Away from Work Policy and Procedure

CHAPTER 16

Performance Evaluation

"What you measure is what you get."   —ROBERT S. KAPLAN

WHEN ED KOCH WAS MAYOR of New York City, he was always asking reporters, "How am I doing?" That is the same question most employees want answered, and it is also a question most organizations want to be able to accurately answer for each of their employees.

Almost every organization has some type of employee performance evaluation procedure. Some are as simple as a form to be completed by the employee's supervisor. Others involve the establishment of objectives and standards, and a later comparison of actual performance to those standards. Regular appraisals provide a basis for many other decisions regarding employment: level of compensation, training, promotion, amount of some benefits, assignments, and at times, even whether an employee is to be terminated.

SUBJECT REVIEW

Performance appraisal at its simplest has two steps. First is the establishment of the criteria against which performance is measured. Second is the comparison of actual performance to desired performance. In some cases, this is a list of competencies or skills. In other situations, there are specific standards to be met by the employee, such as number of items produced, sales made, or applications processed. Other times, broad objectives are established for an employee, such as "improve morale" or "obtain a 10 percent increase in market share." Sometimes, some type of performance test is created.

One thing most of these criteria have in common is a time frame, and at the conclusion of that time frame the appraisal itself (the second step) is made. Appraisals are sometimes conducted by the supervisor; sometimes jointly by the supervisor and employee; and sometimes by the supervisor, the employee, and those with whom the employee works. Some appraisals are based on the completion of forms. Some are two-person interviews and some are group meetings.

When the appraisal is complete, it may be placed in the employee's personnel file, kept by the supervisor, reviewed by others, or destroyed. All of these variations actually depend on the organization's purpose is conducting employee performance evaluations.

POLICY CONSIDERATIONS

Jim Hayes, a former president of the American Management Association, always said that appraisals should be for the primary purpose of "assisting the supervisor in developing the employee and improving performance." However, that is not always the reason an organization conducts appraisals. Some organizations conduct them primarily for compensation purposes. Salary increases are given based on the outcome of the evaluation, or compensation, such as piecework, is tied directly to performance. There are also organizations that conduct appraisals solely to determine whether to retain an employee.

A Minneapolis retail store had its supervisors annually write a memo describing each employee's performance during the year. They were read by the human resources manager and the store manager. Then they were placed in the employees' personnel files.

During an arbitration hearing concerning an employee's termination, both the HR manager and the store manager were asked about the purpose of the appraisals. They did not know. They were asked if the appraisals were ever used for decision making. They said no.

The store manager volunteered: "We just thought we were supposed to conduct appraisals, so we did."

The key question to ask to assist you in writing a policy statement is this: Why do we conduct appraisals? That is, what is the purpose? Whatever your organization's purpose should become your policy statement.

Definitions

Some of the definitions often found in policies and procedures pertaining to performance appraisals are:

Standards. Statements of the results achieved when the job is being satisfactorily performed.

Objective. A broad statement of desired result.

Appraisal. A comparison of desired results to actual results.

PROCEDURES

The employee appraisal procedure should deal with the three basic steps:

❐ Establishing Criteria
❐ Evaluating Performance
❐ Using Results

Establishing the Criteria

Some organizations have established standards of performances for each job. Standards are measurements, so where they exist, they become the criteria for employee performance evaluations. Other organizations develop annual objectives for positions and/or individuals. Objectives are also measurements. Therefore, like standards, objectives provide a basis for evaluating employee performance. Still other organizations use an approach in which an employee and supervisor create and agree to measurements for a specific time period.

Some organizations develop lists of required competencies or behaviors for individual jobs or general employment. These lists are used as a basis for evaluating an employee's performance. Others request each supervisor to write a report describing each employee's performance.

Some jobs and compensation methods provide continual measurements of performance. For example, a salesperson's commission, usually based on sales targets, is an automatic measure of performance. A sewing machine operator who is paid by the pieces of clothing produced has both a goal and a measure.

The time period most often used is one year, so employee evaluations become an annual activity. Sometimes it is for a shorter period, but even with monthly or quarterly evaluations, there is also an annual appraisal. Some organizations evaluate all employees at the same time each year while others stagger the evaluations throughout the year. An employee's birthday or the anniversary of the employee's date of hire or last promotion with the organization are often the dates used for yearly evaluations.

The key questions to answer, then, are:

❐ How are criteria established by your organization for measuring employee performance?

❐ What records of the criteria are maintained?

❐ What time frames are used for employee performance evaluations?

Evaluating Performance

When an employee's actual performance during a time period is to be measured, various approaches can be used. Appraisal interviews are common. Generally, they consist of a two-person meeting—the employee and supervisor. Other times the appraisal is based on a written document prepared by the supervisor. This document may or may not be shared with the employee.

Some organizations use group evaluations in which a number of people familiar with the employee's performance meet and evaluate that performance. Some organizations even invite people outside the organization, such as a salesperson's customers, to participate.

An evaluation technique called the 360-degree review is sometimes used. It combines reviews of the employee's performance from others in the organization with whom the individual has contact. These other employees may be peers, senior to the employee, or at lower levels. Because the feedback comes from all these different points, it is fittingly called a 360-degree evaluation.

Many organizations have the employee sign the final evaluation document to indicate it has been read. Others allow the employee to attach a written statement to the appraisal document either agreeing or disagreeing with the evaluation, and some organizations allow the employee to appeal the evaluation. Key questions are:

❏ How are employee appraisals conducted?

❏ How are evaluation dates determined?

❏ How are employees notified of appraisals?

❏ What type of appraisal is used?

❏ What options are available to an employee who disagrees with an appraisal?

Using Results

Many organizations hold the consensus view that the primary purpose of employee performance evaluations is the development of the employee. Organizations that subscribe to that purpose use the appraisal process as a way to identify training needs for the organization and individual employees. In these situations, one outcome of appraisals is often development objectives for the employee and the communication of training needs to the training function.

Organizations with compensation programs that include pay increases based fully or partially on employee performance use the results of an appraisal as a key element in determining the amount of increase. Some organizations may place an employee on some type of probation if the employee receives a "below required performance" evaluation.

Another consideration is what happens to any written appraisal. Some organizations place it in the employee's personnel file. Some have the employee's supervisor retain the document. Some organizations give employees a copy of their performance appraisal, and some other organizations may share the document with a number of people—generally upper management in the employee's functional area. Key questions are:

❏ How and why are an employee's performance appraisal used (i.e., for what purpose)?

❏ What happens to an employee's written performance appraisal?

❏ What procedures are available for employees who disagree with their appraisal?

Some organizations have a separate appraisal process for newly hired and, sometimes, transferred employees. Often these appraisals are used to determine whether the employee should be retained. In effect, these employees are evaluated at the conclusion of a specified probationary period on a new job.

The key questions to ask are:

❒ What type of appraisal process is in existence for newly hired and/or transferred employees?

❒ How are the results for such a process used?

❒ What type of evaluations are made at the end of an initial period on a new job?

A SAMPLE POLICY AND PROCEDURE

A typical policy and procedure for performance evaluations is presented at the end of this chapter. It is not provided as an example of what your organization's policy and procedure should be. Rather, it is an example of a policy and procedure written in the format suggested in this book, after answering all of the previous questions.

HUMAN RESOURCES PERFORMANCE EVALUATION POLICY AND PROCEDURE

1. POLICY

1.1 Performance evaluation is a continuous process at our Organization with at least one (1) formal appraisal conducted each year.

1.2 The purpose of the performance evaluation is to communicate to employees "how they are doing," identify areas of needed improvement, make specific plans for the employee's development, and acknowledge the employee's contributions.

2. SCOPE

Performance evaluation applies to all employees of the Organization.

3. ACCOUNTABILITY

3.1 Human Resources is accountable for ensuring that each manager is notified at least two (2) months in advance of appraisal dates for the manager's employees; is supplied the appropriate forms and information; and completes and returns the performance appraisal form by its due date.

3.2 All managers who have one or more employees reporting to them are accountable for conducting at least one (1) formal evaluation of performance with each employee each year and submitting the completed Employee Appraisal forms to Human Resources by their due dates.

3.3 Human Resources is accountable for maintaining in the employee's personal file and all completed evaluation forms.

3.4 Human Resources is accountable for ensuring that every manager required to conduct an employee performance appraisal has received training in the techniques of appraisal interviewing and for providing the forms necessary to implement this policy and procedure.

4. DEFINITIONS

4.1 *Anniversary Date*—The employee's date of hire, last promotion, or last transfer, whichever is most recent.

4.2 *Standards*—Statements of the results achieved when the job is being satisfactorily performed.

4.3 *Objective*—A broad statement of desired result.

4.4 *Appraisal or Evaluation*—A comparison of desired results to actual results.

5. FORMS

    5.1 Employee Appraisal forms

6. PROCEDURE

    6.1 Employee performance evaluations are to be based on:

        6.1.1 Position Descriptions—It is the manager's accountability to ensure that all employees reporting to him/her have an up-to-date written description of their job position.

        6.1.2 Standards of Performance and/or Objectives—It is the manager's accountability to ensure that each employee reporting to him/her has annually developed standards of performance and/or objectives.

            6.1.2.1 Standards of performance and/or objectives are to be based on the requirements of the position; are to include a specific measure and completion date; and are to be written and reviewed with the employee at the time the employee begins the job and at each subsequent appraisal.

            6.1.2.2 Any disagreement an employee has with a standard or objective is to be noted. Written copies of standards and/or objectives are signed by the employee and the manager.

    6.2 All managers must monitor their employees' performance throughout the year.

        6.2.1 At least once a quarter, managers should conduct an informal performance appraisal with all employees reporting to them.

        6.2.2 Each review should include how the employee is performing to standard or objective, any barriers the employee is encountering, and any assistance required of the manager.

        6.2.3 If there are any serious performance problems, the manager should use the Employee Appraisal form to so note them.

        6.2.4 Once a year a formal performance appraisal is conducted.

            6.2.4.1 At the annual appraisal, the employee and the manager review the employee's performance to standards or objectives; identify any performance gaps; develop plans to close those gaps; review and, if necessary, revise the standards and objectives; and complete and sign an Employee Appraisal form.

        6.2.5 All completed performance evaluation forms are reviewed and signed by the person to whom the appraising manager reports and are then submitted to Human Resources.

        6.2.6 All performance evaluations must be completed within one (1) month of the employee's anniversary date.

6.3 Performance Ratings

6.3.1 The annual performance appraisal requires the manager to rate the employee's overall performance during the preceding appraisal period (within one year from the previous appraisal or from the employee's entry into the position, whichever is appropriate). The performance ratings are:

6.3.1.1 Outstanding—Outstanding overall performance. The employee consistently performs all tasks at a high level of competency and far exceeds the requirements of all standards of performance and/or objectives.

6.3.1.2 Above Average—High level of overall performance. The employee clearly demonstrates excellence in the position and frequently exceeds the requirements of standards of performance and/or objectives.

6.3.1.3 Good—Good level of overall performance. This is performance that is expected of a typical employee in the position. The employee meets the requirements of standards of performance and/or objectives and occasionally exceeds some of them.

6.3.1.4 Below Average—Minimum level of acceptable overall performance. The employee needs improvement in one or more areas in order to meet the requirements of standards of performance and/or objectives.

6.3.1.5 Unsatisfactory—Unsatisfactory level of overall performance. The employee does not meet the requirements of standards of performance and/or objectives, and/or requires constant direction and supervision.

6.4 Corrective Actions

6.4.1 In situations where an employee is performing at Below Average or Unsatisfactory levels, the manager is accountable for submitting a specific improvement plan with the appraisal and reviewing performance to that plan, in writing, at least once a quarter, until performance is rated at least Good or the employee is no longer in the position.

6.5 Transferred and Promoted Employees

6.5.1 If employees are transferred or promoted to a new position or are to report to a new manager within three (3) months of their last appraisal, no appraisal at the time of transfer or promotion is required.

6.5.1.1 If it has been longer than three (3) months since the last appraisal, the manager conducts a final appraisal at the time of transfer or promotion and submits the completed Employee Appraisal form to Human Resources.

6.5.1.2 Evaluations are not required for transferred or promoted employees who have been in their current assignment less than three (3) months.

6.5.1.3 Whenever an employee is transferred or promoted, the new manager reviews the standards of performance and/or objectives with the employee at the time of transfer or promotion.

6.6 Employee Disagreement

6.6.1 In the event employees disagree with their performance evaluation and cannot resolve the disagreement with the manager conducting the appraisal, employees may attach a written and signed disagreement to the completed appraisal form or request an interview with the person to whom their manager reports, the senior vice president of operations, or the Human Resources manager.

6.6.2 In the event a written disagreement is attached to a completed evaluation, the completed evaluation must be signed by the person to whom the appraising manager reports and the Human Resources manager.

6.6.3 An employee may always use the grievance procedure (see 7.1 Grievance Policy and Procedure).

7. REFERENCES

7.1 Grievance Policy and Procedure

7.2 Compensation Policy and Procedure

CHAPTER 17

Performance Improvement

"My best friend is the one who brings out the best in me."

—HENRY FORD

NOT ALL EMPLOYEES PERFORM AS DESIRED at all times. When they do not, some type of action is required to correct performance—to improve performance—to bring performance to the required level. Performance improvement refers not only to employees accomplishing the elements of their jobs—that is, meeting performance standards. It also refers to following the organization's rules, including those about attendance and dress codes.

Some organizations call this subject discipline or positive discipline. Whatever the actual title, this policy and procedure describes the actions to correct poor employee performance.

POLICY CONSIDERATIONS

Some organizations believe it is solely the employee's responsibility to follow the organization's rules. Those organizations take immediate action in the event of any infractions. Other organizations attempt to correct the employee's performance, and some assign varying degrees of punishment to the employee's actions.

You need to identify your organization's purpose for this type of procedure. Is it punishment or an effort to improve behavior? You also need to determine what type of employee actions such a procedure is intended to correct. Here are a few sample policy statements.

"To assist each employee to perform to the maximum of ability within the organization's guidelines."

"To provide appropriate disciplinary actions for employees not performing within the organization's rules and requirements."

"To encourage correct employee performance through the implementation of an increasingly severe disciplinary procedure."

Definitions

Definitions in this type of policy and procedure usually deal with what are considered the organization's rules and regulations and what the infractions of those rules and regulations are.

PROCEDURES

A procedure for performance improvement generally has three major components: proper or expected employee behavior, actions to improve or correct employee behavior, and the handling of serious offenses.

Proper Employee Behavior

Somewhere, whether in this policy and procedure or another, the organization's rules and regulations for employees need to be published and communicated to all employees. There may be two separate sets of requirements: one for the organization as a whole and one for a specific functional area, department, location, or project.

Generally speaking, an organization's rules typically deal with:

❐ Dress Code

❐ Attendance

❐ Use of Controlled Substances

❐ Use of Firearms and Other Weapons

❐ Verbal and Physical Fighting

❐ Horseplay

❐ Behavior Toward Customers

❐ Refusal to Perform Assignments

- ❏ Communicating or Providing False and Damaging Information
- ❏ Unethical Behavior
- ❏ Improper Use of Organization Equipment and Supplies
- ❏ Stealing
- ❏ Forging Documents and Signatures
- ❏ Yelling, Swearing, and Other Disruptive Behavior
- ❏ Intimidating or Threatening Other People
- ❏ Promoting Political or Religious Points of View in the Workplace
- ❏ Distributing Nonorganization-Approved Literature
- ❏ Gambling
- ❏ Displaying Pornography
- ❏ Violating the Organization's Security Requirements

Other types of improper behavior, such as sexual harassment, discrimination, and making racial and religious slurs, are often handled through separate policies and procedures. That is the case in this book (see Chapter 13 for a policy and procedure for addressing discrimination and sexual harassment).

Key questions to consider are:

- ❏ What organizational rules and regulations are employees required to follow?
- ❏ What other rules and regulations are employees required to follow?
- ❏ What procedures exist for establishing rules and regulations?
- ❏ How are rules and regulations communicated to employees?

Actions to Improve Employee Behavior

Procedures for employee performance improvement generally outline a series of increasingly severe steps to be taken. Most often, the first step is a discussion with the supervisor that does not result in a written document. Later steps deal with documented warnings, specific actions, and eventual discharge. Each step usually includes a time period and a deadline by which employees are expected to change their behavior for the better. Key questions to ask are:

❒   What actions are taken to correct employee behavior?

❒   Who initiates such action?

❒   What type of time limits are involved with each action?

❒   What actions become part of the employee's permanent record?

❒   What procedures exist for removing past actions from an employee's record?

❒   What type of approvals and reviews are made for employee improvement actions?

Serious Offenses

Certain employee actions are usually considered so serious that the normal corrective procedure is not an appropriate remedy. These include such actions as being physically violent, making major threats to others, stealing, purposefully damaging the organization's or other employees' property, and falsifying reports and documents. In these cases, the employee may be immediately subject to one of the later steps of a corrective procedure or even immediate discharge.

Key questions to answer are:

❒   What are considered major offenses requiring specific and immediate action?

❒   How are these requirements communicated to employees?

❒   Who initiates such action?

❒   What type of approvals and reviews are made for employee improvement actions?

A SAMPLE POLICY AND PROCEDURE

This chapter concludes with an example of an employee performance improvement procedure. In this case, the organization's rules and regulations are contained in a separate terms of employment policy and procedure (see Chapter 12), which is referenced in this policy and procedure.

HUMAN RESOURCES PERFORMANCE IMPROVEMENT POLICY AND PROCEDURE

1. POLICY

Our Organization provides a positive procedure to assist employees in meeting position and Organization requirements and conditions of employment.

2. SCOPE

This policy and procedure applies to all employees of the Organization.

3. ACCOUNTABILITY

3.1 All managers are accountable for assisting employees in a positive fashion to meet position and Organization requirements and conditions of employment.

3.2 Human Resources is accountable for coordinating and monitoring the specific actions taken by managers under the terms of this policy and procedure.

3.3 Senior vice president of operations is accountable for approving Step Three performance warnings and terminations as herein described.

4. DEFINITIONS

4.1 *Rules and Regulations*—They are as published in the Terms of Employment Policy and Procedure (see 7.1).

4.2 *Grievance Procedure*—The procedure is as published in the Grievance Policy and Procedure (see 7.2).

5. FORMS

5.1 Performance Improvement

6. PROCEDURE

6.1 Human Resources communicates to each newly hired employee on the first week of employment the Organization's requirements, rules and regulations, and all other conditions of employment.

6.1.1 This communication may be done individually or in a group orientation session.

6.1.2 Human Resources also furnishes each newly hired employee with a copy of the Organization's published employee handbook.

6.2 Each manager communicates to new employees reporting to him/her on their first day of work the requirements of the job, work schedules, and any specific department requirements.

6.3 Human Resources communicates in writing to all employees any revised or newly established Organization requirements and conditions of employment.

6.4 Each manager communicates in writing to all employees reporting to him/her any revised or newly established job requirements, work schedules, and any specific department requirements.

6.5 The manager of each employee is accountable for assisting the employee to meet all Organization and position requirements and conditions of employment.

6.5.1 Assistance is provided through performance evaluations and on-going communication between the manager and the employee.

6.6 When an employee does not meet the Organization's and department's requirements, rules and regulations, and all other conditions of employment, the manager must initiate the Performance Improvement Process, which is a positive and progressive approach to assist the employee to improve individual performance and meet Organization and job requirements.

6.7 Performance Improvement Process

6.7.1 Step One—The manager gathers specific information regarding the employee's performance and meets with the employee to review the information, identify the problem, and develop a plan of corrective action. The manager records the date and time of the meeting, the specific recommendations provided to the employee, and the outcome of the meeting. The manager includes a time for performance correction that should not be more than thirty (30) days.

6.7.2 Step Two—If, by the end of the specified time in Step One or thirty (30) days, whichever is shorter, the employee's performance has not improved, the manager again meets with the employee. Depending on the situation, the manager may elect to repeat Step One or move on to Step Two.

6.7.2.1 Step One may only be repeated twice in any six (6) month period.

6.7.2.2 If the manager elects Step Two, the manager completes a Performance Improvement form. Both the manager and the employee sign it. The form records the date and time of the Step Two meeting, the problem, the date and time of the Step One meeting, and the outcome of the meeting. The form includes the specific actions the employee must take and a time for performance correction of thirty (30) days or less.

6.7.2.3 The employee signs the Performance Improvement form to indicate the employee has read it. The employee's signature does not indicate agreement.

6.7.2.4 The completed form is submitted to the person to whom the manager reports for review and signature.

6.7.2.5 One copy is maintained by the manager and one copy is sent to Human Resources.

6.7.3 Step Three—If by the end of the specified time in Step Two or thirty (30) days, whichever is shorter, the employee's performance has not improved, the manager may elect to repeat Step Two or move on to Step Three.

6.7.3.1 In Step Three, the manager first meets with the person to whom the manager reports, a HR representative, and the senior vice president of operations to review the situation.

6.7.3.2 The manager then meets with the employee with a HR representative and completes a Performance Improvement form with the date and time of the meeting. The employee is advised that failure to correct performance within the time period of Step Three will result in the employee's employment being terminated.

6.7.3.3 The manager, the HR representative, and the employee sign the Step Three form. The form records the date and time of the Step Three meeting, the problem, the dates and times of the Step One and Step Two meetings, and the outcomes of those meetings. The form includes the specific actions the employee must take and a time for performance correction of thirty (30) days or less.

6.7.3.4 The employee signs the form to indicate having read it. The employee signature does not indicate agreement.

6.7.3.5 The completed form is submitted to the person to whom the manager reports for review and signature.

6.7.4 Step Four—If, by the end of the specified time in Step Four or thirty (30) days, whichever is shorter, the employee's performance has not improved, the termination is reviewed by the Human Resources manager and the senior vice president of operations. If all approve termination, the employee is terminated (see Termination Policy and Procedure).

6.7.4.1 If at any point in the process the employee's performance improves to the level required, the process is stopped.

6.7.4.2 If twelve (12) months pass from the time of the last step and the employee has not repeated the behavior that resulted in the step, the process is considered completed and any such future behavior requires the process to begin again.

6.7.4.3 The record of the entire process is maintained in a restricted file by the Human Resources manager. A restricted file is a separate file maintained by the HR manager but whose contents are available only to the HR manager, legal counsel, and the manager initiating the Performance Improvement procedure.

6.7.4.4 If, during the twelve (12) months from the time of the last step, the employee repeats the behavior that resulted in the step, the process is reinstated at the point it was stopped.

6.8 Serious Violations

In the event that an employee seriously, consistently, and/or purposely violates an Organization policy and/or condition of employment and/or position requirement and/or term of employment, such as those described in the Terms of Employment policy and procedure (see 7.1), the Organization may elect to begin the Performance Improvement procedure at other than Step One or immediately discharge the employee. Such action requires the approval of the employee's manager, the Human Resources manager, and/or the senior vice president of operations.

6.9 Employee Disagreement

A grievance procedure is available for employees who disagree with any part of the Performance Improvement Process or feel they have been treated unfairly (see 7.2 Grievance Policy and Procedure).

7. REFERENCES

7.1 Terms of Employment Policy and Procedure

7.2 Grievance Policy and Procedure

CHAPTER 18

Employee Grievance Resolution

"The greatest griefs are those we cause ourselves." —SOPHOCLES

GRIEVANCES CAN BE COMPLAINTS based on both real and imaginary wrongs the employee experienced. In either case, the employee is provided a method for resolving the issue and/or determining the truth. Formal grievance procedures are the typical method used by organizations. Whatever the true reasons for the complaint, a grievance policy and procedure allows employees to bring these issues to management's attention and have them procedurally resolved.

SUBJECT REVIEW

Employee complaints can be about any work-related situations, and sometimes the employee may even file grievances that are not work incurred. Their complaints often stem from disciplinary actions. Other times they may result from actions of other employees, and sometimes by what the employee perceives as the organization violating its own rules and regulations.

Typically, grievance procedures require the complaint to be submitted within a specific time period and in writing. There then follows a series of steps. Each step attempts to resolve the grievance and give the employee the right to appeal. Ultimately, it reaches a final step, often binding arbitration, from which there is no further appeal.

DEFINITIONS

The key definition for this policy and procedure is the one for grievance—that is, a grievance the employee can file. Some organizations limit submitted grievances to complaints involving violations of specific policies and procedures and rules and regulations of the organization. Some limit them to a violation of any condition of employment. Other organizations allow any complaint arising out of the individual's employment, and some others place no limits on the type or subject matter of grievance.

PROCEDURES

The elements of the procedure for grievance filing and resolution are how a grievance is filed, the steps in the process, and the final step from which there are no further appeals. If your organization does not offer such a formal procedure for resolving grievances, you need to discover what exactly is its approach.

Filing a Grievance

The two main considerations here, assuming a grievance has been earlier defined, is how and when a grievance can be filed. For example, if a specific form is required, employees need to know where to obtain the form and where to submit it after they have filled it out. Other key questions are:

❐   What are the steps for filing a grievance?

❐   What time limits exist for filing a grievance?

❐   Who may file a grievance?

❐   What type of evidence must accompany a grievance?

❐   What type of protection does an employee filing a grievance have?

Resolving a Grievance

Most grievance procedures consist of three to six steps, but there are procedures with more or less steps. The first or early steps sometimes involve discussions between a supervisor and employee regarding the issue that occurred prior to a written grievance being completed and filed.

Each of the next steps attempt to resolve the grievance at the lowest possible step. When that fails, the employee appeals to the next step. One or more additional people are usually asked to attend the hearing at the next step. Each succeeding step usually includes someone with increased authority.

The final step may be heard by the senior management position at the location or in the employee's functional area, or it might be a submission of the grievance to binding arbitration. There is no further appeal from binding arbitration, but an employee disagreeing with a senior management decision can file suit. The key questions to answer are:

❐ What are the steps of your organization's grievance procedure?

❐ Who is involved at each step?

❐ What procedural rules govern the hearing of the grievance at each step?

❐ What type of representation can the employee and the organization have?

❐ If the final step is binding arbitration, what is the process for initiating the arbitration?

❐ What are the employee's rights and processes for appealing decisions?

❐ What type of records are maintained after grievances are filed and processed?

A SAMPLE POLICY AND PROCEDURE

The grievance policy and procedure that is presented at the end of this chapter illustrates one approach to employee grievance resolution using the guidelines provided in this book. The policy and procedure, like all examples in this book, is from a real organization.

HUMAN RESOURCES EMPLOYEE GRIEVANCE RESOLUTION POLICY AND PROCEDURE

1. POLICY

The Organization provides a positive procedure to assist employees in resolving problems.

2. SCOPE

This policy and procedure applies to all employees of the Organization.

3. ACCOUNTABILITY

3.1 All managers are accountable for assisting employees in a positive fashion to resolve any problems that impact the employee by fulfilling all terms and conditions of this policy and procedure.

3.2 Human Resources is accountable for administering the resolution procedure for any employee grievance.

4. DEFINITIONS

4.1 *Open Door*—The ability of any employee to speak with any member of management.

4.2 *Complaint*—An employee's verbal description of a real or imaginary wrong or a violation of a policy and procedure.

4.3 *Grievance*—The written statement of an employee's complaint.

5. FORMS

5.1 Employee Grievance

6. PROCEDURE

6.1 Open Door

6.1.1 The Organization maintains an open door policy—any employee may speak with any member of management.

6.1.2 Employees wishing to resolve a problem should do so by first attempting to resolve it with their supervisor and then with the senior manager of the division.

6.1.3 If those discussions fail to resolve the problem, the employee may use the Employee Grievance Procedure (see 6.2 below) or request a meeting with the Human Resources manager and/or senior vice president of operations. Any such meeting is to be scheduled and held at a mutually convenient time for all parties.

6.2 Employee Grievance Procedure

6.2.1 If an employee has a complaint regarding the actions of a direct supervisor, other member of management, and/or other employees, the employee may use a grievance procedure.

6.2.2 In the event the complaint has to do with sexual harassment and/or discrimination, the employee is to use the procedures described in the Equal and Fair Treatment Policy and Procedure (see 7.2).

6.2.3 Step One of the grievance procedure is for employees to discuss the issue with the person to whom they report, in an effort to obtain a satisfactory resolution, and/or with the senior manager of the employee's division (see 6.1 above).

6.2.3.1 If discussions with the direct supervisor and/or the senior manager of the employee's division do not resolve the problem to the employee's satisfaction, the employee may then go to Step Two of the grievance procedure.

6.2.4 Step Two is for the employee to submit the grievance, in writing, on a form provided by Human Resources. The form, signed by the employee and stating the specific problem, must be submitted to the Human Resources manager within ten (10) days of the incident causing the complaint.

6.2.4.1 Within five (5) days of receipt of the grievance, the Human Resources manager meets with the employee to obtain information relevant to the grievance and conducts any required investigation of the complaint.

6.2.4.2 Within five (5) days of meeting with the employee, the Human Resources manager notifies, in writing, the employee and the employee's supervisor of a proposed resolution of the grievance.

6.2.4.3 The employee has five (5) days to accept the Step Two resolution or submit the grievance to Step Three.

6.2.4.4 Within five (5) days of receiving the employee's submission of the grievance to Step Three, the Human Resources manager holds one or more meetings, attended by the employee and any other employees, to explain and clarify the situation resulting in the grievance.

6.2.5 Within five (5) days of Step Three meeting(s), the Human Resources manager notifies, in writing, the employee and the employee's supervisor of a proposed resolution of the grievance.

6.2.5.1 The employee has five (5) days from receipt of the Step Three notification to accept the resolution or submit the grievance to Step Four.

6.2.6 Within ten (10) days of receiving the employee's submission of the grievance to Step Four, the Human Resources manager holds one or more meetings attended by the employee, the employee's supervisor, the senior manager of the employee's division, and the senior vice president of operations. (Other employees may be asked to attend to explain and clarify the situation.)

6.2.6.1 Within five (5) days of Step Four meeting(s), the Human Resources manager notifies, in writing, the employee and the employee's supervisor of a proposed resolution of the grievance.

6.2.6.2 The employee has five (5) days from receipt of the Step Four notification to accept the resolution or submit the grievance to Step Five.

6.2.6.3 If the employee is dissatisfied with the resolution, the employee may file an appeal to the most senior manager of the Organization or the location. That person may reject the appeal, hold a hearing, grant the appeal, or not grant the appeal within ten (10) days, and that person's decision shall be final.

7. REFERENCES

7.1 Terms of Employment Policy and Procedure

7.2 Equal and Fair Treatment Policy and Procedure

7.3 Performance Improvement Policy and Procedure

CHAPTER 19

Termination

"Never complain, never explain." — HENRY FORD II

AT TIMES, EMPLOYEES HAVE TO BE REMOVED from the organization's payroll, sometimes as a result of their own actions and other times as a result of external or internal economic conditions. This is a subject that all employees want to perceive as being fairly and equally handled by the organization.

SUBJECT REVIEW

Termination is the separation of the employee from the organization. This can be voluntary on the employee's part or nonvoluntary. Within these two classifications are many types of terminations. This policy and procedure should simultaneously describe the conditions of termination for each type of termination your organization uses or may use.

The major types of voluntary terminations are resignation, retirement, and contract completion. The major types of nonvoluntary terminations are layoffs, discharge for cause, and a reduction in workforce. How such decisions are made, who approves the terminations, and whether there are any employee appeals are considerations along with the actual termination processes.

Factors to consider in all terminations are benefits, pay, security, and the return of organization property. In addition, exit interviews or follow-up questionnaires are possible elements of the policy and procedure.

DEFINITIONS

Definitions usually deal with the types of terminations the organization uses. For example:

Resignation. An employee's decision to terminate employment with the organization.

Layoff. A temporary termination of employment usually involving more than one employee at a time.

Discharge for Cause. The organization's decision to terminate employment based on some action of the employee.

Reduction in Workforce. A reduction in the number of employees in the organization, a single location, a department, or a functional area. Generally, a reduction in workforce involves more than one employee at a time.

Retirement. Upon reaching a certain age and qualifying for retirement, Social Security, and/or pension benefits, an employee ceases to be employed and uses these programs for income.

Contract Completion. An employee working under a contract with a defined time period concludes the term of the agreement.

POLICY

The policy statement should stress the organization's fair and equal approach to terminations of employment. Organizations may have a separate and detailed employment-at-will policy, which can be referenced in the termination policy and procedure. The following is a policy statement from one such organization:

> Employment at our organization is under an employment-at-will policy, so each employee serves at the pleasure or will of the organization for as long as the employee's services and performance are satisfactory and are needed by the organization. The employment of any employee may be terminated by the organization at any time for any reason, but the organization provides a specific review and approval process for all terminations to ensure all employees are treated equally and fairly.

The main policy questions to consider are as follows:

❏ What does the organization want to accomplish with its termination policy and procedure?

❏ What type of image does the organization want to project in this area?

❏ What opportunities are available to terminating employees for reemployment?

Procedures

This procedure should deal with those factors applicable to all terminating employees, such as exit interviews, return of company property, security, and benefits. In addition, each type of termination needs to have its specific conditions and processes detailed.

Exit Interviews

There are a number of factors to review with any terminating employee. Some organizations have these covered by the employee's supervisor. Others have them covered in a meeting with another person—quite often a human resources representative. Other times it is a combination of interviews.

The factors that most often need to be covered in an exit interview are:

Benefits. The employee needs to know when benefits terminate and what types of conversion privileges are available based on the type of termination. Also, the disposition of funds and vesting in any pension and retirement plan must be explained to the employee. If the terminating employee is retiring, there have probably been other interviews and meetings prior to actual termination. If not, retirement benefits, if any, need to be reviewed at this time and the appropriate forms executed.

Organization Property. Any organization property in the possession of the employee needs to be returned or accounted for. At times, a later return date may be established. If invoices for such items as company credit cards and cell telephones are outstanding, arrangements should be made for account terminations and payment.

Security. Depending on the level and type of security in your organization, items giving the employee access to organization files, computers, and premises need to be returned. In addition, all identifying cards, badges, and keys should be returned. The employee needs to be told what will happen to assigned passwords, codes, e-mail, and voice mail.

Pay. Details about the final pay period—the amount and when it will be made—should be described. This should include pay for any earned but unused vacation and other paid time, such as sick days for which the employee is eligible. If the employee is receiving pay beyond the termination date, the employee needs to know if it is being assigned to a specific period since this can affect any unemployment benefits for which the employee may otherwise be eligible.

Questions. Many organizations view the exit interview as an ideal time to ask terminating employees about their perceptions of the organization and its conditions of employment. These questions are sometimes asked by the interviewer; other times, a follow-up questionnaire may be used.

Employees being laid off will typically request to know the possibility and date of reinstatement. Another question often asked by terminating employees concerns how the organization will respond to any future reference requests for the employee. Some organizations offer letters of reference. Others provide a name and telephone number for inquiries. Most organizations state exactly what information they will provide. That information is often limited to only dates of employment, positions held, and final rate of pay.

In creating an exit strategy procedure, then, the questions you want to answer are:

❒   What types of exit interviews are conducted and by who?

❒   What subjects are covered in each exit interview?

❒   What types of materials are given to the terminating employee?

❒   Have your benefits for terminating employees been checked to ensure they meet all government requirements?

❒   How is organization property for return identified?

❒   What constitutes final pay, and when is it paid?

❒   What procedures are there for paying bonuses or continuing pay for a specific period after termination, or for offering pay in lieu of notice?

❐ What security procedures are there for disabling employee identification cards and access privileges?

❐ What procedures exist for requesting information on the employee's perceptions of the organization and its conditions of employment?

Resignations

Most organizations request or sometimes require advance notice of resignations. Those that do generally identify two weeks or one pay period as the required minimum time. Some organizations suggest different times for different types of employees. For example, a production worker may be asked to give at least one week's notice and a senior manager one month's notice.

Though most organizations desire advance notice, once received, an organization may ask the employee to no longer report for work. For example, an employee giving a two-week notice may be asked to depart the work premises immediately, but will be paid for the two weeks.

Key questions are:

❐ How much advance notice does your organization request for resignations?

❐ What procedures does your organization follow once resignation notice is received?

Contract Termination

Some organizations contract employees for a specific period of time. Such contracts usually require action on the part of the employee and organization either to renew them or, in some cases, stop them from automatic renewal. When either or both parties elect not to renew the contract, it is usually treated as a voluntary termination. The key questions for creating a procedure for contract terminations are:

❐ What types of employment contracts does your organization use?

❐ What are the requirements for renewal?

Layoffs

Layoffs general imply an eventual return to work. For example, an automobile manufacturer may require a month's closing in order to retool for a new model, so it lays off its production employees with the plan to return them as soon as the retooling is completed.

Since layoffs imply rehiring, benefits and length of service are often continued for all or part of the layoff. Some organizations allow other conditions of employment to remain in effect, such as allowing laid-off employees to participate in organization-related activities.

Layoffs also usually ensure the laid-off employee will receive any offer of a future job before new candidates are considered. Some organizations allow employees scheduled to be laid off to "bump" or replace other employees with less length of service.

When creating procedures for addressing layoffs, key questions to answer are:

❒ What are the factors that determine a layoff?

❒ What is the maximum length of time for a layoff?

❒ What benefits will employees receive during a layoff?

❒ How is the employee's length of service affected during a layoff?

❒ What procedures are there for an employee subject to a layoff to replace another employee?

Discharge for Cause

At times it is necessary to terminate an employee for specific reasons. It could be due to the performance improvement (disciplinary) policy and procedure. It could be the employee's inability to perform the requirements of a job.

As a general rule, employees discharged for cause are immediately terminated regardless of the length of the period for which they are paid. There is usually a stated procedure for any such discharge to be approved. This procedure may include reviews by human resources, the manager of the employee's supervisor, and a senior manager. Sometimes there is also a procedure for the employee to appeal the decision. Key questions are:

❒ Under what conditions can an employee be discharged for cause?

❒ What process is used to obtain the required approvals for such a discharge?

❏ What documentation is required for such a discharge?

❏ What right of appeal does an employee have?

Reduction in Workforce

A reduction in workforce (sometimes referred to as an RIF) is similar to a layoff in that it generally includes a number of employees. However, an RIF does not imply an opportunity for the employee to be rehired, so all benefits are terminated as if it was a resignation.

Quite often, employees terminated as a part of a reduction in workforce are paid in lieu of notice. The schedule for such payment is many times included in the policy and procedure. Key questions are:

❏ What are the factors that determine a reduction in workforce?

❏ What type of pay in lieu of notice is involved?

❏ How is the amount of pay in lieu of notice calculated (e.g., according to length of service, position, or some other factor)?

❏ How is any such paid made and assigned?

❏ What procedures are there for an employee subject to a reduction in workforce to replace another employee?

A SAMPLE POLICY AND PROCEDURE

A sample termination policy and procedure is presented at the end of this chapter. It was written using the guidelines provided in this book and makes reference to other policies and procedures, including those related to time away from work (Chapter 14), performance improvement (Chapter 17), and terms of employment (Chapter 12).

HUMAN RESOURCES TERMINATION POLICY AND PROCEDURE

1. POLICY

1.1 Employment at our Organization is under an employment-at-will policy, so each employee serves at the pleasure or will of the Organization for as long as the employee's services and performance are satisfactory and are needed by the Organization.

1.2 The employment of any employee may be terminated by the Organization at any time for any reason.

2. SCOPE

This policy and procedure applies to all employees of the Organization except those with contracts that include termination procedures that differ from the terms herein contained.

3. ACCOUNTABILITY

3.1 All managers are accountable for fulfilling the terms of this policy and procedure when terminating an employee.

3.2 Human Resources is accountable for processing all employee terminations and ensuring that the proper procedures are followed and the proper documentation maintained to protect both the employee and the Organization.

4. DEFINITIONS

4.1 *Voluntary Termination*—Termination that is initiated by the employee.

4.1.1 *Resignation*—An employee's decision to terminate employment with the organization.

4.1.2 *Retirement*—Upon reaching a certain age and qualifying for retirement, Social Security, and/or pension benefits, an employee ceases to be employed and uses these programs for income.

4.2 *Involuntary Termination*—Termination that is initiated by the Organization.

4.2.1 *Layoff*—A temporary termination of employment usually involving more than one employee at a time.

4.2.2 *Discharge for Cause*—The Organization's decision to terminate employment based on some action of the employee.

4.2.3 *Reduction in Workforce*—A reduction in the number of employees in the organization, a single location, a department, or a functional area. Generally, involves more than one employee at a time.

4.3 *Termination in Good Standing*—At the time of termination, the employee's overall performance is rated as Good or better; there are no current Performance Improvement procedure steps; and the employee is not being terminated for a violation of the Organization's terms of employment.

4.4 *Termination Not in Good Standing*—At the time of termination, the employee's overall performance is rated as Below Average or Unsatisfactory and/or there are current Performance Improvement procedure steps.

5. Forms

5.1 Employee Status Change

5.2 Exit Interview

6. Procedure

6.1 When an employee is terminated for any reason, the employee's manager completes an Employee Status Change form, has it signed by the person to whom the manager reports, and submits it to the Human Resources manager, along with a cover memo and all supporting documentation.

6.2 The effective date of termination is the last day worked, or if the employee is on vacation or not at work for any paid reason, the last day paid.

6.3 Reasons for Termination

6.3.1 Disability—An employee who is away from work due to a disability caused by a nonwork-associated accident or illness is maintained on the payroll as an employee on a medical or disability leave of absence until it is evident the employee can never return to work or six (6) months pass, whichever occurs first.

6.3.1.1 At that time, the employee will be placed on permanent leave of absence for up to another six (6) months.

6.3.1.2 If the employee is still unable to return to work, the employee's employment is terminated.

6.3.2 Nonreturn from Military Leave—Employees who do not return from military leave as required are considered to be voluntary terminations.

6.3.3 Employees who voluntarily join the military service are considered to be voluntary terminations.

6.3.4 Nonreturn from Leave of Absence—Employees who do not return from approved leaves of absence as required by their leaves are considered to be voluntary terminations.

6.3.5 Death—The termination date for deceased employees shall be the date of death. Any expense reimbursement and wages due the employee at the time of the employee's death are paid to the legal heir of the deceased employee.

6.3.6 Performance Improvement Procedure—The termination is based on implementation of the Organization's Performance Improvement Procedure (see 7.2) or the serious violation of one of the Organization's terms of employment (see 7.4).

6.3.7 Unable to Perform Job—The termination is due to the employee's inability to perform the essential functions of the job.

6.4 Termination of Benefits

6.4.1 All benefits terminate the effective date of employment termination. However, the employee shall have insurance conversion rights as per federal and state law.

6.4.2 Any unused paid vacation, personal days, and sick days are handled as per the Time Away from Work Policy and Procedure (see 7.3).

6.5 Severance Pay

6.5.1 Any employee involuntarily terminated (layoffs excepted) who is in good standing at the time of termination receives pay equal to one full pay period in lieu of notice.

6.5.2 An employee with at least six (6) months of service but less than five years (5) who is involuntarily terminated (layoffs excepted) in good standing is paid an additional two (2) weeks severance pay in lieu of notice.

6.5.3 An employee with at least five (5) years who is involuntarily terminated (layoffs excepted) in good standing is paid an additional week severance pay in lieu of notice for each year of service. Six (6) months or more in the same calendar year is considered a year.

6.6 Organization Property

6.6.1 Money

6.6.1.1 If at the time of termination, the employee owes the Organization any money such as loan repayment or advance repayment, that amount is subtracted from the employee's final pay.

6.6.1.2 If the final pay is not adequate for full recovery, a separate arrangement for payment of the balance is made.

6.6.2 Property

6.6.2.1 If at the time of termination, the employee has possession of any of the Organization's property, that property is to be returned in good condition at a time agreed by Human Resources.

6.6.2.2 If the property is not returned by the time established by Human Resources, the value of the property may be deducted from the employee's final pay or the Organization may take other legal action.

6.6.3 Security

6.6.3.1 At the time of termination, the employee shall return all security items to the Organization such as keys, badges, and identification cards.

6.6.3.2 If the security items are not returned by the time established by Human Resources, the Organization may take other legal action.

6.7 Exit Interviews

6.7.1 Human Resources conducts an exit interview with all terminating employees on their last day of employment.

6.7.2 The results of that interview are documented and placed in the terminating employee's personal file in the HR department.

7. REFERENCES

7.1 Benefits Policy and Procedure

7.2 Performance Improvement Policy and Procedure

7.3 Time Away from Work Policy and Procedure

7.4 Terms of Employment Policy and Procedure

CHAPTER 20

Training and Development

"Whoever desires constant success must change his conduct with the times."

—NICCOLÒ MACHIAVELLI

A TRAINING AND DEVELOPMENT POLICY and procedure has two major focuses. First, there is the need to train employees in the specific skills required by the organization. Second is the development of employees for the future.

SUBJECT REVIEW

Training has become increasingly important to organizations as new processes, equipment, and techniques have been developed. In addition, organizations are challenged by new government regulations and customer requirements, and many people seeking jobs, although otherwise qualified, lack the basic language and mathematical skills required. Moreover, many organizations have unique requirements. Often it is difficult, if not impossible, for organizations to locate employees with the needed skills and knowledge. The solution becomes providing that training.

In addition to present training requirements, organizations look to their future needs. It seems safe to assume that the rate of innovation will at least remain the same, but more likely it will increase. The complexities of jobs will also increase. In recognition of these realities, and the belief that better-educated employees improve the ability of an organization to succeed, the development of employees is generally viewed as a benefit to both employees and the organization. That is true even when the educational program an employee pursues does not directly relate to the employee's current position or organizational requirements.

POLICY CONSIDERATIONS

Since this subject matter has two components, organizations often have two policy statements. One is for training, and the other is for employee development. For example:

> "The organization provides employees with all training required for them to fulfill their job responsibilities."

> "The organization believes in supporting the development of its employees and encourages educational activities designed to improve their overall performance and potential."

Other organizations create broad policy statements that cover both components. For example:

> "The organization believes in the development and training of its employees and encourages both internal and external training, creation of career paths, and promotion from within whenever possible."

Here are some questions to consider:

- ❏ What type of training does the organization provide?
- ❏ What type of education does the organization provide?
- ❏ What type of organizational support does the organization provide?

DEFINITIONS

The following terms generally require definition. The typical definitions are:

Education. Acquiring knowledge and understanding of a subject.

Training. Developing skill and knowledge in a job requirement.

Tuition. The charge (cost) for participation in an external educational course or program.

PROCEDURES

The procedure for this subject usually deals with three topics: internal training, external training, and tuition reimbursement. There are also several additional considerations that in this chapter are classified as "other."

Internal Training

Internal training is that training offered and conducted by the organization. It is usually job-related and paid for by the organization. However, sometimes the actual cost is charged to the employee's individual department or functional area. If not covered elsewhere, new employee orientation is often included in this policy and procedure. Key questions to answer are:

❑ What type of internal training does the organization offer?

❑ How are an employee's internal training needs determined?

❑ What are the requirements for employee participation?

❑ What constitutes successful completion of the training?

❑ What are the enrollment procedures?

❑ How is the training paid for?

❑ What type of compensation does the employee receive while in training?

External Training

This type of training is also job-related, but an external source—such as a local school or college, association, or consulting firm—conducts the training, rather than the organization itself. Because of the external nature of the training, additional costs are associated with it, such as travel, lodging, and meals. At times, these costs are dealt with in a policy and procedure on travel and entertainment. Other times they are handled within the training policy and procedure. Key questions are:

❑ What type of external training does the organization offer?

❑ How are an employee's external training needs determined?

❑ What are the requirements for employee participation?

❏ What constitutes successful completion of this type of training?

❏ What are the enrollment procedures?

❏ How are the training and related charges paid for?

❏ What type of compensation does the employee receive while in training?

Tuition Reimbursement

Tuition reimbursement programs are designed to encourage employees to pursue additional education outside the organization. Major elements of such a policy relate to eligibility, payment, and successful completion of the course or educational program.

Eligibility refers not only to which employees are eligible for tuition reimbursement, but also what courses are eligible. Some organizations allow reimbursement for any external training, whereas others limit tuition reimbursement to courses of study that are job- or organization-related.

Payment also varies. Some organizations pay a percent of tuition. Some pay the actual charge in full, plus additional expenses to cover any taxes the employee will have to pay. Some organizations pay only for tuition; others pay for all related costs, including books and lab fees.

Some organizations advance payment at registration time. However, most seem to make payment when evidence of satisfactory completion of the course is submitted. At minimum, that means whatever the school considers satisfactory completion of the course. Some organizations, though, may stipulate a specific grade, such as a C or better in undergraduate courses and a B or better in graduate courses. Nonacademic courses often issue pass or fail grades. In those instances, a passing grade is acceptable.

Key questions to consider are:

❏ Who is eligible for tuition reimbursement?

❏ What courses or courses of study are eligible?

❏ How is payment made?

❏ When is payment made?

❏ What evidence of costs and course completion are required?

❏ What is the process for dealing with employees who leave the organization before course completion or start with the organization after beginning a course of study?

Other Issues

There are numerous other ways in which organizations may support employee training and development. Some common ones are listed here with definitions:

Career Pathing. The organization may establish a sequence of jobs that form a career path for an employee.

Counseling. An internal service assists employees to create individual development plans.

Internship. This arrangement allows a student to work part-time or full-time with the organization while completing a course of study.

Degree Support. An employee is allowed to take the necessary time-off to pursue a specific degree on a full-time basis. Sometimes the organization pays all costs, and often there is an agreement with the employee to remain at the organization for a specific period of time following attainment of the degree.

On-the-Job Education. At times, organizations offer and pay for regular educational courses. For example, college credit courses and high school equivalency courses may be given on the organization's premises while the employees are being paid.

If your organization offers any of these programs or others related to training and development, you need to ask questions such as:

❒ What are the purpose and details of the program?
❒ Who is eligible for the program?
❒ What type of costs are paid for by the organization?
❒ What are the procedures for participation in the program?

A SAMPLE POLICY AND PROCEDURE

A training and development policy and procedure, written in the format suggested in this book after answering all of the previous questions, is presented at the end of this chapter. Like all examples in this book, the sample policy and procedure is taken from a real organization.

HUMAN RESOURCES TRAINING AND DEVELOPMENT POLICY AND PROCEDURE

1. POLICY

The Organization believes in the development of its employees and encourages both internal and external training.

2. SCOPE

This policy and procedure applies to all employees of the Organization.

3. ACCOUNTABILITY

3.1 All managers are accountable for fulfilling the terms of this policy and procedure.

3.2 Human Resources is accountable for providing development counseling, processing all tuition reimbursement applications, and maintaining files of externally offered training.

4. DEFINITIONS

4.1 *Education*—Acquiring knowledge and understanding of a subject.

4.2 *Training*—Developing skill and knowledge in a job requirement.

4.3 *Tuition*—Charge for participation in an external educational course or program.

5. FORMS

5.1 Tuition Reimbursement Application

6. PROCEDURE

6.1 Tuition Reimbursement

The Organization will reimburse any full-time permanent employee in good standing for eighty percent (80%) of the cost of tuition and books for successful completion of an external course that is required for a job-related course of study.

6.1.1 Tuition reimbursement is limited to no more than $10,000 per employee per calendar year.

6.1.2 A Tuition Reimbursement Application is completed by the employee prior to the start of the course and submitted to the employee's supervisor. The application states the course, job relatedness, tuition cost, estimated cost of books, and scheduled dates.

6.1.2.1 If the supervisor approves the Tuition Reimbursement Application, it is submitted to Human Resources for approval.

6.1.2.2 If the supervisor does not approve the application, the employee may then submit it directly to Human Resources for approval.

6.1.2.3 If Human Resources approves the application, a copy of the approval is returned to the employee.

6.1.2.4 If the Human Resources manager does not approve the application, the employee may appeal the decision to the senior vice president of operations.

6.1.2.5 The senior vice president of operation's decision is final.

6.1.3 If the employee completes the course with a passing grade, the employee submits evidence of the passing grade and tuition and book costs to Human Resources. (In a traditional A through F marking system, a C or better is considered passing. Other grading systems such as "pass" and "fail" will be accepted.)

6.1.3.1 Once approved by Human Resources, it is sent to payroll for payment.

6.1.4 Tuition reimbursement will not be paid to employees:

6.1.4.1 Who are no longer employed at the time the course is completed.

6.1.4.2 Who are involved in one or more steps of a Performance Improvement procedure.

6.2 Organization-Required Training

If the Organization requires an employee to participate in a training course or seminar, the Organization will pay one hundred percent (100%) of all costs, including any required travel, lodging, meals, tuition, and books.

6.2.1 If such a course is conducted during the employee's scheduled work time, and it is impossible to alter the employee's schedule, the employee's base pay will be paid and the time will be considered time worked for calculation of overtime, benefits, and any time-off with pay.

6.3 Development Counseling

Every manager is encouraged to assist employees with their development. This can be accomplished through the annual appraisal process and as part of the ongoing communication between managers and their employees.

6.3.1 Human Resources will assist in this process whenever requested by the employee or the manager.

6.3.2 Human Resources will also provide educational and development counseling if requested by the employee or the manager.

6.3.3 Human Resources maintains current files and sources of available job-related courses and catalogs from regional and national organizations offering seminars and courses that could benefit all employees.

6.4 Career Paths

Every manager is encouraged, with the assistance of Human Resources, to identify logical career paths of positions within the department and Organization and to communicate these identified career paths to employees and candidates for employment, along with the requirements of each position in a career path.

CHAPTER 21

Code of Business Conduct

"Ethics pays."

—JOHN SHAD

IF THERE WAS EVER A DOUBT about the importance of ethical business conduct and the dangers of unethical business conduct, the past few years have well demonstrated its importance to individuals and organizations.

SUBJECT REVIEW

Business conduct traditionally has covered such areas as:

- ❏ Ethical Behavior
- ❏ Outside Employment
- ❏ Financial Investments and Dealings in Securities
- ❏ Fiduciary Responsibilities
- ❏ Confidential and Proprietary Information
- ❏ Disclosures
- ❏ Loans and Gifts
- ❏ Giving and Receiving Political Contributions
- ❏ Relationships with Competitors
- ❏ Standards of Conduct
- ❏ Protection of the Organization's Assets

As a result of some of new legislation and the concerns raised by well-publicized corporate scandals, organizations have added protection of whistle-blowers to this list.

Not all these areas apply to all classes of employees. For example, senior executives and hourly production workers do not have the same opportunities, influence, and information to protect. In such instances, the organization will develop different policies and procedures and accompanying implementation approaches.

POLICY CONSIDERATIONS

Most organizations insist on ethical behavior from all employees. A typical policy statement might read as follows:

The organization holds its employees and itself to the highest standards of business conduct. To provide employees with guidance in identifying business situations that create (or have the potential to create) legal and ethical problems, or the appearance of such, and to provide direction in handling actual and potential situations, the organization has developed a Code of Business Conduct.

DEFINITIONS

Specific elements in this type of policy and procedure require definition, especially as they relate to competitors, gifts, loans, whistle-blowers, and confidential information. Here are a few such definitions:

Competitors. Any organization or individual dealing with the same third parties and providing similar services and/or products.

Gifts. Any item, service, cash, or meal valued in excess of $25.00 that is received or given by the employee from or to another employee or an external business contact.

Loan. Any item, service, or cash received or given by the employee from or to another employee or an external business contact on the condition of repayment at a later time, whether or not payment of interest is involved.

Whistle-Blower. Any employee reporting unethical and unlawful behavior of the organization or any of its employees to an external party or individual.

Confidential Information. Information that is the sole property of the organization and crucial to its operations, whether or not it is protected by trademark, copyright, and patent.

PROCEDURES

To create this procedure, all areas of the organization's operations should be scrutinized to determine what specific rules apply and what is considered unethical behavior. Once determined, the procedure can be written. It should include a method for communicating requirements to covered employees and ensuring their understanding and compliance.

As previously mentioned, separate procedures may be required for different classifications of employees. These questions should be asked for each type of employee covered by a code of business conduct:

- ❐ What is considered ethical behavior in your organization?
- ❐ How are ethical requirements communicated to employees?
- ❐ What type of training is made available to employees regarding ethical requirements?
- ❐ What type of behavior auditing and record keeping is there to ensure employees are meeting ethical requirements?
- ❐ What type of follow-up communication and reinforcement is there for employees regarding ethical requirements?
- ❐ Does the organization's code of ethics and enforcement meet all legal requirements?
- ❐ What actions and sanctions are taken when employees do not meet ethical requirements?

A SAMPLE POLICY AND PROCEDURE

At the end of this chapter is a sample policy and procedure written in the format suggested in this book, after answering all of the previous questions. This code of business conduct covers outside employment; personal financial interests; confidential information; gifts and loans; whistle-blower protection; and disclosures of conflict of interest, among other subjects. It also references other policies and procedures, including those detailing the equal and fair treatment of employees (Chapter 13) and the external selection of candidates to fill job positions (Chapter 9).

HUMAN RESOURCES CODE OF BUSINESS CONDUCT POLICY AND PROCEDURE

1. POLICY

1.1 The Organization holds its employees to the highest standards of business conduct.

1.2 To provide employees with guidance in identifying business situations that create or have the potential to create legal and ethical problems, or the appearance of such, and to provide direction in handling actual and potential situations, the Organization has developed a Code of Business Conduct.

1.3 The Organization intends to operate in full compliance with all laws, so all employees are to conform their business conduct to the requirements of local, state, and federal laws.

1.4 The Organization's Code of Business Conduct requires faithful compliance with all laws by all employees, even if an employee believes noncompliance does not present ethical implications.

1.5 Compliance with local, state, and federal laws does not eliminate the necessity for employees to consider the business ethics of their activities. All employees must be cognizant of the fact that a legal business practice can still present an ethical problem.

1.6 It is critical to avoid even the appearance of any illegal or unethical behavior. Employees must behave in a fashion that retains the trust of our clients, other employees, stockholders, and the public.

2. SCOPE

The conditions of employment contained in this policy and procedure apply to all departments and employees of the Organization.

3. ACCOUNTABILITY

3.1 Human Resources is accountable for obtaining at time of hire, and updating each calendar year, a Code of Business Conduct statement signed by the employee indicating the employee's understanding and agreement with the Organization's Code of Business Conduct.

3.2 Every employee is accountable for performance that fulfills the specific terms and conditions of the Organization's Code of Conduct as well as its intent.

3.3 All managers are accountable for ensuring their employees operate within the specific terms and conditions of the Organization's Code of Conduct as well as its intent.

4. DEFINITIONS

4.1 *Associate*—For purposes of the Code of Business Conduct, an associate is a member of an employee's immediate family, a trust of which an employee is a trustee, or a trust in which a member of the employee's immediate family has a beneficial interest.

5. FORMS

5.1 Code of Business Conduct statement for employee signature

6. CODE OF BUSINESS CONDUCT PROCEDURE

6.1 Any question regarding whether a specific behavior is covered by the Code of Business Conduct should be presented to Human Resources, which will have the question reviewed by the appropriate parties (generally a senior manager and the Organization's general counsel) and return an answer to the employee.

6.2 Outside Employment

6.2.1 As a condition of employment, all employees are expected to devote their full professional efforts to the Organization's business.

6.2.2 Therefore, outside employment should not be accepted if it in any way interferes with job requirements or performance.

6.2.3 It is recommended that employees notify their manager prior to accepting any such outside employment, and the manager will advise the employee of any possible conflict with Organization employment.

6.3 Personal Financial Interest

6.3.1 Employees are expected to exercise their judgment and discretion in the best interests of the Organization and to avoid any conflict of interest or appearance of conflict of interest.

6.3.2 Employees and their associates should not have a direct or indirect interest and/or investment in any business enterprise that is doing or seeking to do business with the Organization, other than minor ownership of publicly traded stock.

6.3.3 Employees (and their associates) in positions to influence, make, or carry out investment or purchasing decisions should avoid investment in any business enterprise in which the Organization has an investment, from whom the Organization may or has or is making a purchase, and from whom the Organization is receiving products or services.

6.4 Confidential and Proprietary Information

6.4.1 During the course of employment, employees may obtain access to information with respect to the Organization's business or the business or personal affairs of its customers or other employees. All such information must be kept confidential, and employees must adhere to all local, state, and federal privacy laws.

6.4.2 This responsibility continues after an employee is no longer employed by the Organization, and the Organization will pursue all available legal remedies to prevent current and former employees from benefiting or misusing such confidential Organization information.

6.5 Organization Opportunities

6.5.1 No employee may appropriate, for his/her own or any associate's personal profit or advantage, any business venture, opportunity, or potential opportunity discovered or developed in the course of employment that is in any way related to any business in which the Organization is or may become engaged.

6.5.2 No employee may, directly or indirectly, compete with the Organization in the purchase or sale of any property, right, interest, or information, nor may any employee or associate knowingly acquire, directly or indirectly, anything of probable interest to the Organization without the prior written consent of the Organization.

6.6 Dealings in Securities

6.6.1 Federal law prohibits security transactions based on nonpublic information.

6.6.2 Generally, such laws apply to a person when purchasing, selling, or otherwise trading the securities of, or any other proprietary interest in, any business or enterprise in which the person participating in the transaction is in possession of material information concerning the transaction, including:

6.6.2.1 Information that relates in any way to the business or financial condition, present or prospective, of such business or enterprise; to its products, services, or facilities, whether presently available or in the process of development; to the market for its securities; or to the Organization's investment intentions with respect to such business or enterprise.

6.6.2.2 Information that has not been made generally known to the public.

6.6.2.3 In the case of any such action taken by an employee or any associate of an employee on the employee's or associate's behalf, information that has been obtained in the course of such employee's employment with the Organization.

6.7 Gifts, Entertainment, Loans, and Other Favors

6.7.1 All transactions between the Organization and customers, suppliers, and vendors must be based solely on the merits of each decision.

6.7.2 Employees and associates may not accept or give gifts, entertainment, loans, or other favors from any business, enterprise, organization, or person that is doing business or seeking to do business with the Organization, which is a competitor of the Organization, or with which the Organization is considering investing.

6.7.3 The prohibition against loans does not apply to loans made in the ordinary course of business from established banking or financial institutions.

6.7.4 The prohibition against the giving and receiving of gifts and other favors does not apply if the gift, entertainment, or other favor is of such nominal value (less than $25.00) that it could not be reasonably regarded as placing the recipient under any obligation to the donor.

6.7.5 The prohibition against the giving and receiving of entertainment does not apply if it is prior approved by the Organization; reflects normal business practices; is of nominal value; is legal under applicable law; meets generally accepted ethical standards; and would not embarrass the Organization if disclosed.

6.8 Political Contributions

6.8.1 Federal and state laws regulate the conditions under which political contributions may be made or an Organization may ask its employees to make such contributions.

6.8.2 Except as allowed by law, the Organization forbids the use of Organization funds or resources for contributions to any political party or committee or candidate or office holder of any government—federal, state, and local.

6.8.3 Employee will not be reimbursed by the Organization for any individual political contributions.

6.8.4 The Organization may authorize resources to defray administrative expenses of an Organization-affiliated political action committee to the extent clearly permitted under law.

6.9 Protection of Organization Assets

6.9.1 Employees share the responsibility to protect Organization property—both property specifically assigned to an employee as well as common property and property assigned to other employees.

6.9.2 No employee shall take, sell, lend, or give away any Organization property, regardless of its condition or value, without prior written authorization.

6.9.3 No employee has the right to receive or give away Organization services, information, use of information, use of facilities, or use of equipment without prior written authorization.

6.10 Relationship with Competitors

6.10.1 An employee's knowledge of the Organization's business and information is one of the Organization's most valuable assets, so employees may not render advice or give service, gratuitous or otherwise, to any organization or individual engaged in the same business as the Organization without prior written authorization.

6.10.2 No employee shall at any time enter into a written or oral understanding or agreement, expressed or implied, or participate in any plan or scheme, formal or informal, with any competitor concerning prices, offers, information, terms, conditions, contracts, contacts, sources, or any other information.

6.10.3 No employee shall engage in any other conduct that, in the opinion of the Organization's legal counsel, violates any antitrust law.

6.11 Standards of Conduct

6.11.1 The Organization maintains internal standards of conduct that seek to protect employees from harassment and from discrimination (see 7.1 Terms of Employment policy and procedure).

6.11.2 Similarly, employees who represent the Organization in activities or in business transactions involving nonemployees should conduct themselves in strict compliance with the same standards of conduct.

6.12 Disclosure

6.12.1 The following procedures have been established to allow disclosure of any material interest, affiliation, or activity on the part of any employee that conflicts with, is likely to conflict with, or may appear to conflict with the duties of any employee, the Organization, or the Organization's Code of Business Conduct.

6.12.1.1 On an annual basis, Human Resources will distribute to all management a questionnaire to elicit disclosures of conflicts or possible conflicts.

6.12.2 Human Resources will distribute to each newly hired management employee at time of employment a questionnaire to elicit disclosures of conflicts or possible conflicts.

6.12.3 Any employee who, in the course of a year, becomes aware of a potential conflict should immediately contact the Human Resources manager to obtain and complete a questionnaire.

6.12.4 All completed questionnaires are returned to the Human Resources manager, who forwards them to the Organization's general counsel for determination of any that indicate a possible conflict.

6.12.5 All information reported by questionnaire is treated as confidential, except to the extent necessary for the protection of the Organization's interests or as required by law.

6.12.6 Employees not subject to the disclosure procedure, as represented by completion of a questionnaire, are not excused from the Code of Business Conduct.

6.12.7 On an annual basis, Human Resources will distribute to every employee a Code of Business Conduct and a memo stating the Code of Business Conduct was previously signed by the employee and is still in full force and effect.

6.12.8 Human Resources will obtain a signed Code of Business Conduct from each newly hired employee at time of employment.

6.13 Whistle-Blower Protection

6.13.1 Any employee knowing of an illegal act of the Organization or any of its officers or employees is encouraged to bring it to senior management's attention.

6.13.2 At any time and instead of bringing such information to the attention of senior management, the employee may contact federal, state, or local authorities with the information.

6.13.3 There shall be no retaliation by any employee of the Organization as a result of such disclosure.

6.14 Sanctions

Any infraction of the Organization's Code of Business Conduct or requirements of this policy and procedure may subject the employee to disciplinary action, including termination of employment.

7. REFERENCES

    7.1 Terms of Employment

    7.2 External Selection

    7.3 Equal and Fair Treatment

CHAPTER 22

Other Policies and Procedures

"If you don't ask 'why this' often enough, somebody will ask 'why you?'"

—TIM HIRSHFIELD

THIS BOOK HAS DEALT WITH THE MOST COMMON human resources policies and procedures as identified by an advisory board of HR professionals. However, as mentioned in the Introduction, it is impossible to cover all possible HR policies and procedures.

Several subjects are not included in this book, though most organizations have policies and procedures related to them. However, they do not always fall under the umbrella of human resources. More often, these are financial, facilities, legal, or security policies and procedures. These subjects are:

❏ **Travel and Entertainment.** Generally, the financial requirements for reimbursement and prepayment of employee travel and entertainment expenses are formulated by the finance function of the organization. Also, there are federal laws that apply to what expenses are allowable for tax purposes.

HR policies and procedures for this subject tend to deal with travel and entertainment guidelines for employees. For example, employees need to be informed about the class of air travel that may be reimbursed, what qualifies as an eligible travel expense, and what type of ground transportation may be used (e.g., taxi, rental car, or limousine). Also covered are guidelines for entertainment expenses, such as what type of meals are eligible and what type of gifts, if any, may be given.

The evidence required for an eligible expense is also described. The evidence required by the company may exceed federal and financial function requirements. For example, federal requirements allow some expenses of under $25 to be paid without a supporting receipt, and many finance functions repeat that requirement. However, some HR travel and entertainment policies and procedures stipulate receipts must be presented for all eligible expenses in excess of $5.

Each of the policy and procedure summaries in this chapter provide some of the questions to consider. But for these subjects, you will need to discover the questions that are applicable to your organization. Here are some for a travel and entertainment policy and procedure:

❒ What type of travel and entertainment expenses are eligible for organization payment?

❒ Who approves employee travel and entertainment expenses for organization payment?

❒ What are the procedure for travel and entertainment approval and payment?

❒ What documentation is required for organization payment?

❒ Does the organization provide credit cards in its name?

The accompanying disk provides an example of one company's approach to this subject.

❒ **Relocation of Household.** Typically, there are three situations that could require relocation of a household: A new employee is hired and has to be relocated; an existing employee is transferred to another location; and a retiring or terminating employee is being returned to a former location. Not all organizations offer relocation for all of these situations. If they do, they may have the same policy and procedure for all situations, or the organization can have different policies and procedures for each.

In all three instances, rules are needed to determine what will be moved; how it will be moved; how existing houses are sold and new ones purchased, what types of visits for acquiring a new home are permitted; and what types of (and how many) family visits and moves are allowed. As with travel and entertainment, there are laws and regulations covering much of this subject, so the finance function also needs to be involved.

Some questions to consider here are:

❐ What constitutes a move that is eligible for organization payment?

❐ What moving expenses are eligible for organization payment?

❐ What is the procedure organization payment of relocation expenses?

❐ What are the tax implications for the employee?

The sample policy and procedure on the accompanying disk provides a template for the types of inclusions to consider.

❐ **Safety and Health.** A policy and procedure in this area has to be coordinated with federal and state laws, your insurance company's requirements, and the specific type of operations your organization conducts. There are federal and state laws that apply to most organizations, and then there are some safety and health laws and regulations that cover specific products, materials, and industries.

Generally, a safety and health policy and procedure covers such topics as: personal protection; safety training; maintenance of a healthy environment; optional personal safety protection; safety inspections, safety rules and regulations; accident reporting; and emergency treatment. You can expect a company working with hazardous materials and machinery to have a more extensive policy and procedure than one whose operations are restricted to office administrative work.

A safety and health policy and procedure usually describes who is accountable for the various implementation and reporting requirements, and in many organizations, it describes the creation and operation of a safety committee.

The sample policy and procedure on the disk is from a manufacturing firm. It is a basic form whose context will assist you in developing a safety and health policy and procedure for your specific organization. Be sure to seek the advice of your insurance company and someone knowledgeable about the laws and regulations (as well as any dangers) applicable to your organization's operations.

In this area, questions to consider include:

❐ Who is accountable for ensuring organization and employee safety and health?

❐ Who is accountable for ensuring compliance with safety and health regulations and laws?

❐ What provisions have been made for accidents and emergencies?

❐ What provisions have been made for first aid and medical attention?

❐ Who is accountable for accident reporting?

❐ How are accidents investigated?

❐ How and when are safety and health inspections and tests conducted?

❐ What type of safety and health training is provided?

❐ What type of protective devices are provided?

❐ What type of safety drills are conducted?

❐ **Security.** A security policy and procedure can deal with many topics. Most of these policies and procedures cover subjects such as: facility security, employee identification, security checks, government security levels, product and materials security, information security, and employee records security. More recently, these policies and procedures include actions in the event of a terrorist attack or threat and violence in the workplace.

In some situations, the policy and procedure is extended to the parking lot, employee travel, and employees living in foreign countries. Sometimes, security policies and procedures also deal with explosions, natural disasters, and fires. Other times these subjects may be covered in a safety and health policy and procedure.

Like safety and health, this is an area where requirements vary depending on the type of operation, so coordination with your insurance company and someone with knowledge of applicable laws and regulations is vital. The sample policy and procedure on the disk can be used as a starting point.

Some of the questions regarding security are:

❐ Who is accountable for ensuring security of the organization facilities, employees, and records?

❐ Who is accountable for ensuring compliance with security regulations and laws?

❐ What type of identification is provided employees?

❐ What security procedures are in place for visitors?

❐ What provisions have been made to control facility access?

❐ What provisions have been made for any breaches of security?

❐ What provisions have been made for duplicate record storage?

❐ What type of emergency evacuation drills have been conducted?

❐ How and when are security inspections and tests conducted?

❐ What type of security training is provided?

❐ **Labor Relations.** Generally, labor relations policies and procedures are published by organizations if at least some of their employees are unionized. However, some organizations without unions also have labor relations policies and procedures that establish a structure for when (and if) employees become unionized and a format for dealing with any organizational attempt.

Where unions exist, they are responsible for negotiating conditions of employment for their members. So, to a large extent, the contract between the organization and the union becomes a combination policy and procedure manual and employee handbook.

Generally, a labor relations policy and procedure deals with the organization's approach to the union relationship—for example, it identifies who is accountable for labor relations and who represents the organization at contract negations, arbitration hearings, and grievance meetings. The sample policy and procedure on the disk describes a typical organizational relationship with an existing union and the unionized employees.

Labor relations questions include:

❐ Who is accountable for labor relations?

❐ Who is accountable for negotiating labor agreements?

❐ Who is accountable for conducting grievance and arbitration hearings?

❐ What role do labor attorneys have?

❐ What are the procedures for union organizational attempts?

❐ **Employee Discounts on Purchases of Organization Products and/or Services.** Many organizations, but not all, make their products and/or services available to employees at a reduced price. Some also provide a payroll deduction plan for payment of such purchases. This policy and procedure describes employee eligibility for discounted purchases, the method of purchase, and payment procedures. Some organizations (such as some automobile manufacturers) make this benefit available to the employee's family.

Questions in this subject include:

- ❒ What products and/or services are eligible for employee discounts?

- ❒ What types of discounts are offered to employees?

- ❒ Which employees are eligible for discount purchases?

- ❒ Which relatives of employees are eligible for discount purchases?

- ❒ Are there limitations on employee use of discounted products and/or services?

- ❒ What type of payment is required?

❒ **Memberships.** For an organization that pays for all or any portion of employee professional, health, and social memberships, this policy and procedure should describe eligibility, approval procedures, membership payment, organization and individual memberships, percent covered, and membership conditions at the time of employee termination.

Here, questions are:

- ❒ For what memberships does the organization pay?

- ❒ For what type of membership does the organization pay (individual, group, organization)?

- ❒ Who can use organization memberships?

- ❒ How are memberships selected and approved?

- ❒ What happens to memberships on employee termination?

❒ **Subscriptions.** Like memberships, a policy and procedure is required to describe what subscriptions the organization will obtain for distribution and what subscriptions the organization will obtain for individual employees. It should also clarify conditions at the time of employee termination.

Questions to consider are:

- ❒ For what subscriptions does the organization pay?

- ❒ For what type of subscriptions does the organization pay (individual, group, organization)?

❐ How are subscriptions selected and approved?

❐ Are organization-paid subscription publications distributed?

❐ **Contributions.** There are several types of contributions with which an organization may become involved. Sometimes, there are federal laws and regulations as to what contributions are eligible for tax deduction.

This policy and procedure can deal with monetary contributions as well as contributions of equipment and services. It should identify who is accountable for determining what contributions are made and describe development of a contribution budget. It should explain what types of contributions are not allowed. Other areas to consider are prohibitions of solicitations of contributions on company property, and matching contributions.

Your marketing and sales areas also may become involved in contributions and sponsorships related to customers and public relations. If so, guidelines should be included.

Questions to answer include:

❐ What type of contributions does the organization make?

❐ Are contributions annual or ongoing?

❐ What is the contribution recommendation and approval procedure?

❐ Who is accountable for making organization contributions and decisions?

❐ What limitations are there on organization contributions?

❐ What type of contribution matching plan does the organization offer employees?

Although they are not dealt with in this book, sample policies and procedures on all these subjects are included on the accompanying disk. The disk also contains all of the forms and policies and procedures used or mentioned in this book. They are provided in a format that allows you to print and use them and/or revise them.

Keep in mind that all these examples are abbreviated and generalized to meet the needs of the widest range of organizations as possible. Also, remember they are not offered as the correct policies and procedures for your organization, but rather as a starting point for you to develop the policies and procedures your organization actually requires.

PART FOUR

Policy and Procedure Administration

CHAPTER 23

Communication and Publication

"Tell them the truth, first because it is the right thing to do and second, they'll find out anyway."

—PAUL GALVIN

WHEN A POLICY AND PROCEDURE IS COMPLETED—written and approved—the final step is to publish and communicate it. This means ensuring everyone affected by the policy and procedure knows its contents, knows how it is to be implemented, and knows how it affects them.

PUBLISHED FORMATS

Since one of the key objectives of policies and procedures is to ensure consistency and equal treatment of employees, communication is important. For management, there should at least be a policy and procedure book provided to each manager and supervisor. More important is that all managers and supervisors receive training in how to implement the policies and procedures and know when and where to obtain any needed assistance.

For employees, an employee handbook covering all conditions of employment from their point of view is ideal. If the policy and procedure being published is new or consists of significant revisions, then employees, too, will need training. However, their training is generally more of an orientation and description.

These two documents—the supervisor's manual and the employee handbook—although basically serving the same purpose, are constructed and written in entirely different formats. Their audiences are different with different needs.

RECORDS

The finished set of policies and procedures also requires several record-keeping formats. Each format is designed for a different audience and purpose. The typical formats are:

❒ Master Copy
❒ History File
❒ Precedent File

Master Copy

The master copy is the current final product of your efforts. It may be in electronic memory or in a traditional paper file. Often it takes the form of a series of file folders—one for each policy and procedure. Each folder contains not only the actual document of the current policy and procedure, but also previous editions of it and sometimes development information. Wherever it is and in whatever format, the master copy represents the controlling document.

History File

This is a file containing all of the information collected and used to create each policy and procedure. There is a separate file folder or folders for each one. As time passes and policies and procedures are revised to meet changing needs, new materials are added to these files. Generally, each file is organized by time periods or editions of a policy and procedure.

Precedent File

No matter how thorough the initial development process, new questions may arise that may not be covered by a policy and procedure. Other times changes, both within and outside the organization, may occur that were not anticipated when a policy and procedure was developed and may require it to be rewritten.

Some of the issues that may arise do not allow sufficient time for research and rewriting. They require an immediate answer. For example, assume your organization has a published policy and procedure covering discharges and absences. It states:

Employees not reporting for work as scheduled for three consecutive days and not notifying their supervisor of the reason for the absence will be considered an automatic quit.

One of your employees is absent for three days without calling. He is removed from the payroll. A week later, his father calls to tell you the employee was in a coma after an automobile accident. His father says he did not know of the notification requirement. If he had, he would have called. The policy and procedure did not address this type of situation. Consequently, you make a new rule:

If an employee is unable to call due to a physical condition, his family or representative may call within two weeks and the employee will be retained.

When you make that type of decision you have established a precedent. You have created a new policy and procedure. That is okay, but you have to be consistent.

Now, assume it is six months later. Another employee is absent for three days without calling. A week later he reports back to work claiming he was in a motorcycle accident and was too injured to call. He also claims he lives alone, so there was no one to call for him. You are on vacation, so someone else has to make a decision. The rule from the first instance was recorded, so it is now part of the policy and procedure. It applies to all employees. This employee is considered a voluntary quit (since no one contacted the organization on his behalf).

This is a relatively simple and obvious example, but if the decision had not been recorded, the second employee might have been treated differently. A file should be maintained for each policy and procedure, and whenever a decision is made regarding it, a record of that decision is placed in the file. That creates a source for reference when possible similar situations develop, and it provides input for the next time the policy and procedure is reviewed for possible revision.

SUPERVISOR'S MANUAL

This manual contains copies of all policies and procedures and is provided to each person within the organization who manages or supervises employees. These documents become the supervisor's and manager's reference for decision making.

Most organizations seem to publish these manuals in $8^1/_2'' \times 11''$ loose-leaf binders so individual policies and procedures can be replaced, removed, or added without having to republish and redistribute the entire manual. Some organizations include the policy and procedure heading, with a page number, on each page. They can then revise and issue individual pages as necessary.

Some organizations print on two sides of each page. Others print on only one side—the odd-numbered page. When placed in the binder, the back of a page becomes the even-numbered page opposite an odd-numbered page. Supervisors are encouraged to make notes and write questions on these blank pages that relate to the contents on the opposite page.

Since these manuals are the basis for many supervisory decisions, it is important that they contain the latest editions of all policies and procedures. Many organizations number these books and have the supervisor sign to acknowledge receipt of the original book and any revisions and additions. Some organizations actually have a person from human resources physically update each book whenever there is a revision or addition. That way they can remove any outdated policies and procedures.

Some organizations publish these manuals electronically. If your supervisors have ready access to PCs and are comfortable with this format, it is one to consider because it allows for faster updating and communication. Whatever format you select—print or online—it should be one that is most useful to your supervisors.

EMPLOYEE HANDBOOK

Policies and procedures cover the conditions of employment that apply to employees, so employees also need to have a reference source. However, policies and procedures are written from management's viewpoint, and the implementation procedures are meant to meet management's needs. Employees generally have different needs.

For example, a supervisor needs to know how to balance vacation time for all employees in her department. An employee needs to know how to obtain approval for his vacation time. The same rules apply to each, but they each need to know them from a different point of view.

An employee handbook describes all elements of the policies and procedures as they apply to employees. It is usually written in a less structured format and also includes information other than policies and procedures that a new employee might need, such as key telephone numbers, supervisor's name and telephone number, and organizational history. Like the supervisor's manuals, employee handbooks are often published as loose-leaf binders, so revisions can be easily accomplished. However, employee handbooks are often of a smaller size. The $5\frac{1}{2}'' \times 8\frac{1}{2}''$ format is common.

Employee handbooks often include a disclaimer, such as:

> This handbook is a summary of the organization's policies and procedures that apply to employees. Any difference between this handbook and the actual human resources policy and procedure is governed by the policy and procedure.

If you use a disclaimer, it should be reviewed by your attorney or legal department.

Some organizations treat employee handbooks as they do policy and procedure manuals issued to supervisors. They number the books and have employees sign acknowledgments of receipt of the original and any revisions. Some organizations also have employees sign acknowledgments of the disclaimer statement.

Some organizations publish employee manuals electronically. If your employees have ready access to PCs and are comfortable with this format, it may allow for faster updating and communication. Whatever format you select—print or online—it should be one that is most useful to your employees.

PUBLICATION DATE

Policies and procedures have an effective date, so they must be published or at least communicated to the appropriate employees in advance of the effective date. That means allowing adequate time for final preparation— the printing, the addressing of mailing envelopes or labels, and the distribution of the documents. If, for any reason, they are not published and communicated by their effective date, you will have to make exceptions in their implementation.

A local government agency in Arizona changed the number of allowable personal days off from six to five. However, the revised policy and procedure was not communicated by its effective date, and one employee took a sixth personal day off after the effective date but before the communication of the change.

The employee was disciplined by her supervisor. She was given three days off without pay.

The employee filed a grievance under the available grievance procedure. Her grievance was denied and eventually went to arbitration. The arbitrator ruled in the employee's favor. The employee received back pay with interest. However, the worse result of this situation was the other employees' perceptions of the unreasonableness of management's decision.

TRAINING

So far we have been considering the publication of documents and their distribution, but to be effective there needs to be appropriate training. People do not always read or understand written materials.

Training generally takes two forms. Supervisors and managers participate in a formal session in which they learn the policies and procedures and practice their implementation. Often this training occurs when the new or revised manuals are to be distributed. All supervisors receive their manual as a part of the training course.

Employee training takes the form of an orientation. Each new or revised policy and procedure is explained, questions are answered, and any required forms to be completed by employees are introduced.

The supervisor training often becomes part of the training a new supervisor attends. The employee orientation becomes part of new employee training.

CONCLUSION

The final consideration for the development of your organization's policies and procedures is the establishment of a system to keep them current. That is the subject of the next chapter.

CHAPTER 24

Maintaining Relevance

"Avoid organizational rigor mortis. Change is inevitable and the organization—and its people—must accommodate change."

—JOEL E. ROSS AND MICHAEL J. KAMI

THE ONLY THING CONSTANT IS CHANGE. It is ever with us and at times seems to be accelerating. Change is not only caused by internal actions but also by external ones. Laws change. Contracts change. Economics change. These are but a few of the changes an organization encounters, and many of these changes require new or revised policies and procedures.

In 1999, the American economy was booming. There were more jobs than people seeking them. A Washington plastics manufacturer departed from its usual employment practices in order to obtain sufficient workers. "If we hadn't changed our hiring policy and procedure," the president said, "we would not have stayed in business due to a lack of employees."

After the tragedy of September 11, 2001, the economy slumped. Suddenly instead of no candidates, the company had too many candidates for very few jobs. It had to change its hiring policies and procedures to recognize this new reality.

PRECEDENT FILE

The importance of maintaining a precedent file was mentioned in the previous chapter. This is the file in which you place a record of any decisions and interpretations regarding a policy and procedure. This file can also be used for other decisions and actions that may affect the policy and procedure.

New and revised laws and regulations, contracts, licenses, and memberships can all generate the need for policy and procedure revisions. Another item that may be added to the precedent file is a new or revised form used in implementing the policy and procedure.

It is also helpful to have a separate folder in which you place suggestions and requests for new policies and procedures. However, sometimes such requests require action before a regular review occurs.

All of this information creates a basis for the review and possible revision of your policies and procedures. For example, the file may have a newspaper article about an applicable law that has been revised. It does not give you all the information you need, but prompts you to obtain the actual revision to the law.

WHAT TO REVIEW

When you are ready to review the status of your organization's existing policies and procedures, you can use the process introduced in this book. You can use the questionnaires provided, or use the meeting or interview techniques also described. Your policies and procedures should also be reviewed by your attorney or legal department for advice on any changes you should be considering.

If you review the status of your policies and procedures fairly regularly, then a questionnaire, a review by your attorney, and an examination of the precedent files are probably sufficient. However, eventually you will have to do a thorough review and check for possible newly required policies and procedures.

WHEN TO CONDUCT A REVIEW

How often should you review the status of your existing policies and procedures? To a large extent, the answer depends on your organization. A few factors may suggest that you need a yearly review. For example:

❑   Your organization is in a highly regulated industry.
❑   The organization is physically moving locations or is establishing new operations.

❏   The organization encountered employee problems in recent months.

❏   The organization received negative employee feedback from an employee opinion survey indicating dissatisfaction with existing policies and procedures.

❏   The organization is undergoing major changes.

On the other hand, if your organization is in a stable industry, is experiencing little change, and has few employee problems, you do not have to conduct a review as often. In such instances, the basic guideline may be to review policies and procedures every three years unless there is an identified need to do it more frequently. Some organizations review each policy and procedure two years after the effective date of its last revision. Some organizations do a quick review every two years and a full review every five years.

A Connecticut insurance company assigns a human resources person to each functional area of the company to serve as the HR representative for that area. As a part of the assignment, the HR person attends the area's monthly staff meetings. Each month the HR person raises questions regarding one policy and procedure. There are twenty-four HR policies and procedures, so each one is discussed once every two years.

Whenever it is suggested that changes are required, HR conducts a thorough review of that policy and procedure throughout the company. Every three years it conducts a general review of all policies and procedures.

WHO DOES THE REVIEW

Just as in any kind of planning, there has to be an assignment of accountability for this activity. Someone needs to maintain the precedent files, stay in touch with the attorney, collect information on possible new policies and procedures, and conduct reviews. The person is probably someone in human resources. Whoever it is should have clear knowledge that this delegated task requires thorough attention.

CONCLUSION

This book has covered the process for developing a comprehensive set of HR policies and procedures. It has explained a flexible process that can be adapted to policies and procedures for other areas of the organization as well. Your next step is to put the process to use and create the necessary HR policies and procedures for your organization.

Related Reading

OTHER AMACOM BOOKS FOR HUMAN RESOURCES PROFESSIONALS

Arthur, Diane. *Recruiting, Interviewing, Selecting & Orienting New Employees, Third Edition*. ISBN: 0-8144-0401-4.

Branham, F. Leigh. *Keeping the People Who Keep You in Business: 24 Ways to Hang On to Your Most Valuable Talent*. ISBN: 0-8144-0597-5.

Downey, Diane, Tom March, and Adena Berkman. *Assimilating New Leaders: The Key to Executive Retention*. ISBN: 0-8144-0645-9.

Falcone, Paul. *96 Great Interview Questions to Ask Before You Hire*. ISBN: 0-8144-7909-X.

———. *The Hiring and Firing Question and Answer Book*. ISBN: 0-8144-0640-8.

———. *101 Sample Write-Ups for Documenting Employee Performance Problems*. ISBN: 0-8144-7977-4.

Fitz-enz, Jac. *The 8 Practices of Exceptional Companies: How Great Organizations Make the Most of Their Human Assets*. ISBN: 0-8144-0348-4.

———. *The ROI of Human Capital: Measuring the Economic Value of Employee Performance*. ISBN: 0-8144-0574-6.

Galbraith, Jay, Diane Downey, and Amy Kates. *Designing Dynamic Organizations: A Hands-On Guide for Leaders at All Levels*. ISBN: 0-8144-7119-6.

Grote, Dick. *The Complete Guide to Performance Appraisal.* ISBN: 0-8144-0313-1.

————. *The Performance Appraisal Question and Answer Book: A Survival Guide for Managers.* ISBN: 0-8144-7151-X.

Johnson, Larry, and Bob Phillips. *Absolute Honesty: Building a Corporate Culture that Values Straight Talk and Rewards Integrity.* ISBN: 0-8144-0781-1.

Manas, Todd M., and Michael Dennis Graham. *Creating a Total Rewards Strategy: A Toolkit for Designing Business-Based Plans.* ISBN: 0-8144-0722-6.

Masters, Marick F., and Robert R. Albright. *The Complete Guide to Conflict Resolution in the Workplace.* ISBN: 0-8144-0629-7.

McConnell, John H. *Auditing Your Human Resources Department: A Step-by-Step Guide.* ISBN: 0-8144-7076-9.

————. *How to Design, Implement, and Interpret an Employee Survey.* ISBN: 0-8144-0709-9.

————. *How to Identify Your Organization's Training Needs: A Practical Guide to Needs Analysis.* ISBN: 0-8144-0710-2.

Sartain, Libby, et al. *HR from the Heart: Inspiring Stories and Strategies for Building the People Side of Great Business.* ISBN: 0-8144-0756-0.

Thomas, R. Roosevelt, Jr. *Beyond Race and Gender: Unleashing the Power of Your Total Work Force by Managing Diversity.* ISBN: 0-8144-7807-7.

————, et al. *Building a House for Diversity: A Fable About a Giraffe and an Elephant Offers New Strategies for Today's Workforce.* ISBN: 0-8144-0463-4.

Zemke, Ron, Claire Raines, and Bob Filipczak. *Generations at Work: Managing the Clash of Veterans, Boomers, Xers, and Nexters in Your Workplace.* ISBN: 0-8144-0480-4.

To order, please call 1-800-714-6395.

Index

About the Author

JOHN H. MCCONNELL is president of McConnell-Simmons and Company, Inc., a management consulting firm located in Morristown, New Jersey. The firm specializes in human resources products and services. Prior to establishing his current company in 1974, McConnell held a number of human resources executive positions with Capital Holding, Garan, Inc., and Wolverine Tube Division of Calumet and Hecla. He has undergraduate and graduate degrees from Wayne State University in Detroit, Michigan. He has written more than thirty books on management and human resources, including *Auditing Your Human Resources Department, How to Identify Your Organization's Training Needs*, and *How to Design, Implement, and Interpret an Employee Survey*. The author has been a frequent speaker at American Management Association seminars, the AMA Management Course, and national and international human resources conventions.